Director of production: Susan M. Moyer
Project manager: Tracy Gaudreau
Developmental editor: Doug Hoepker
Copy editor: Cynthia L. McNew
Dust jacket design: Kerri Baker
Photo editor: Erin Linden-Levy

Interior photos of baseball cards courtesy of The Topps Company, Inc.

ISBN: 1-58261-190-4

Printed in the United States

Sports Publishing L.L.C.
www.sportspublishingllc.com

To my wonderful aunt, Phyllis Glouberman,
who prefers lox to Marlins and Royalty to Scrabble,
and is still the best writer in the family at age 100.

—Dan Schlossberg

Contents

Foreword

By DAVE BARRY
The Miami Herald

[This originally appeared as a syndicated column run in *The Miami Herald* on October 10, on the eve of the 2003 NL Championship Series between the Florida Marlins and Chicago Cubs.]

I'm a huge Marlins fan. I've been following this plucky team ever since they beat the San Francisco Giants, which was, what, nearly a week ago. I live and die by this team! When they win, I drink champagne and dance all night. This is also what I do when they lose, because there is no point in wasting champagne. But I dance in a more subdued manner.

The last time I was a huge Marlins fan was October 18 through 26, 1997, which happens to be exactly when the Marlins won the World Series against the Cleveland Native Americans. I'm not taking all the credit for that victory: many Marlins players were also involved.

But I was in the stands for Game 7 and when the score was tied in the bottom of the 11th inning, with two out and the potential game-winning Marlin run on third base, I decided that if I buttoned a certain button on my shirt, it might cause the Marlins to get a base hit. A bold tactical gamble? Yes. But it paid off, and the Marlins won, and South Florida erupted in a joyous celebration that lasted until 2:30 the following afternoon, at which time owner Wayne "The Antichrist" Huizenga sold all the good players.

But that is the distant past. Today South Florida is, once again, totally and permanently united, for the time being, behind this spunky young Marlins team and its plucky players, including one named "Pudge" and another one named "Spooneybarger."

You'd think everyone would be rooting for this spunky team, but you'd be wrong. Everyone else in the entire world (including, in a formal statement released today, the Pope) is rooting for the Chicago Cubs. Why? Because, historically, the Cubs stink. They have not won anything for centuries. They are the only team in the National League that fought for the South in the Civil War. So now everybody is making a big deal about the Cubs, and their fans who've been loyally supporting them through decade after decade of losing—as if we should applaud them because they wasted generations of perfectly good fan energy rooting for a team that traditionally had as much chance of winning the World Series as the von Trapp Family Singers, with Julie Andrews pitching.

Does this make any sense? Let's say you're at a restaurant, and you see a man stagger away from the bar and walk directly into the wall, mistaking it for a door, banging his face and falling down, only to pick himself up and walk into the wall again, and then again, over and over. Would you say to yourself: "I admire that man! He is loyal to the tactic of walking into the wall, in the hope that it will eventually turn into a door!"

No! You'd say: "He must be a Cubs fan."

Ha ha! I'm kidding, of course: a true Cubs fan would never leave the bar. But my point is that we South Florida fans deserve some credit for displaying discretion. Yes, we're loyal to our local teams. But if, after a reasonable period of loyalty—generally two days—we perceive that a given local team is unlikely to win a national or world championship, we drop that team like a used napkin and move on to another team, or another sport, or a mall.

But for now, we're committed to our Marlins, and we'll be out rooting for them this weekend in Formerly Joe Robbie Stadium. Oh, sure, it's not historic Wrigley Field, with the ivy growing on the walls.

This is actually a sign of poor maintenance, but it causes baseball writers—who spend their entire lives in dingy press boxes where the only green organic thing they ever see is relish—to spurt little prose orgasms. Wow! Wall vegetation!

Listen, baseball writers: if you like wildlife, South Florida has way more wildlife than Chicago! It would not surprise anybody down here if, during a game, a third-base coach was eaten by an alligator.

But it's no use arguing South Florida's merits: nobody wants us to win, except us.

So let's do our part; let's go out to Formerly Stadium and root, root, root for our Marlins. Go "Pudge!" Go "Spooneybarger!" Go "whoever the other Marlins players are!"

If they don't win, it's the mall.

Preface

By JEFF CONINE
Florida Marlins

I was sitting in a bus on an airport tarmac in Seattle when I got the news: I was going home. Back to South Florida. Back to the Marlins. Back to a playoff race.

At the time, of course, it was impossible to know that I was also being dropped into a unique moment in history; perhaps the most dramatic, heart-stopping, improbable World Series run ever.

And the most enjoyable two months in my baseball career.

But as I sat in the back of the bus with Jim Beattie, my general manager in Baltimore, it was hard not to feel conflicted. I loved Baltimore—loved my teammates, loved the city. And oh that ballpark. Every player who ever puts on a big-league uniform should have the privilege of playing at least one series at Camden Yards in front of those great Orioles fans. I feel blessed to have been able to play there for five years!

But the Orioles were rebuilding and I was getting a chance join a team that was winning now in the city where I really established myself as a major league player. I had won a world championship in Miami and played in two all-star games as a Marlin before I and a number of my teammates were sent packing in the infamous fire sale that followed the 1997 World Series. A new owner, Jeffrey Loria, was making a run at another title now and one of his star players, Mike Lowell, had gone down with a broken bone in his hand the night before. He wanted me to come back for the stretch drive.

However there was a catch: the deadline for setting postseason rosters was less than six hours away and the Marlins wanted the deal done before then. The Orioles were about to get on a plane for the

East Coast, my agent Michael Watkins was on another plane headed to the West Coast and we had a lot of things to negotiate.

As soon as we took off, I grabbed an airphone and called Michael's wife and told her what was up. Michael knew nothing of the trade until he landed, but he immediately got in touch with Marlins general manager Larry Beinfest and they started working out a deal. Both sides were motivated—the Marlins wanted me and I wanted them. Still, it was nerve-wracking to be flying 35,000 feet over the Great Plains while two guys on opposite ends of the country were on cell phones determining my future.

By the time the Oriole charter touched down in Baltimore, I was a Marlin. In a sense, though, I guess I've always been a Marlin—an original Marlin. I was one of the first players the organization selected in the expansion draft that brought the franchise into being. And I was in left field when Charlie Hough threw the first pitch in Marlin history. I went four-for-four that day and became the first Marlin to steal a base. I've stolen a grand total of 39 in the 10 years since then, which would be a good month for Juan Pierre.

The next year I bought a house in South Florida and I've lived there ever since. Although I'm a Southern California transplant—everybody in South Florida is from somewhere else, it seems—the community has really embraced me and my family. Even during the five years I was with the Orioles I was known in Miami as "Mr. Marlin." And not just by the fans. On my first day back in a Marlins uniform, as I stood on the top step of the dugout for the national anthem, I could hear Dontrelle Willis saying to himself "Man, I'm standing next to 'Mr. Marlin.'"

That was a little embarrassing for me, but Dontrelle was sincere. Dontrelle, by the way, is sincere about everything. People who haven't had the pleasure of meeting him ask me if he's always smiling, always that enthusiastic, always that upbeat. I guess we're all a little cynical. But with Dontrelle, the answer is yes, he is. His mother did a fantastic job raising him by herself.

When I first heard Dontrelle, that's when I knew that this team was different. These guys were fighting for a playoff berth but it felt like we were just a group of neighborhood kids who had gotten together for a pickup game at the vacant lot on the corner.

The guys on the bench—Andy Fox, Mike Redmond, Brian Banks and Todd Hollandsworth—kept everybody loose with their joking and cheerleading. They had me in stitches my first day there. I think I laughed more in the those first three or four innings than I had in 10 big-league seasons combined. I was just cracking up, having a good old time and thinking this is like my Pony League days.

It wasn't that we didn't know what kind of situation we were in or understand the importance of what was at stake. We did. We just went about it in a happy-go-lucky manner. Like our manager, Jack McKeon, always said, "Winning is fun and it's fun to win." We were winning and it was fun.

The World Series team I played on in 1997 had fun too, but that was a veteran team that went about things in a much more businesslike way. We had a different mindset then. For one thing, we were expected to win in 1997.

The 2003 team caught everyone by surprise. We got key contributions from two rookies, Dontrelle Willis and Miguel Cabrera, who had never played above Double A before 2003. Dontrelle used to say that "Every day in the major leagues is a good day." And that's the way we played. Why get upset about a loss today when we know we get to play again tomorrow?

I'm convinced that attitude was a big part of our success. It was literally like you were thrown back to the days when baseball was meant to be fun. And sometimes in this game, especially in the big leagues and in places where you're supposed to win, it's not fun. There's too much negativity and people saying, "Well, you guys are supposed to be better than this." But this was just pure baseball. It was refreshing to see the game in that light again, to experience that passion again. These guys definitely had a passion for the game that was infectious. And it was probably the most fun I've ever had on a baseball field.

In fact, that was probably the only thing that kept me sane my first two weeks with the Marlins. I knew the team was counting on me with Mike Lowell sidelined. And they had gone to such great lengths to get me. I really wanted to reward their confidence.

I was only in the clubhouse for about 15 minutes before Jeffrey Loria, the team's owner, came up to introduce himself.

Can you believe it? Here's a guy who's paying me a lot of money to lead his team to the playoffs and all he wants me to do is have fun. That made me even more determined to do well. But after two weeks I was batting .178 with four RBI as we left for Philadelphia and a key showdown with the Phillies. In that series, I had four hits, including a home run, three RBI and a pretty decent catch on a ball hit by Jim Thome, and that kind of turned things around for me. Then I was fortunate enough to hit a home run in the win that clinched the wild-card berth for us.

But what happened next is still a blur two months later. We played three series in the postseason and we trailed in every single one of them. In the National League Division Series, we won three in a row to eliminate the San Francisco Giants, a team that won 100 games in the regular season. What a series!

Then we go to Chicago, and let me tell you there is nothing like playing a playoff series at Wrigley Field. To take nothing away from our fans, the 39,000 that packed Wrigley for the games we played there were every bit as loud as the 65,000 we drew at Pro Player Stadium.

And those fans had a lot to cheer about. In the N.L. Championship Series we were five outs from the end of our season when we scored eight runs to force a seventh and deciding game against the Cubs. After that comeback, as we went up to the clubhouse, all the guys were saying "What just happened there? Did we just score eight runs in the eighth inning to beat them?"

I can tell you now that I knew we'd win that final game right then. But that was still a tiresome series. It was so close, so up and down, so much offense. Emotionally, it was really draining. And don't forget that there would have been no eight-run eighth inning—probably no sixth game at all—if Josh Beckett had not pitched one of the greatest games in playoff history to beat the Cubs 2-0 in Game 5. Amazing! So we won three straight to beat the Cubs, just as we did against the Giants.

Now we go to Yankee Stadium! The monuments, the history. But once again, we fell behind two games to one—and we've got to face Roger Clemens, perhaps the greatest pitcher of the generation in Game 4. But, as you know by now, we would never lose again. Alex Gonzalez won that game in typically improbable Marlins fashion, hitting a 12th-inning walk-off home run.

Gonzo was in a horrible slump but he never quit. In fact, he probably won the first game of the World Series with two big defensive plays, then he won Game 4 with his bat. The next night Brad Penny came up huge again, winning his second game of the Series to give us the lead going back to Yankee Stadium.

I think by then it was clear that we were a team of destiny. And when Jack McKeon put the ball back in Josh Beckett's hand, well, let me tell you the feeling in our clubhouse was electric.

Alex Gonzalez scored the only run Beckett would need with one of the most amazing slides I've ever seen, and I was fortunate enough to score an insurance run an inning later. Once again we'd won three straight games to win a series. Think about how tough it is to sweep a three-game series during the regular season. And we'd won three in a row three times in the postseason.

I'm thankful I was able to contribute, leading the starters with a .367 batting average in the postseason. My throw to Pudge Rodriguez led to the final out of the first series, then I scored the final run of the season in the World Series. Afterward, in the bedlam that enveloped the Marlins clubhouse, my teammates handed me the World Series trophy. That meant a lot to me.

The Miracle Marlins. It was something unique. I don't know if it can ever happen again. But there will always be that memory.

Acknowledgments

This book would not have been possible without the urging of my publicist, Bob Ibach, who called the day after the World Series ended. Making that call took courage, since Bob lives in Chicago and actually spent eight years working for the Cubs as director of public relations and publications.

Bob's contacts helped enormously; his long-standing friendship with Bill Beck, director of team travel for the Marlins and former publicist for the Padres, resulted in Jeff Conine's consent to become a contributing author, sharing his memories of both Florida world champions as well as personal thoughts about his uniformed and non-uniformed colleagues. It was Bill Beck's personal appeal that turned Mr. Marlin's words into print.

Thanks also to Kevin Baxter, national baseball writer for The Miami Herald, who went above and beyond the call of duty, responded instantly to a barrage of e-mail, and offered many services not specified in the original agreement.

As for Conine himself, he couldn't have been more kind. He spent hours yielding his insights on every aspect of the Florida season, posed for pictures, and gave generously of his time and thoughts. He'll make a fine manager someday if a TV network doesn't grab him first.

Two Sports Publishing figures also stepped up to the plate: Bob Snodgrass, who showed sincerity and flexibility in negotiating the complicated contract, and Developmental Editor Doug Hoepker, who accepted ideas about titles, graphics, and design that others might have rejected. It's to his credit that this book isn't called *These Fish Don't Stink*, one of several proposed titles.

We also appreciate the cooperation of syndicated humor columnist Dave Barry and his capable assistant Judi Smith; and Pat Courtney and John Blundell, public relations officials from Major League Baseball.

The sage counsel of Doug Lyons, a jovial attorney friend from the Society for American Baseball Research, and the good-natured jabs of Ed Lucas, a blind sportswriter with more vision than anyone I know, also made it easier to write this book. Thanks also to Bob Nesoff for his quick wit, Debbie Mirandi for her banter-filled aerobics classes, and Mitch Packer for his loyal friendship. Too bad they're all Yankee fans who may find it painful to read the pages that follow.

Thanks also go to Lewis Grabel, who provided the unused New York City Transit Authority poster for the Yankee victory-parade-that-wasn't; Bill Jacobowitz of Skybox Baseball Cards, who found many of the Marlins baseball cards featured in the pages that follow; and Clay Luraschi of Topps, who gave us permission to reprint them.

And a final big thank you to my daughter Samantha and the rest of the family and friends who knew not to call during the stress-filled days and nights while this book was being written. I owe you guys!

—Dan Schlossberg
Fair Lawn, NJ

Prologue

BY KEVIN BAXTER
The Miami Herald

The stadium lights had been turned off, the television cameras were all put away and most of the newspaper stories had already been filed when the Florida Marlins took the field at Yankee Stadium.

It had been nearly two hours since pitcher Josh Beckett had charged off the mound to field Jorge Posada's weak grounder and tag the Yankee catcher out, making the Marlins baseball's most unlikely champions in a generation. But there they were, back on the field, as if to make sure this wasn't some cruel joke.

The Florida Marlins, world champions? There must be some mistake.

Coaches and players lined up to have their pictures taken on the mound, as if the photographs would somehow prove it wasn't a dream. The team cheered as owner Jeffrey Loria, his hair and clothes reeking of champagne, dashed—well, OK, dawdled—around the bases before touching home, something no Yankee had been able to do that night.

Back in the clubhouse pitcher Carl Pavano stood stunned in the middle of the room, his mind stuck between shock and disbelief. In the far corner, the double play combination of Alex Gonzalez and Luis Castillo wept while Andy Fox grabbed anyone who came near and confessed "The Florida Marlins, world champions. That still doesn't sound right."

No one disagreed.

For Beckett, winning the World Series seemingly meant nothing more than a day off after the longest season of his career.

"I can't believe we don't have a game tomorrow. That's kind of the weird thing right now," he said. "Not to say that winning the world championship is not a big thing, but like we just—we don't have a game tomorrow. …It's kind of a relief to get to go dear hunting now."

In other words, After slaying the Yankees it was time to hunt some really big game.

But that's the kind of season it was for the Marlins—one so wild and wacky and so laughably unbelievable that even when it was over, no one wanted it to end. And with good reason, for it's unlikely any team will ever duplicate the mysterious and magical run of the miracle Marlins of 2003.

It was a summer when the improbable became predictable, the impossible became infallible, the irrational became irresistible. And the Marlins became invincible.

What a white-knuckle ride it was.

From spring training, when the Marlins were losing a pitcher a week, to the World Series, when they found out they really only needed two—as long as their names were Brad Penny and Josh Beckett.

From early April, when Marlins' baserunners were stealing everything in sight but a win, to late October, when they were stealing the heart and soul of the venerable Cubs and Yankees.

There were many turning points, of course, but none stand out more than the early morning hours of May 11, when the team fired manager Jeff Torborg and replaced him with Jack McKeon, the closest thing baseball has to a human lawn gnome.

Reliever Braden Looper summed up the team's attitude best when, awoken from a deep sleep and told McKeon was his new manager, he asked "who?"

The 72-year-old McKeon entered that morning's press conference clutching a cigar before taking a seat behind a microphone, his feet barely reaching the floor. He squinted into the TV lights, cupped an ear with his hand and strained to hear as each question was repeated. Then he worked the room like a stand-up comic, mispronouncing words, getting names wrong and laughing at his malapropos.

He had us at "Hello."

Sure he was more George Burns than George "Sparky" Anderson and, at first, hardly seemed capable of turning the Marlins around. But, like Burns, he could play God when he needed to. Compared to the easy-going Torborg, McKeon's wrath was of Biblical proportions—and few Marlins were spared his ire.

There was no generation gap when the Geritol Generation met Generation X, McKeon made sure of that. Twice he chewed out Dontrelle Willis on the mound; both times Willis responded with victories. In early June he threatened to send an underachieving Penny to the bullpen; Penny won 13 of his last 20 decisions, including two in the World Series.

"He expects a certain amount out of you and if you don't give it to him, I think his way of motivating, if you're pitching like shit or something, he won't even talk to you," said Beckett, who was a favorite target of McKeon's. "It's to get under your skin, but it's also to motivate. He's awesome to play for, he really is."

Many of McKeon's moves were illogical or at least inexplicable —like wearing a polka-dot tie to his first meeting with owner Jeffrey Loria and repeatedly addressing him as Jerry. But from May 23 on the Marlins went 86-55, the best record in baseball.

As for memories, it's unlikely any team packed more spine-tingling moments into a six-month season than the Marlins jammed into 2003. In the N.L. Division Series, there was Pudge Rodriguez scoring the go-ahead run in a collision at the plate, then retiring J.T. Snow for the final out in another home-plate collision half an inning later. In the N.L. championships, the Marlins were four outs from elimination when they staged an improbable eight-run eighth-inning rally. And then there was the 23-year-old Beckett, with a 17-17 lifetime record, finally living up to his promise by shutting out the Cubs and Yankees with the first two complete games of his career.

But I'll remember other things as well. When I think of the summer of '03, I'll remember Tommy Phelps making his major league debut after 10 seasons in the minors—and striking out Jim Thome with the bases loaded. I'll remember third base coach Ozzie

Guillen and closer Ugueth Urbina gathering the Marlins' Latin players together after every game to school them about life in a pennant race—or, in the case of 20-year-old rookie Miguel Cabrera, to school them simply about life.

I'll remember backup catcher Mike Redmond twice taking batting practice in the nude in an effort to break the team out of a slump and I'll remember the uncommon character of outfielder Todd Hollandsworth, who lost his starting job to Cabrera in June then went on to become the team's best pinch hitter.

I'll remember centerfielder Juan Pierre, the first one to arrive at the ballpark every day, patiently rolling balls down the baselines, studying which way his bunt would break.

I'll remember Willis, frozen in the lobby of the Chicago Westin Hotel at the All-Star Game, saying, "I feel like a kid in a candy store with a $100 bill. When I was in high school, I remember seeing these guys on TV. Now I'm in the same lobby with them." And I'll remember him ending an interview with writers after a tough August loss by saying "you guys be careful and drive home safely"—and meaning it.

I'll remember the courage and grace of Mike Lowell, tearfully describing a second brush with cancer in July, then quietly biting his lip and accepting his benching at the start of the playoffs, proving that his hand may have been broken but not his spirit.

And I'll remember a clubhouse of some of the toughest, most macho men in sports not being the least bit ashamed to repeatedly profess their love for one another. That kiss Rodriguez gave Urbina after Game 1 of the World Series? It wasn't the first.

When it was over, there were no shortage of people willing to stand up and tell you they'd predicted the Marlins would win. Don't believe them; in April, that was a bet even Pete Rose wouldn't have taken.

"I didn't even think we'd have a winning record this season," Penny said when it was over.

The Florida Marlins world champions? Hey, stranger things have happened.

Just not very often.

Introduction

By Dan Schlossberg

I admit it. I laughed every time the Florida Marlins made a player move last year.

Pudge Rodriguez? Why would a budget-conscious team take a $10 million gamble on a man coming off three straight injury-riddled seasons?

Ugie Urbina? How did the Marlins outbid a half-dozen other clubs, contenders and pretenders, without giving up a major-leaguer in return?

When A.J. Burnett went on the shelf, and then Josh Beckett, I figured Florida wouldn't be a factor in the National League East, or even in the wild-card race. If any NL East team was going to take the wild card, it would probably be Philadelphia, fortified by Jim Thome and Kevin Millwood. Or so it seemed.

Frankly, Florida had a track record of putting payroll considerations above winning percentage. Whenever a player's contract became too pricey, the Marlins managed to ship him off, usually for a package of prospects. That tradition started under H. Wayne Huizenga, the self-made billionaire who brought baseball to South Florida, spent a fortune to buy a world championship in 1997, and then dismantled the club because it was costing him millions.

Another owner, John Henry, lasted only two years, giving way to a New York art dealer named Jeffrey Loria. In his first year, there was no inkling things would be different.

The list of ex-Marlins was long: Moises Alou, Kevin Brown, Ryan Dempster, Cliff Floyd, Charles Johnson, Al Leiter, Robb Nen, Mike Piazza, Edgar Renteria, Gary Sheffield, and Preston Wilson, among others. But trading a virtual All-Star team is one thing; acquiring quality prospects in exchange is another.

Under Dave Dombrowski, their original general manager, and then under successor Larry Beinfest, the Marlins quietly assembled an army of blue-chip prospects culled from other organizations. Since bottom-feeding clubs pick first in the amateur draft, they also got to choose the choicest plums from an untouched salad bar. Josh Beckett is just one example.

Emphasizing scouting, trading, and bargain hunting, Florida found a formula that worked: pitching, speed, and defense, with a touch of power and a ton of youthful enthusiasm. Kids came up from the minors and clicked. Veterans crossed league lines in time to make major contributions. Injured pitchers recovered in time to lead a stunning stretch drive. And an old man, virtually forgotten by the baseball world, gave up retirement on the farm to lead these kids to the world title.

Jack McKeon may not have been the second coming of Moses, but he parted the Red Sea and drowned seven rivals for the NL's wild-card berth, the Giant juggernaut of Barry Bonds, the long-deprived Cubs, and finally the overconfident Yankees. Constantly underestimated by the experts, Florida found ways to win, capitalizing on errors, staging two-out rallies, and destroying the myth of home-field advantage.

The only team in the majors that banked heavily on the running game, the Marlins rebounded from 10 games under .500 to post the best record in the majors for the final four months. This is the story of that improbable run, of a team that celebrated its diversity, and a group that wouldn't quit, even when trailing in all three rounds of postseason play.

The Marlins won because they refused to lose. They didn't care if they had two outs, two strikes, and nobody on base. Florida flourished frequently with black clouds on the horizon.

Miracle Over Miami is an answer to those who said the Marlins should be contracted—that Florida is only good for spring training. The 2003 Marlins spent the winter hearing a very different message from their fans.

Jeff Conine is congratulated by teammate Derrek Lee, left, after belting a three-run homer against the Phillies on September 23 to lead Florida to a 5-4 comeback victory.
AP/WWP

Chapter 1

WILD ABOUT THE WILD CARD

The wild card is a great thing. Since its inception, it's given fans so much more to be enthusiastic about, right down to the last day of the season. To come into a wild-card race in 2003 with five teams within a game and a half or two games, that was crazy. You know there are good quality teams behind you and you're going to have to play some great ball down the stretch to get into the playoffs.

I don't know how confident I was, coming into the last month, thinking we would be able to do it. But every night we found a way to eke out a win. It was fun. We did a lot of scoreboard watching, every night as you take your position in the field, to see what the other scores were.

Being able to be thrust into a battle like that was so exciting, to get back into the playoff hunt which I hadn't been in for six years. To come over here and have every game mean so much was great. Every inning, every pitch, every at-bat could mean the difference between a win and a loss.

When you amplify it like that, that last month seemed like I was here for the whole season.

—Jeff Conine

Two world titles. A 6-0 record in postseason series. Zero divisional crowns.

No wonder Florida is wild about the wild card.

Babe Ruth would not recognize the term, a Bud Selig brainstorm conceived to promote parity, sustain fan interest, and raise revenues through smaller divisions and larger playoffs.

In 1994, four years before Selig became the first owner-turned-commissioner, each of the two 14-team leagues changed from a two-division format to three. Divisions that had been the same size, with seven teams each, suddenly had a 5-5-4 configuration, making it easier for teams in the smallest divisions to finish first (the National League is now 5-5-6, with two new teams added in 1998).

Three divisions meant three champions and the need for a playoff before the playoff. Enter the Division Series, pitting the team with the best record against a "wild-card" opponent, the second-place team with the best record. The other two division winners would also face off, with the winners of each league's two Division Series advancing to the Championship Series.

Adding another round of playoffs infuriated baseball purists, who said such a device increased the odds that the best teams might not reach the World Series. But Selig, who spent six years as chairman of baseball's Executive Committee while allegedly searching for a full-time commissioner, insisted fan interest would linger longer in multiple cities, not just those of the likely divisional champions.

After the 1994 postseason was cancelled by a player strike, Selig's theory proved true in 1995 when the Colorado Rockies, in their third season, won the National League wild-card chase and reached the playoffs. They didn't last long, but their success showed almost anybody could win.

Two years later, the Florida Marlins took the idea further. They not only swept the Division Series from the San Francisco Giants but beat the Atlanta Braves in the Championship Series and the Cleveland Indians in the World Series. Though they finished nine games behind during the regular season, the Marlins had become the first wild-card team to win a world championship.

Six seasons later, they did it again. After a dreadful start that cost manager Jeff Torborg his job, the Marlins closed with a rush, posting baseball's best record over the final four months. Ten games behind the Braves in the NL East, they again beat the Giants in the first round, then needed seven games to beat the Chicago Cubs and six to knock off the New York Yankees to earn their second world championship.

One year after *two* wild-card winners had reached the World Series for the first time, every team insisted on taking its shot.

Florida had hoped to follow in the footsteps of the San Francisco Giants and Anaheim Angels, the two wild-card winners of the previous year. But it had given no hint of challenging for a wild-card berth prior to July.

After losing their March 31 opener to Philadelphia, the Marlins ambled through April at a .500 pace (14-14). The bottom fell out in May, when the team endured two six-game losing streaks even though it changed managers in between.

"This is a better team than we've shown," general manager Larry Beinfest told *USA Today Sports Weekly*. "This team should be in the pennant race. Right now we're not. There's enough time to turn it around and get back in it. That's part of the reason for making the change now."

The kind, gentle Torborg was out, and crusty old Jack McKeon was in. Despite McKeon's reputation for always having a trick up his sleeve, the change didn't help right away.

On May 22, after suffering a sweep in Montreal, the Marlins were 19-29. Eight days later, still five games under .500, their 26-31 record left them essentially tied for last place, 12 games behind the Braves. They were also last in the eight-team scramble for the wild card, eight games behind the front-running Expos.

A 16-11 mark in June helped the Marlins reach .500, but their 42-42 record left them last in the wild-card standings, five and a half games behind Philadelphia.

Things changed as the weather warmed. The return of injured starter Josh Beckett, the acquisition of veteran closer Ugueth Urbina, and the continued success of rookies Dontrelle Willis and Miguel Cabrera helped the Marlins emerge as a serious wild-card contender.

No fewer than eight National League teams were still alive by July 4th weekend, and the lead kept switching back and forth, like a squirrel trying to cross the street. Only four games separated the Crazy Eight, with the Philadelphia Phillies (47-38) and Arizona Diamondbacks (48-39) leading the pack.

Also in the wild, wild race were the Montreal Expos, St. Louis Cardinals, Chicago Cubs, Houston Astros, and Los Angeles Dodgers. With Atlanta and San Francisco comfortably ahead in both the East and West, the Cubs and Astros, barely over .500 at 44-43, were bidding for both the NL Central crown and the wild card, while the entire group was keeping a watchful eye on the surging Marlins, rejuvenated by their rookie sensations.

After sweeping a late-July series in Philadelphia, Florida stood three games behind the wild-card leaders and captured the attention of Phillies manager Larry Bowa.

"Florida played like we had been playing," he said. "They got key hits, moved runners, and created things."

Though McKeon saluted his charges with a "We're on a roll" announcement, inwardly he was cautious. He remembered 1999, when his Cincinnati Reds dropped two of three to struggling Milwaukee over the final weekend, forcing a one-game playoff against the Mets for the wild-card berth. Al Leiter threw a two-hit shutout, and the Reds, on the verge of winning the NL Central, wound up with nothing.

"At the first meeting I had with the players, I told them we could make the playoffs," McKeon confided. "All they had to do was dig deeper, work hard, give 100 percent, and play unselfish baseball."

With a 17-7 record during the month, the team moved into second place, a game and a half behind the Phillies in the wild-card standings, though still 12 games behind Atlanta in the division.

"We've had some growing pains," said Mike Lowell, the slugger who survived a half-season of trade rumors to remain with the team, "but right now everything is coming together."

Realizing the race was serious, Marlins management made major moves to bulk up the potential postseason roster. Chad Fox, Rick Helling, and Lenny Harris were signed as free agents, and Jeff Conine, an original Marlin, returned from Baltimore at the end of August to replace the injured Mike Lowell. But the dog days proved too difficult as Florida floundered with a 14-14 record.

The Expos had been hot, with 11 wins in 15 games, but the Marlins, Phillies, and other pretenders to the throne had stumbled around the far turn before entering the final month. The August 29 sports section of *USA Today* even had a headline that read "NL wild card: You take it; no, it's yours."

Entering September, Florida was tied for first in the wild-card standings with a 73-63 mark, matching Philadelphia's mark but a game and a half up on the Dodgers. Even an August-ending sweep of the Expos didn't do much for Florida's fading title chances in the NL East; the Braves had entered September with a 14-game lead. But every time the Marlins looked up, they saw the wild-card prize hanging like mistletoe over a doorjam.

Because so many teams were involved, the ninth National League wild-card race was more prolonged and more involved than any previous one. By Labor Day weekend, seven clubs were still alive, with just two games separating them from top to bottom.

The youthful Marlins started the final month by finishing off the Expos, who had entered the four-game series tied for tops in the wild-card standings. Florida stayed as hot as the weather, parlaying potent pitching, dynamic defense, and timely hitting into an 18-8 record, best in the division that month. But it wasn't a cakewalk.

On September 15, Philadelphia beat Florida, 14-0, to pull within a half game. The Marlins bounced back to win the following night, 11-4, but dropped the series finale, 5-4, before heading south to Atlanta.

"We had the lead but just didn't hold it," said McKeon, whose team blew leads of 3-0 and 4-3 in the game. "When you get a three-run lead, you've got to close them out."

Some critics contended the manager should have used Braden Looper or Ugie Urbina, while others charged he had already used Looper too much. But no one on the Florida staff seemed capable of stopping the red-hot Jim Thome, who homered for the Phils in all three games. His last home run, against Chad Fox in the eighth inning of the finale, proved to be the game winner.

The Atlanta series opened on a Friday night that meant nothing to the Braves and everything to the Marlins. But Josh Beckett and the Fish ran into Russ Ortiz, who pitched a 1-0 shutout—only the second shutout of his six-year career—for the Braves. Florida won two of the next three games, however, before returning home for the remainder of the season.

The Marlins opened against Philadelphia on Tuesday night, September 23. Kevin Millwood, Philadelphia's ace, worked six scoreless innings before the Marlins answered back. A five-run seventh, highlighted by a three-run Jeff Conine homer, gave the Marlins a 5-4 win and increased the team's wild-card lead to two. It went up to three the next night, when Florida survived a five-run Philadelphia eighth to win, 6-5.

Then, on Friday night, September 26, Florida clinched when Ugueth Urbina saved Carl Pavano's 4-3 win over the last-place New York Mets. The final wild-card standings showed the Marlins with a four-game lead over Houston, five over Philadelphia, and six over both St. Louis and Los Angeles.

Refusing to give anything away, the Marlins had won nine of their last 11 games, played nine consecutive errorless games from September 7-17, and specialized in beating NL East rivals.

Florida compiled a .631 winning percentage and won a club-record 48 games against divisional rivals, finishing with a flourish by taking 15 of its last 21 games and six of its last seven. The team had never won more than 15 games in the month of September.

For the season, Florida was 10-9 against Atlanta, 13-6 against Philadelphia, 13-6 against Montreal, and 12-7 against New York. They struggled against Central Division teams, posting winning records only against the lowly Reds and Brewers, and against NL West opponents, losing more than they won against all but Arizona and San Diego.

The schedule had worked in Florida's favor: with the exception of a three-game Pittsburgh series early in the month, their September itinerary listed games only against NL East rivals, including six games versus Philadelphia. Winning four of those six helped the Fish finish their march to October.

The Marlins would not have reached the postseason without the wild card.

"This one might be a little sweeter because nobody thought we could do this," said Jeff Conine at the conclusion of the regular season. He should know, as he's the only man to play for both Florida world champions.

Although the 1997 Marlins were the first wild-card team to reach the World Series, three of the last four World Series contestants also got there via the wild-card route.

"Winning the wild card makes you big-game ready," said Marlins first baseman Derrek Lee.

Not that the concept isn't without its naysayers.

"Critics accused us of cheapening the pennant races and the World Series," Bud Selig admitted. "Now, nearly a decade after we implemented the wild card and three-division play, it has worked out even better than we thought it would."

That's especially true in South Florida.

Shortstop Edgar Renteria is carried off the field by teammates Livan Hernandez, left, and Gary Sheffield after driving in the 1997 series-winning run in the bottom of the 11th.

Chapter 2
THEN
AND NOW

Right from the get-go in '97, we knew we had something special. We were 26-5 in spring training. It was a joke. We knew we were going to make the playoffs.

On the flip side of that, I came back to a team that had a lot of question marks and so many unproven players, unproven pitchers and guys who hadn't played a full season in the big leagues.

The '97 team had so much confidence because we had proven veterans who had been in the playoffs before. That was our motivation then. This time it was youthful enthusiasm, kids who didn't care about pressure or big games. They cared about playing baseball. They went out there, they had fun, we laughed, and we had a good time.

It was all business—like in '97—but this was more fun. Like sandlot ball, kids grabbing some sticks and putting a bunch of tape together and having a tapeball game on the street corner. That's the way it felt sometimes.

It was funny, one of the first nights I was here, I was standing on the top step of the dugout next to Dontrelle for the National Anthem. And he just looks at me and says, "Man, I'm standing next to Mr. Marlin! Mr. Marlin! That's unbelievable." It showed his enthusiasm for the game and respect for the players who have played it and his gratefulness just to be there. It was so refreshing. We didn't have that in 1997.

—Jeff Conine

The Florida Marlins are the only playoff team that has never lost a postseason series. In both 1997 and 2003, the team reached the playoffs via the wild-card route, then pulled off a trio of upsets against heavily favored opponents.

Though the world championships occurred within a seven-year span, the two Florida winners were as different as grapefruits and oranges. Other than Jeff Conine, who played for both clubs, the only things they had in common were their black and teal uniforms.

The '97 edition was the best team money could buy, at least in the eyes of H. Wayne Huizenga, the man who brought big-league baseball to South Florida in 1993. Pitchers Kevin Brown, Al Leiter, Livan Hernandez, and Alex Fernandez, third baseman Bobby Bonilla, and outfielders Devon White and Moises Alou were all signed as free agents, along with versatile reserves Jim Eisenreich and John Cangelosi. Slugging outfielder Gary Sheffield, infielder Craig Counsell, valuable subs Cliff Floyd and Darren Daulton, and closer Robb Nen arrived in trades.

Of the major players, only shortstop Edgar Renteria, signed out of Colombia as a nondrafted free agent, and catcher Charles Johnson, Florida's first pick in the 1992 amateur draft, had never played for another major league team. Even first baseman Jeff Conine, acquired from Kansas City in the first round of the 1992 expansion draft, had 37 games of big-league experience before joining the Fish.

On Opening Day of the 1997 season, Florida's lineup looked like this:

1. Luis Castillo, 2B
2. Edgar Renteria, SS
3. Gary Sheffield, RF
4. Bobby Bonilla, 3B
5. Moises Alou, LF
6. Devon White, CF
7. Jeff Conine, 1B
8. Charles Johnson, C
9. Kevin Brown, P

All but Castillo, who was sent to the minors on July 28, were major players in the postseason.

The Marlins got there by posting a 92-70 record, nine games behind Atlanta in the National League East but good enough for the wild card. They swept San Francisco in the Division Series, needed six games to beat the Braves in the NLCS, and stretched the World Series beyond normal limits, beating the Cleveland Indians in the 11th inning of the seventh game.

Florida found some help in unexpected places.

The Division Series format then in vogue allowed the Marlins to play the first two games at home, with the final three on the road. They won the first pair of games 2-1 and 7-6, scoring the winning run in the bottom of the ninth both times, before shifting to California with the Giants in an 0-2 hole. Even good teams seldom survive such a deficit in the best-of-five round, and the Giants weren't good enough. A sixth-inning grand slam by Devon White gave the Marlins a 6-2 win and a pass into the next round, against Atlanta.

After the two teams split the first four games, Livan Hernandez pitched the game of his life, aided by the overly generous strike zone of home-plate umpire Eric Gregg. He finished with two walks and 15 strikeouts, an NLCS record, plus a 2-1 win over Atlanta ace Greg Maddux. Two starts later, with Randy Marsh working the plate, Hernandez posted eight walks and only two strikeouts.

The Marlins carried their momentum back to Turner Field, where they beat Tom Glavine with a four-run first in Game 6, 7-4. The heavily favored Braves had won four of the previous five NL pennants.

Florida's autumn surprise continued against Cleveland. The Marlins won, 7-4, then lost, 6-1, before beginning one of the strangest games in World Series annals. Playing at Jacobs Field, the teams took a 7-7 tie into the top of the ninth. The Marlins suddenly exploded for seven runs, doing most of the damage against a pitcher whose surname suggested the sound of the Indians' sinking title chances. Eric Plunk yielded two hits, two walks, and the first four runs. Cleveland contributed three ninth-inning errors.

Here's what happened.

Bonilla walked. Daulton singled to center. Marquis Grissom, trying to nail Bonilla at third, made a bad throw, allowing Bonilla to score and Daulton (who had reached second on the throw) to take third. Three batters later, with runners at the corners, Plunk's pick-off attempt got by Jim Thome for an error, scoring Daulton. Johnson, still batting, singled to put runners on the corners.

New pitcher Al Morman induced a Counsell grounder to second, but Tony Fernandez, usually a sure-handed fielder, made the third error of the frame. Floyd scored, giving Florida a 10-7 lead. Sheffield and Bonilla followed with consecutive two-run singles. Seven runs, four hits, three errors, and a 14-7 Florida lead.

The Indians, embarrassed by their fielding foibles, recovered in time to post a four-spot against Robb Nen in the bottom of the ninth. But it wasn't enough. The Marlins won, 14-11, in the wildest postseason game since the Toronto Blue Jays beat the Philadelphia Phillies, 15-14, in the fourth game of the 1993 World Series. The 15-14 game had consumed a record four hours and 15 minutes, only three minutes longer than the third game of the 1997 Series.

Cleveland evened the series with a 10-3 triumph over southpaw Tony Saunders, but Florida survived a three-run ninth to take Game 5 by an 8-7 score.

With both remaining games in Florida, the Marlins loomed as likely champions. But Indian pitcher Chad Ogea, winner of Game 2, postponed the celebration with a 4-1 win in the sixth game. He yielded only four hits in five innings, then relied on solid work from the Cleveland relief corps to preserve the victory.

In the first seventh game since the Worst-to-First World Series of 1991, the Indians received more good pitching. Jaret Wright, the hard-throwing rookie righthander who had won Game 4, nursed a 2-0 lead into the seventh. A one-out homer by Bobby Bonilla, only the second hit surrendered by Wright, cut the lead in half. The pitcher then fanned Johnson for his seventh whiff but walked Counsell on four pitches. With Cliff Floyd announced as a pinch hitter for Dennis Cook, Cleveland manager Mike Hargrove called for curveball specialist Paul Assenmacher.

He and two other relievers held the lead until the ninth, when closer Jose Mesa was inserted. Singles by Alou and Johnson put runners on the corners with one out. Counsell, who would finish the World Series with a .182 batting average, then did something totally unexpected from a No. 8 hitter. He sent a rocket to right, forcing Manny Ramirez to make an over-the-shoulder catch near the warning track.

Alou scored easily as Counsell, acquired from Colorado on July 27, jumped up and down, celebrating the sacrifice fly that tied the World Series.

Cleveland's last hurrah came in the 10th, when Renteria's throw home nailed Sandy Alomar, Jr., attempting to score on a Grissom grounder.

An inning later, Renteria became an even bigger hero. After Bonilla singled, Counsell sent a slow grounder to Fernandez at second base. The veteran infielder, whose third-inning single had plated both Indian runs, let it roll under his glove. Eisenreich drew an intentional walk, loading the bases with one out, and White's grounder to Fernandez produced a forceout at home. Renteria, who had previously poked a game-winning single in the Division Series opener, delivered again, victimizing erstwhile starter Charles Nagy.

The 3-2 victory made the Marlins the quickest World Series winners of any expansion team, reaching the top of the baseball world in their fifth season, erasing the 1969 New York Mets, world champions in their eighth season. The 2001 Arizona Diamondbacks have since topped both with a fourth-year crown.

Even the first winning season in Marlins history failed to conjure up the fan support needed to sustain the heavy payroll. With attendance down 700,000 from the club's initial season, Huizenga ordered general manager Dave Dombrowski to unload his well-paid stars immediately—if not sooner.

Almost everyone went, with Alou, White, Conine, and Nen departing so quickly that they were still feeling the buzz from the clubhouse champagne party. Bonilla, Sheffield, Eisenreich, and Charles Johnson all left in the same trade, a May 15, 1998 block-buster that brought Dodger veterans Mike Piazza and Todd Zeile to the Marlins. The implications were obvious: the Marlins were laying the groundwork for another swap.

It came exactly a week later, when the Fish packaged heavy-hitting catcher Piazza, a prospective free agent that fall, to the Mets for Preston Wilson, Ed Yarnall, and Geoff Goetz.

The Marlins were in for a dramatic fall during the '98 season: the team went 54-108, posted an embarrassing .333 "winning" per-centage, and finished dead last, 52 games behind the front-running Braves. Even the first-year expansion team—the '93 Marlins—had done better, posting a 64-98 mark, .395 winning percentage, and 33-game deficit. The '99 team was almost as abysmal and finished last again.

By then, '97 World Series manager Jim Leyland was gone. The plunge from first to worst had taken the starch out of the highly respected pilot, who had managed the Marlins to their best and worst seasons in his two years on the job.

Floridians are famous for their ability to rebuild after hurri-canes, though the Marlins offered a bigger challenge than most. It took a while, but a few silver clouds started appearing on the hori-zon.

Dombrowski's deals, ostensibly designed as salary dumps, were laying the foundation for a new and better generation of Fish. Derrek Lee arrived from the Padres, Preston Wilson and A.J. Burnett from the Mets, Mike Lowell from the Yankees, Braden Looper from the Cardinals, and Brad Penny from the D'backs. And that last-place finish in 1998 allowed the Marlins to draft second in the following year's amateur draft. They chose a hard-throwing Texas righthander named Josh Beckett.

Once the new administration took over in 2002, new deals added Dontrelle Willis, Juan Encarnacion, Carl Pavano, and Mark Redman, plus free agents Pudge Rodriguez and Todd Hollandsworth. There was even a complicated three-team trade that netted Juan Pierre.

All that maneuvering allowed the Marlins to open the 2003 campaign with this lineup:

1. Luis Castillo, 2B
2. Juan Pierre, CF
3. Ivan Rodriguez, C
4. Derrek Lee, 1B
5. Mike Lowell, 3B
6. Juan Encarnacion, RF
7. Todd Hollandsworth, LF
8. Alex Gonzalez, SS
9. Josh Beckett, P

Except for Rodriguez, a 10-time Gold Glove receiver during his tenure with the Texas Rangers, none of the 2003 Marlins had been in the big leagues long. In fact, the contrast between the veteran-heavy world champions of 1997 and the youth-oriented 2003 model could not have been more pronounced.

Here's how they compared at each position:

CATCHER—Charles Johnson (1997) versus Pudge Rodriguez (2003). Although Johnson led the '97 Marlins with 10 World Series hits, including a Game 1 homer against Orel Hershiser, I-Rod could have swept MVP honors in all three rounds of the 2003 postseason. Florida's best player in the Division Series, where no MVP is awarded, Rodriguez won the honor in the NLCS and keyed the World Series win with hard-nosed defense and expert handling of the young pitchers. The edge goes to Rodriguez.

FIRST BASE—Jeff Conine (1997) versus Derrek Lee (2003). Lee provided Gold Glove defense and more power during the regular season than Conine, who hit .242 with 17 homers during the '97 season. But Conine also hit .364 in the '97 Division Series to help engineer the first Florida flag. Conine formed a right-left platoon with Darren Daulton in the World Series. Daulton hit .389 with two doubles, a home run, and two RBI, while Conine's .231 average included three singles and two runs batted in. Lee hit just .208 in the '03 playoffs. We'll call it a tie.

SECOND BASE—Craig Counsell (1997) versus Luis Castillo (2003). A switch-hitter with speed, Castillo had a 35-game hitting streak in 2002, when he led the majors with 48 steals, and a team-best .314 average in 2003, when he made the All-Star team for the second straight season. Counsell, a pesky hitter who had opened 1997 in the minors, plated the tying run in World Series Game 7 and scored the winner two innings later. But his Series batting average was only .182. He can't compare to Castillo, on offense or defense.

SHORTSTOP—Edgar Renteria (1997) versus Alex Gonzalez (2003). Renteria led the '97 Fish with 32 stolen bases, 90 runs scored, and 171 hits. Then he batted .290 in the World Series with three RBI, including the Series winner in the 11th inning of the seventh game. Because of his solid fielding at shortstop, his anemic averages in the other two playoff rounds hardly mattered. Gonzalez showed more pop, with 18 homers, but disappeared during the postseason except for a 12th-inning homer that won Game 4 of the World Series. He batted .256 during the season but .161 in October. If not for his steady defense, Gonzo would have been gonzo from the lineup. Renteria wins this match up.

THIRD BASE—Bobby Bonilla (1997) versus Mike Lowell (2003). Even though he missed the last month with a broken hand, Lowell led the Marlins with 32 homers and 105 RBI, both career highs, and posted the highest fielding percentage of any NL third baseman. Still recuperating, he contributed a pair of key postseason homers, including a pinch-hit shot that won Championship Series Game 1 against the Cubs. Bonilla, a switch-hitter who couldn't carry Lowell's glove, led the '97 team with a .297 average and 39 doubles while knocking in 96 runs, second to Alou on the club. His solo homer in the seventh inning of World Series Game 7 cut Cleveland's 2-0 lead in half, and his leadoff single to center in the 11th ignited the winning rally. Bonilla, who had 10 postseason RBIs, was good against the Giants (.333 with a homer and three RBIs) and okay against the Braves (.261, four RBIs), but he's no Mike Lowell, a team leader and All-Star the last two years. The edge goes to Lowell.

LEFT FIELD—Moises Alou (1997) versus Miguel Cabrera (2003). In '97, Alou, now with the Chicago Cubs, led the Marlins with 23 homers, 115 RBI, and 265 total bases, numbers which Cabrera may soon be able to better. Alou also hit .321 with two doubles, three homers, and a team-best nine RBIs during the World Series. Cabrera, promoted from the minors on June 20, hit .268 with 12 homers during the regular season and .265 with 12 RBI and a club-best four home runs during the postseason. His versatility made him valuable, as he opened the playoffs at third base, later moved to left, and played right before moving back to left again. During the regular season, Cabrera played 55 games in left field and 34 at third, pinch hit once, and pinch ran once. Despite this versatility, Alou was the more valuable player.

CENTER FIELD—Devon White (1997) versus Juan Pierre (2003). This is a no-brainer. Pierre, at the top of his game, was Florida's most valuable player during the regular season and continued his catalyst role in October. Amazingly consistent, he hit .305 during the 162-game schedule and .301 in postseason play, providing plenty of speed at the top of the lineup (best-in-baseball 65 steals). Pierre was one of four Marlins to score at least 10 postseason runs, along with Conine, Cabrera, and Rodriguez. White wasn't quite the same player. A fading veteran who was pushing 35, he hit just .242 against the Indians, fanned a club-high 10 times, and failed to hit .200 in either the NLDS or NLCS, though he did hit a grand slam against San Francisco in the first round. Pierre wins hands down.

RIGHT FIELD—Gary Sheffield (1997) versus Juan Encarnacion (2003). Sheffield's numbers don't jump off the page: he hit .250 with 21 homers and 71 RBI . But he had 121 walks and only 79 strikeouts. In other words, he was on base a lot. A terror against the Giants, with a .556 average in Florida's three-game sweep, Sheffield was less devastating in the next two rounds, hitting .235 against Atlanta and .292 against Cleveland. But he did manage to homer in all three postseason matches. Encarnacion, a .270 hitter with 19 homers and 19 steals during the 2003 season, hit two post-season homers but batted only .184, earning himself a seat on the bench in Florida's home World Series games (played without a DH). Sheffield gets the nod.

DESIGNATED HITTER—Jim Eisenreich (1997) versus Jeff Conine (2003). Like Craig Counsell, a latecomer to the 1997 Marlins, Conine came along in time to make major contributions down the stretch and throughout the postseason. Though he hit just .238 in 25 games for the Fish, he had numerous big hits during the hard-fought stretch drive. Conine continued his fine work in post-season play, leading the Marlins with 22 hits (tied with Juan Pierre) and a .367 batting average. He also proved his versatility, serving as a part-time DH in the World Series after making a game-saving throw to end the NLDS with an exclamation mark. Although the defensively challenged Bobby Bonilla would have made a better DH, manager Jim Leyland listened when the veteran third baseman killed the idea, saying "I'm 0-for-the-world as a DH." Instead, Leyland used a cartel consisting of Jim Eisenreich, Darren Daulton, and Cliff Floyd from the left side and Kurt Abbott from the right. Conine wins this match up with ease.

BENCH—1997 versus 2003. Dave Dombrowski's late-season acquisitions of Darren Daulton and Craig Counsell gave the 1997 Marlins a deep and experienced bench: Cliff Floyd, John Cangelosi, Jim Eisenreich, Alex Arias, and Gregg Zaun were already there. All but Arias, who batted righthanded, and the switch-hitting Zaun and Cangelosi, batted from the left side, making the Marlins extraordi-narily tough in the late innings of tight games. The 2003 Marlins countered with Todd Hollandsworth and Mike Mordecai, both heroes of the upset NLCS victory over the Chicago Cubs, plus Brian

Banks, Mike Redmond, and Lenny Harris, the lifetime leader in
pinch hits. But Jack McKeon didn't use his reserves as freely as Jim
Leyland had six years earlier. Hollandsworth, who had opened the
season as Florida's leftfielder, came off the bench to deliver four hits
and two RBIs in six at-bats against Chicago, while Mordecai
smacked the three-run double that capped Florida's eight-run uprising in the eighth inning of NLCS Game 6. 1997 was a superior
bench to 2003.

ROTATION—Even. Too tough to call. Veterans or kids? In
1997, the rotation mainstays were free agent signees Kevin Brown,
Alex Fernandez, and Al Leiter, plus rookies Livan Hernandez and
Tony Saunders. The 2003 Marlins roared down the stretch with the
under-30 quintet of Josh Beckett, Brad Penny, Carl Pavano, Mark
Redman, and Dontrelle Willis. Brown led the '97 team with 205
strikeouts, 237 innings pitched, six complete games, and a 2.69
ERA, while Fernandez topped the staff with 17 wins. But
Hernandez, a rookie that year, stole the show in October, winning
MVP honors in both the NLCS and the World Series. He was 2-0
in the Fall Classic after he and Brown both posted 2-0 marks against
the Braves in the NLCS. In 2003, Willis, Redman, and Penny finished with a staff-best 14 wins, Redman led with three completions,
and Beckett had the best ERA (3.04) and most strikeouts (152) even
though he missed two months with elbow problems. Penny picked
up a staff-high three wins in the postseason, Pavano posted the best
October ERA (1.40), and Beckett had the most strikeouts (47, tying
a Randy Johnson record). Beckett's two complete-game shutouts,
plus his yeoman relief work, saved two series.

BULLPEN—1997 is the victor in this comparison. Robb Nen
was 27 when he came out of the Florida bullpen to save 35 games
during the 1997 regular season, plus two more in each of the three
postseason rounds. Nen, who did not yield an earned run in the first
two playoff rounds, had only one World Series meltdown: a four-run
Indian revolt that narrowed Florida's Game 3 margin of victory to
14-7. He received solid support from Jay Powell, whose 74 appearances led the '97 Marlins, fellow righthander Antonio Alfonseca, and

lefties Dennis Cook, Ed Vosberg, and Felix Heredia. Last year's combination of Braden Looper and midseason arrival Ugie Urbina nearly matched Nen, posting 34 regular-season saves plus five more (four by Urbina) in the postseason. Except for Chad Fox, however, the supporting cast in the postseason was so shaky that the Marlins relied heavily on getting good relief from pitchers normally used as starters. Looper, like Powell, worked a team-high 74 times during the season and Rick Helling, who started 1997 with the Marlins before his trade to Texas, posted a team-best 0.55 ERA in his 11 late-season outings.

MANAGER—Dead even. Both Jim Leyland and Jack McKeon were minor-league catchers not good enough to play in the majors but sensational as managers. After winning three straight Manager of the Year awards in the minors, Leyland reached the majors in 1982 as third base coach of the White Sox under Tony La Russa. Three years later, he parlayed La Russa's recommendation into the manager's post in Pittsburgh, a team plagued by drug scandals and free agent defections. He rebuilt the club, winning three consecutive NL East titles (1990-92) and two Manager of the Year awards. With the team paralyzed by free agency following the 1996 season, Leyland resigned to join the Marlins. Buoyed by the signing of a half-dozen veteran stars, the Marlins not only had their first winning season but won the wild card and all three postseason series. After ownership ordered the payroll slashed, Leyland suddenly became a teacher instead of a leader. The team finished last and he left to join the Colorado Rockies, where he stayed one year before retiring.

McKeon thought he had retired too: the Cincinnati Reds, his fourth team, fired him in 2000, sending him back to his North Carolina farm before Florida located him. A manager since 1973, McKeon had a knack for quick turnarounds, proving the point in Kansas City, San Diego, and Cincinnati before resurrecting the moribund Marlins last May. Capable of carrying a big stick or patting players on the back, McKeon found his grandfatherly ways resonated with his young players. Responding to his discipline as well as his penchant for laughter, Florida rebounded from an enormous deficit to win the wild card and the postseason, even though it had to win key games on enemy turf. McKeon, the NL Manager of the Year with the 1999 Reds, won the award again.

SUMMARY—Neither the 1997 nor the 2003 Marlins believed that statistics serve as an accurate barometer. Both teams used the wild card as their ticket to postseason play and overcame long odds once they got there.

Both Florida world champions beat San Francisco in the first round, holding the much-feared Barry Bonds at bay and giving the clubs the momentum they needed to go all the way.

In the '97 playoffs, Atlanta got by Houston in the first round and outplayed Florida in the second, out-hitting the Marlins (.253 to .199), slugging more home runs (6 to 1), and posting a better earned run average (2.60 to 3.57). But Florida still took the series.

Last year, a combination of cold weather and hot pitching enabled the Cubs to eliminate the Braves early. But Florida found a new formula to beat the odds: a barrage of two-out hits. In nine of their 11 postseason wins, the Marlins scored the tying, go-ahead, or winning runs with two outs. In fact, their five straight hits against Roger Clemens in the first inning of the fourth game were the most consecutive two-out hits in *any* World Series inning, dating back to 1903.

Asked to compare the two champions, Jeff Conine has a ready answer:

"The 1997 team was built for a purpose," he says. "In 1997, they expected us to get to the playoffs, expected us to be in the World Series."

The 2003 Marlins, he suggests, sneaked up on people. That's surprising, since the Marlins finished the season on a 21-12 (.676) dash. The team's winning percentage with Miguel Cabrera, the rookie slugger recalled on June 20, was almost as good. With Cabrera, the won-lost record was 61-35, good for a .635 mark.

Such percentages win pennants, or at least division titles. Getting beyond that depends upon a combination of good fortune, good managing, and good play.

Marlins owner Jeffrey Loria hoists up the World Series trophy as he and his wife Sivia
enjoy the parade honoring the champion Florida Marlins.
AP/WWP

Chapter 3
MUSICAL OWNERS

I was in the clubhouse probably 15 minutes before I met our owner. I never met my owner in Baltimore face to face in the five years I played there. That means a lot to a player, knowing that basically the commander in chief has an interest in what's going on with his team. And Jeffrey Loria was there every step of the way. We saw him all the time. He was enthusiastic. He was generous. And he came to me and said, "Listen, I don't care if you fall on your face or you do great. I'm really, really happy that you're here. The fans are happy that you're here. ...Just go out there and have fun." This guy cares about his players—cares about what they do. I think his enthusiasm rubs off on us too and helps us play better.

—*Jeff Conine*

Groucho Marx once said that he refused to belong to any club that would have him as a member. Baseball team owners would be wise to consider the concept.

During the 100 years that the National and American leagues have coexisted, owners have ranged from Hollywood stars (Gene Autry, Danny Kaye, even Hope & Crosby) to beer barons (Augie Busch), TV moguls (Ted Turner), and ship builders (George

Steinbrenner). They've fined each other, elected and deposed commissioners, awarded new franchises, authorized shifts of existing teams, and changed the size of the leagues, length of the postseason, and rules of the game. One former owner, Allan H. (Bud) Selig, even told another, George W. Bush, that an owner should not become commissioner of Baseball.

Of all the strange moves made by the mostly male ownership fraternity, nothing topped the three-team trade finalized just before spring training in 2002.

John W. Henry, owner of the Florida Marlins for only two seasons, sold his team to Jeffrey Loria, owner of the Montreal Expos, for $158.5 million. That allowed Henry and TV executive Tom Werner to purchase the Boston Red Sox for $660 million. It also allowed Loria to switch teams without losing a dime. Loria not only sold the Expos to Major League Baseball for $120 million but paid the rest of his bill to Henry with a $38.5 million loan from MLB. To cement the deal, Loria won assurances that the loan would be forgiven if the Marlins failed to win approval for a new ballpark.

The third Florida owner in the nine-year history of the franchise, Loria brought along a boatload of front office personnel and equipment, plus his field manager, coaches, scouts, and a few players. He even won approval for a swap of spring training camps, with the Expos heading north to Space Coast Stadium in Viera and the Marlins moving closer to home, relocating to Jupiter's Roger Dean Stadium, newest and swankiest of the spring training facilities in Florida.

Had the game of musical owners occurred earlier, the site swap would have been immediate. Instead, it was put off for a year—long enough for a smoother transition but not long enough for the Expos to paint over the Marlin teal on their new spring digs. As a New York art dealer, Jeffrey Loria would have cringed at the contrast between the red, white, and blue Montreal logo and the leftover color of the previous occupant. But he had more serious things to think about—like filling seats.

The new regime immediately promised to put a winner on the field and keep it in South Florida. But fans, told the same thing by both previous owners, weren't buying it.

"We said we weren't asking for people's trust," said team president David Samson, stepson of the owner. "We wanted our actions to speak more loudly than our words."

Samson's actions seemed impulsive. Before the 2003 season started, he predicted the Marlins would win 91 games. Since the team had topped .500 only once in 10 previous tries, the odds against that goal seemed prohibitive.

Adding to the cacophony, Loria unveiled a $2.5 million promotional and marketing campaign called *Why Not Us? Why Not Now?* The new initiative seemed preposterous for a team that just a year earlier had no programs and too few hot dogs on Opening Day, didn't buy the stadium flags that show current standings, seldom advertised, banned cover sheets for outgoing faxes, and almost routinely dumped high-salaried veterans.

Even management hedged its bets; it buttressed Billy the Marlin, the club's mascot for 10 years, with a team of curvaceous young women (Marlins Mermaids) whose chief assignment was distracting fans by dancing on the dugout and partying with them in baseball's only hot tub. Somebody in the front office must have remembered Bill Veeck's old adage, "Give 'em a show if you can't give 'em a ballclub."

The Marlins *still* played in a park designed for football, with crazy configurations and no roof. That might have been fine during football season but not for summer baseball in South Florida.

In Montreal, a dome protected against rainouts (though falling ceiling debris posed more serious problems). In Florida, where the Marlins play in Pro Player Stadium, summer showers were an omnipresent threat. During the 1999 season, for example, there were three postponements and 16 rain delays, totaling 19 hours and eight minutes.

The $115 million ballpark, constructed entirely with private funds raised by the leasing of executive suites and club seats over a 10-year span, hosted its first game on August 16, 1987, when the Dolphins battled the Chicago Bears in an NFL exhibition game. The first baseball game was played there on March 11, 1988, when the Baltimore Orioles faced the Los Angeles Dodgers in an exhibition. The field measures 330 feet to left, where a wall stands 26 feet high, 345 feet to right, and 434 feet to dead center with the power alleys at 385. The stadium's synthetic warning track is built to absorb water, but not the mini-floods that frequently afflict Florida during the summer. And fans don't feel like sitting in sweat-soaked clothes when they could be watching the games in the air-conditioned comfort of their living rooms.

"Ultimately, we need a baseball-only venue," said Loria, remembering the chopped-up turf left behind whenever the Dolphins used the stadium for football.

Loria is just one of several Florida owners who have tried to convince local lawmakers to fund a new ballpark, preferably in a downtown location with easy access. But fan interest has been muted. Only in 1993, the first year the Marlins existed, did attendance top three million.

Even a 1997 world championship failed to keep the turnstiles spinning, forcing then-owner H. Wayne Huizenga to dump virtually all of his high-priced talent. Crushed when the team followed its World Series win with two last-place finishes, fans stayed away in droves.

Last year, the average attendance at a Marlins home game was 16,290, ahead of only the nomadic Expos, who played 22 "home" games in San Juan, and the Tampa Bay Devil Rays, who never had a winning season. Florida's figure would have been worse if not for a late-summer realization that the team might return to the playoffs for the second time in its history. When it did, Pro Player Stadium—the largest in the majors—was packed with more than 65,000 spectators per game.

"They've accomplished a lot," said former general manager Dave Dombrowski, "but the problem is that the fans have had their hearts broken so many times. Now they're in a position where they can see they're being romanced again."

South Florida weather, benign in October, is decidedly different during the long, hot summer. That's why ownership has been pushing for a new park since day one.

The Orange Bowl, where 57,713 turned out for a 1956 International League game featuring Satchel Paige as starting pitcher and Cab Calloway as pre-game entertainment, was even more of a football field than Pro Player Stadium. And all of the area's spring training parks were too small.

Before 1993, spring training was the only baseball South Florida had. Although the Marlins, Cardinals, Orioles, and Mets train there now, many other clubs previously pitched their camps in the area. The list includes the Athletics, Braves, Browns, Giants, Pirates, Reds, and Yankees.

Miami hosted minor league baseball as long ago as 1912, where the Miami Magicians played in the East Florida State League, a Class D circuit. On the eve of the Second World War, the Florida East Coast League featured four local clubs: the Miami Beach Flamingos, Miami Wahoos, Fort Lauderdale Tarpons, and West Palm Beach Indians. Miami Stadium, opened in 1949 with 9,000 seats, had played host to such teams as the Miami Sun Sox, managed by Pepper Martin, and the Fort Lauderdale Lions, who wore shorts during the 1953 season.

Three years later, when the Triple-A Syracuse franchise shifted to Miami under legendary promoter Bill Veeck, the Marlins nickname appeared for the first time. Although the team moved to San Juan in 1960, the nickname resurfaced when the Florida State League placed a team in Miami. Subsequent clubs were called the Miami Orioles, the Miami Miracle, and the Miami Amigos, an Inter-American League team that lasted half a season.

Although the pros often struggled to survive under the South Florida sun, the college game thrived. For more than 30 years, the University of Miami Hurricanes, managed by Ron Fraser, parlayed good promotions with good ballclubs to pack the stands.

In 1997, pitcher Alex Fernandez became the first person to play high school, college, and major league baseball in South Florida. He got that chance because Major League Baseball, after considering six sites for two spots, awarded a franchise to Wayne Huizenga.

Florida's journey from the Grapefruit League to the National League followed a circuitous route. In 1989, baseball club owners decided to add two new NL teams, giving both circuits 14 members. A year later, the National League revealed a list of possible sites that included Buffalo, Denver, Orlando, South Florida, Tampa Bay, and Washington, D.C.

To help eliminate competing ownership groups in South Florida, Huizenga paid $30 million for 15 percent of the Miami Dolphins and a 50-percent stake in their home park, then called Joe Robbie Stadium.

After a pair of 1991 exhibition games between the Yankees and Orioles drew a combined 215,013 fans, owners okayed one group from Denver and the group from South Florida. Huizenga, who owned Blockbuster Video and Waste Management as well as a stake in the Dolphins, paid his expansion fee in cash. One of his first moves was hiring Dave Dombrowski, the highly regarded young general manager of the Montreal Expos, as GM in Florida.

Nigel Wilson, the team's first pick in the 1992 expansion draft, never amounted to anything (0-for-16 with Florida) but two prominent players from the first-edition Marlins made it to the 1997 World Series: Jeff Conine, a first-round draft choice off the Kansas City roster, and Gary Sheffield, obtained by trade from San Diego in midseason.

After his team posted losing records in their first four seasons, Huizenga tried a new tack: he was going to win fans back by buying a pennant. Florida inked eight veteran free agents, plus highly respected manager Jim Leyland, topped .500 for the first time, and became the youngest expansion team (at that time) to reach the World Series. Victories over San Francisco, Atlanta, and Cleveland in the postseason made the upstart Marlins into world champions.

But the magic soon turned to mud. Although the Marlins drew 2,364,387 fans that season and did especially well as the postseason approached, Huizenga claimed huge losses and ordered the team dismantled. GM Dave Dombrowski obliged, with predictable results: just a year after posting a 92-70 mark, the team plunged to the depths of the division in with a 54-108 record, 52 games behind the Atlanta Braves.

"There was no choice," Dombrowski told *USA Today* last October. "After I went through all the emotions attached to the decision, from anger to self-pity to why is this happening, I decided I could tackle it one of two ways, as a professional and try to do the best job I could to rebuild the organization as quickly as I possibly could, or quit."

The GM chose to stick it out and start over. Although many of his deals laid the foundation for Florida's resurgence, many fans felt he was just the hatchet man for Huizenga. Once adored for bringing Greater Miami a big-league franchise, Huizenga was suddenly the most villified man in Florida, with the possible exception of Yasir Arafat.

Fans felt he could have built a new ballpark himself instead of seeking funds for a publicly financed stadium with a dome, and they were mortified at his dismantling of the first winning team in franchise history. To Marlin fans, Huizenga was indeed a blockbuster, the destroyer of a dream minutes after it materialized.

Even Jim Leyland agreed: the manager resigned after the 1998 season, though he noticed some sunshine on the Florida horizon.

"I think about how tough it was for the kids," said Leyland, who moved on to manage the Colorado Rockies before retiring. "For first- or second-year players, a lot of the kids held their heads above water. But no matter what we did, the results were bad. The kids weren't ready, but the ability was there. They just needed time to get acclimated to the majors."

Huizenga finally hung up his spikes, not to mention his hatchet, in January 1999. That was the month he sold the team to John W. Henry, a prominent commodities trader who once rooted for the St. Louis Cardinals. With a one percent stake in the New York Yankees, Henry had learned that nothing is more limited than being a limited partner of the Yankees under George Steinbrenner.

"The Yankee partner meetings were some of the greatest times of my life," he told Hal Bodley of *USA Today*. "We had a filial relationship, like we were all George's kids."

Once he bought the Marlins, Yankee meetings were out and stadium talk was in. But, like Huizenga, his appeals to local lawmakers fell on deaf ears. In three years under Henry, the Marlins went 64-98, 79-82, and 76-86. Building for the future, they even gave a $7 million contract to a high school pitcher named Josh Beckett. But Henry couldn't wait.

"I worked awfully hard there," he said, "but eventually threw up my hands and said, 'This is not going to work.'"

Jeffrey Loria had the same feeling in Montreal, a hockey town that had little regard for the Expos and less for the poorly constructed, poorly located Olympic Stadium. He had taken over the Montreal ownership on December 9, 1999, a month before John Henry bought the Marlins.

By allowing both owners to move on, Baseball Commissioner Bud Selig believed he could condense two problems into one. Musical owners was the solution, with Henry heading the new Boston group, Loria leaping from Montreal to Florida, and the Expos operating under the aegis of Major League Baseball until a permanent solution (i.e., home) could be found for the franchise.

As expected, Boston thrived and Montreal struggled, even playing 22 "home games" in San Juan, Puerto Rico to generate some operating revenue. The great unknown was Florida.

The first year under Loria, the Marlins went 76-86, next to last in the NL East, and drew only 813,111 fans, an average of 10,038 per game. John Boles, the second and fourth manager in Marlin history, was fired and replaced by assistant general manager Tony Perez. He lasted the rest of the season, but there was speculation the team might not.

The Marlins were on the short list of teams, along with the Twins, Expos, and Devil Rays, that were considered for contraction by Major League Baseball. That talk ended only when a new four-year Basic Agreement between labor and management prohibited MLB from contracting any franchise before the 2006 end of the pact.

At the same time, Jeffrey Loria was getting his feet wet. His front office team, virtually all part of the same exodus from Montreal, included team president Samson, his stepson, and vice-chairman Joel A. Mael, a Canadian-born investment banker whose long working relationship with Loria had earned him the owner's confidence.

Twice an all-city second baseman at Stuyvesant High School in his native Manhattan, Loria once turned an unassisted triple play. On the next play, he was spiked on the back by a runner.

In addition to the scar, which remained, Loria has deep New York roots for other reasons. His dad even pitched against Lou Gehrig in high school (yielding home runs on the only two pitches he threw). Loria saw his first game at Yankee Stadium in 1950, the year Whitey Ford was a rookie. The future Marlins owner used to needle Red Sox rightfielder Faye Throneberry from his seat in the first or second row of the bleachers. After Throneberry threw a handful of outfield grass in his direction, Loria's dad warned he'd better get used to such treatment if he persisted in ragging rivals.

"I wasn't good enough to play professionally," said Loria, who also ran track and boxed at the YMCA. "Baseball was in my blood from age six or seven when my father first took me to Yankee Stadium.

"I hurt one of my knees at the end of high school and didn't play in college. But I went to lots of games, enjoyed it, and loved it. And I studied it all the time."

Loria studied other things too. After graduating from Yale in 1962, Loria returned to New York to earn an MBA from Columbia. He then started dealing in international art, especially major paintings and sculptures by 20th century masters.

"I like to have a challenge in front of me all the time," said Loria, who does not collect baseball art but has some cards he enjoys. "I used to do that in my art business and I do it now in the baseball business. Putting together all the elements of a championship team and then watching it, guiding it, and cheering for it, is no different than helping a client build a world-class art collection.

"They're two separate worlds, but they do come together when you talk about quality of players and quality of art. The difference is paintings don't get injured and don't end up on the DL."

When he thought about changing managers last May, Loria sifted several names before applying his philosophy of art to his baseball interests.

"I kind of acquaint [Jack McKeon] to the painting world of an Old Master," the owner said. "He's been around for awhile and he's got a sense of it. He's not perfect and he's not right every day. But he certainly does give guidance.

"He knew more than people thought he knew. He had been down to spring training (with his son) and seen some games. He watched games on television. And he is such a student of the game. He was the right guy. I know I was criticized soundly the first day I brought him into the clubhouse. People thought either it was my father or I had lost my mind. But I felt and the organization felt there was a fairly strong possibility he could turn the team around."

The author of *Collecting American Art*, Loria also kept active in baseball, owning the Oklahoma City 89ers, a Triple-A team, from 1989-93. He even won an award as American Association Executive of the Year in 1992, when the club won the Triple-A championship.

Two months after the Marlins gave him another championship, Loria remembered his first exposure to the executive level of the game.

"I bought the team to see if I would enjoy ownership," he said. "Lo and behold, I discovered that I liked the camaraderie. I liked needling the players occasionally.

"I'm a big fan of the game. I'm involved because I want the challenge of putting it together and making a championship team and then sitting back and watching it work. Hopefully. It doesn't always work, but it worked for us this year."

Loria never lost his taste for winning. In Montreal, he gave long-term contracts to Jose Vidro and Javier Vazquez, among others, to help build a competitive ballclub. He did the same for the Marlins, although fans initially criticized him as the latest in a string of owners concerned purely with profits. That perception started to change when Loria agreed to go over budget for the late January signing of catcher Ivan Rodriguez, a former MVP and 10-time All-Star.

Even with I-Rod on board, the Marlins finished the season with a payroll of $53,987,955, ranking ahead of only nine other teams. But that was more than enough to win Loria a title.

"I have a good relationship with him," said Rodriguez of the owner during the World Series. "He's always in the clubhouse. He talks to everybody in the clubhouse. When you have an owner who is always there, supporting you, giving you 100 percent effort, it's nice. Loria likes to do that.

"He got mad whenever we lost, but at the same time, he went in the clubhouse and said, 'Let's go tomorrow, tomorrow is another game' and 'Keep positive, stay high.' A lot of players want to be on that team because he's the owner. He loves baseball. He loves to see the team performing well in the field. He's a real fan."

Friends insist Loria watches more games than any other owner, attending virtually all home games and many on the road. Although he has an owner's box at Pro Player Stadium, he prefers dugout-level seats near the Marlins bench. During the World Series, he bypassed the visiting owner's box for his long-held Yankee Stadium season tickets.

"I went to Yankee Stadium by myself from the age of 10 on," he said. "Those were the days when you got on the subway by yourself.

"I had a very surrealistic feeling during the World Series, sitting there watching my team play the Yankees, the team I had rooted for as a kid. I spent a lot of time during the last game looking over behind third base, where I sat when I went for my first game at Yankee Stadium with my father. A lot of memories passed that night."

It was Loria's willingness to loosen the purse strings that made that Marlins resilient enough to reach the Fall Classic.

"I promised the players that if we were right there, we would bring in some additional help," he said. "When we needed somebody to help us in the bullpen, we put Urbina's name on the table. Everybody had an interest in pursuing [him]. I remember it was a Monday and I told Larry [Beinfest], 'You've got to get this deal done today.' There was hesitation about giving up some of the players we traded but I said, 'We're talking about a World Series here and Ugie is going to be a big help. Get it done today before somebody else does it.' Larry got it done and [Urbina] was a major presence."

Three weeks earlier, Miguel Cabrera had been promoted from the minors despite dissenting opinions in the Florida front office.

"Some of our guys were not happy about bringing him up as soon as we did," Loria revealed. "He had been playing third base. Larry and I had a discussion and he said, 'Well, what do you think we ought to do?' I said, 'Let's put him in the outfield. Todd Hollandsworth isn't doing the job. The kid can play third base, he can play the outfield, he can play shortstop. People are interchangeable if you give them a chance.

"I've never been able to blow my own horn and I won't do it now but prompting people is what I'm all about. Prompting people, encouraging them, and making them do things that maybe they might not have thought about doing is part of the plan. And I'm surrounded by terrific people."

A hands-on owner who is involved in every decision involving the team, Loria operates his club like a corporate CEO, providing direction and leading by consensus. When he intervenes, he does it gently, according to friends.

"I can make a unilateral decision," he explained, "but I choose not to most of the time because it's best to have the input of the great organization you put together. Why have them if you don't use them as a resource?"

Loria also has his own views on dealing with players.

"It's not about beating them up," he said. "It's about complimenting them when they're due for compliments and letting them know you're still behind them on the day they fail."

It's also about providing the proper guidance, at least from Loria's point of view.

According to the owner, "The first day our players went out to Yankee Stadium, they were in great awe of the ballpark. They were mostly young kids who had never played there before. Some of them had never been to the Bronx before. They were excited and they went out to see the monuments. When they came back to the clubhouse and were talking about what they had seen, I said to them, 'Hey, guys. Get it out of your system. Those players you have been admiring out there are all dead. They're not playing tomorrow night.'"

Loria made a point of surprising his personnel. En route to Pittsburgh after a bad West Coast road trip in August, the owner ordered the charter to make a pit stop in Las Vegas. The players partied for several hours before reboarding. Two months later, Loria gave Jack McKeon a new Mercedes convertible as a gesture of appreciation.

The owner once wrote a book called *What's It All About, Charlie Brown?* To Jeffrey Loria, it is all about maintaining a quality product on a quality stage without burning the bankbook. Thanks to the latest world championship, talk of finding that new stage has never been louder.

"We feel we know something about baseball and the business of baseball," Loria said. "I focused on the big picture. I focused on the direction and I helped mold this team to the vision we had. How we got there was a result of using all the talents of all the good people in the operation upstairs to produce the people who performed on the field downstairs."

Chapter 4
THE
ARCHITECT

After every step of the way—especially after we clinched the wild card, after we clinched the Division Series, after we clinched the National League Championship Series, and after we won the World Series—and amidst all the celebration, Larry (Beinfest) came up to me and said, "Hey, thanks for coming." And I looked at him and said, "Hey, thanks for having me."

What can you say? He orchestrated and put together a team no one expected could win. Or would win. I think he's got a sense of not necessarily putting talent together, but putting people together. And knowing what kind of people will make the best team, because not necessarily the most talented team will win. Having better people on a team gives that team a better chance of winning than a more talented team without better people.

In 1997, we had a great "better people" team. Everybody was a great guy. There were no people you didn't like to be with or you avoided. It was the same way this past year. We just had a great bunch of guys. They use that word chemistry a lot. And they often use it loosely. But I think there's a lot to it. Our guys had great chemistry."

—Jeff Conine

Like Jack Benny, Larry Beinfest believes life begins at 39.

That was his age when he made maximum mileage out of limited resources, sparking the Florida Marlins to one of the least likely world championships in baseball history.

The second general manager in team history, he succeeded Dave Dombrowski on February 12, 2002, four months after his appointment as interim general manager in Montreal. Beinfest, assistant general manager of the Expos for two previous seasons, made the move as part of a mass exodus triggered by a three-way transfer of ownership: John Henry went from Florida to Boston and Jeffrey Loria from Montreal to Florida while the Expos became wards of the state, owned by the other 29 teams in Major League Baseball.

Maybe that's where Beinfest learned the art of the three-way deal.

On November 18, 2002, after more than a month of negotiations, he sent catcher Charles Johnson, slugging centerfielder Preston Wilson, pitcher Vic Darensbourg, and infielder Pablo Ozuna to the Colorado Rockies for swift leadoff man Juan Pierre and lefthanded starting pitcher Mike Hampton. Two days later, after agreeing to pay $23 million of Hampton's huge contract over the next three seasons, he sent the southpaw to the Atlanta Braves for reliever Tim Spooneybarger and righthander Ryan Baker.

For the Marlins, the complicated, three-team transaction was the key deal of a busy winter. Pierre, a contact hitter with blinding speed, took over the top spot in the batting order and succeeded the whiff-prone Wilson in center field. Pierre and Luis Castillo, who dropped to second in the batting order, provided a go-go tandem not seen since Vince Coleman and Ozzie Smith headed the St. Louis lineup 16 years earlier.

Two months later, Beinfest gambled that Ivan (Pudge) Rodriguez, a 10-time All-Star and former MVP who lived in Miami Beach, had recovered from three years of injuries. Signed for a relatively cheap $10 million deal that was mostly deferred, he gave the young Marlins a veteran presence and enjoyed his peak production during postseason play.

The GM also hoodwinked rivals by landing Mark Redman, a lefty who had gone 8-15 for Detroit but nearly reversed that record in Florida, and righthanded closer Ugueth Urbina, the American League leader in saves when shipped to South Florida on July 11.

The cost was prospects Rob Henkel, Gary Knotts, and Nate Robertson to the Tigers and Adrian Gonzalez, Ryan Snare, and Will Smith to the Rangers.

The off-season maneuvers were part of a master plan, according to Beinfest. That plan started taking shape during the 2002 campaign.

"There was nothing scientific," the GM said. "We said, 'What are our strengths? Where do we play? How are we going to be successful?'

"We had most of the season to look at the team and evaluate it. We looked at our strengths and our deficiencies. We wanted to tailor the club to our ballpark, to put pressure on opponents and maximize the dimensions of the ballpark.

"We thought speed played in the ballpark and we thought pitching played in the ballpark. The team was not built to win on the three-run homer."

Seeking to reverse his team's propensity for frequent strikeouts, Beinfest set out to secure speed, defense, and pitching. He wanted hitters who would put the ball into play.

"When we made the trade with Colorado, we added speed and reduced strikeouts," he said. "We wanted to add pitching depth, add a lefthanded bat, and improve the bench. We stayed with our plan. In January, our payroll was at its threshold. We were done."

Not exactly.

Late in the month, the GM read in the papers that Pudge Rodriguez, unable to find a team that would pay fair value to a 10-time All-Star, was considering joining a Japanese club.

Pudge Rodriguez? The same Pudge Rodriguez who lives in Miami Beach?

Beinfest called his owner for permission to negotiate. Loria agreed to open his pocketbook one more time, inflating his payroll by $3 million, with another $7 million deferred.

"That was the one time we deviated from the plan we thought we had executed," Beinfest said.

While the front office partied, the local press howled.

Miami Herald columnist Dan LeBatard complained, "This rotting Marlins franchise is so blindly desperate for something positive, anything, that management spent $10 million Wednesday to buy some good PR. It wasn't the best way to spend that much money, or even a smart way, but it passes for improvement around here, where spending poorly beats the other gruesome alternatives—like paying Mike Hampton $23 million to pitch for your division rival.

"It makes you wonder, though, about the competence of Florida's baseball people when the blueprint is so meandering and stupefyingly inconsistent that the Marlins will save a few pennies by firing the mascot but blow the budget on a catcher they don't need."

Beinfest saw the situation differently. Like King Midas, everything he touched turned to gold, perhaps with a tinge of teal. All of a sudden, Florida featured fleet table-setters at the top of the lineup, flawless infield defense, a stronger, more versatile bench, plus a deeper rotation and better bullpen. The Marlins also had a strong, signal-calling quarterback who commanded respect behind the plate and in the clubhouse.

"Players can make you look good or make you look bad," Beinfest said. "These players made me look good."

The Redman trade was a prime example.

Though he had lost 15 games for the Tigers, Redman also had received the worst run support of any American League pitcher. Beinfest reasoned he could get him cheaply and change him into a winning pitcher. "That move really paid off," the GM said.

According to Derrek Lee, a holdover from the horrible Marlin team that lost a club-record 108 times the year after the last world title, "They had an idea [about] what they wanted to get done and they went after it. It was the first year they had that much movement since 1998."

The mass movement continued into the 2003 campaign. In the first month alone, Beinfest made 13 moves involving their pitching staff. In May, the month he changed managers, the GM reached deep into the farm system for Dontrelle Willis, a pitcher whose arrival energized the Marlins like the crackling key on Ben Franklin's kite. Another call up a month later allowed Miguel Cabrera to give the same jolt-start to the offense.

When incumbent third baseman Mike Lowell was lost with a broken hand just before Labor Day, Beinfest pulled a rabbit out of his hat by landing original Marlin Jeff Conine from Baltimore. Again, he yielded only prospects, pitchers Denny Bautista and Donald Levinski.

"It was a big blow," Beinfest said of Lowell's injury, which occurred in the eighth inning on the night of August 30, little more than 24 hours before the deadline for finalizing postseason roster elgibility. "It was a gut-wrencher. We had come so far, and we were heading into the stretch run."

Beinfest worked the phones more feverishly than a solicitor on a public television beg-a-thon. He called other clubs even while doctors were looking at Lowell's hand.

"Conine was our first choice," he said later. "We thought he was a durable guy with a veteran's presence."

The trade cost the Marlins Levinski, one of the promising pitchers plucked from the Expos in the Cliff Floyd deal of the previous summer, and Bautista, a cousin of Pedro Martinez.

The GM had previously inked relief pitchers Rick Helling and Chad Fox for the stretch drive and signed Lenny Harris, the career leader in pinch-hits, when no one else seemed interested.

Todd Hollandsworth, a one-time NL Rookie of the Year who started 2003 as the regular leftfielder, was another who found the Fish through free agency. Projected to provide punch from the left side, Hollandsworth was pushed to the bench when Cabrera was promoted from the minors. Like Willis a month earlier, Cabrera had come up with less than half a year of Double-A seasoning. Although their *combined* ages matched the season-ending age of Yankee pitcher Roger Clemens, Beinfest was willing to go for broke. He was willing to do whatever worked, no matter how unorthodox, as long as it was within the confines of his conservative budget.

Beinfest opted to take chances on rejects. Fox, a bust with Boston, was out of work nine days after his release by the Red Sox. There was a 20-day span between the time the Cubs released Harris and the Marlins signed him. Both men prospered the minute they donned black and teal.

Manager Jack McKeon, who had trouble pronouncing his GM's surname, said, "Larry did a tremendous job assembling this club. All I tried to do was just mold it, get it going in the right direction, and stay out of the way.

"In my opinion, Larry is the executive of the year, hands down. He made deals that helped this club more than any other club to get to the World Series."

Beinfest's boldest move may have been his May 11 hiring of McKeon, a 72-year-old baseball lifer who had been languishing on his North Carolina farm before Bill Beck, the Marlins traveling secretary, recommended him. Beck, who had worked for the San Diego Padres when McKeon was there as manager and general manager, whispered McKeon's name into the ear of owner Jeffrey Loria after the owner indicated he might be in the market for a new manager. Instead, he got an old one: McKeon, at 72, suddenly became the oldest manager in the major leagues. But "Jack & the Beinfest" would sow the seeds that had already been planted.

Many of the Marlins McKeon molded into champions were there before the Beinfest regime began. But a significant number arrived under his watch.

On March 6, 2002, lefthanded pitcher Tommy Phelps, a career minor leaguer, signed as a free agent.

Exactly three weeks later, minor league lefty Dontrelle Willis arrived from Chicago with catcher Ryan Jorgensen and pitchers Julian Tavarez and Jose Cueto in a deal that sent starter Matt Clement and closer Antonio Alfonseca to the Windy City.

That deal, derided as a salary dump, didn't cause as much commotion as a three-team swap announced on the same day four months later. Florida foisted the hefty contract of erstwhile pitching ace Ryan Dempster on the Cincinnati Reds for outfielder Juan Encarnacion, infielder Wilton Guerrero, and pitcher Ryan Snare. Then they packaged Guerrero, pitcher Claudio Vargas, and slugging outfielder Cliff Floyd to Montreal for pitchers Carl Pavano, Graeme Lloyd, Justin Wayne, and Don Levinski plus infielder Mike Mordecai. In retrospect, both deals look like they came from the bargain basement.

All the other key figures in Florida's second world championship came during the Dombrowski reign. Luis Castillo and Alex Gonzalez, the intrepid double-play combination, both signed as nondrafted free agents, in 1992 and 1994, respectively. So did backup catcher Mike Redmond. Michael Tejera, Blaine Neal, and Kevin Olsen arrived in the amateur draft, along with Josh Beckett, the nation's No. 2 pick (but Florida's No. 1) in the amateur selection of June 1999.

There were four key trades, all made within an 18-month span:

• Derrek Lee, a first baseman with power at the plate and polish in the field, came from San Diego with pitchers Rafael Medina and Steve Hoff for Kevin Brown, Florida's top starter, on December 15, 1997.

• A.J. Burnett, who would later throw a no-hitter, arrived from the New York Mets on February 6, 1998 with fellow pitchers Jesus Sanchez and Brandon Villafuerte, and outfielder Cesar Crespo for lefthanded starting pitcher Al Leiter and second baseman Ralph Milliard.

• Relievers Braden Looper and Armando Almanza were next, coming from St. Louis with infielder Pablo Ozuna on December 14,

1998 in exchange for shortstop Edgar Renteria, author of the winning hit in the 1997 World Series.

• In a reversal of fortune deal, the Marlins landed third baseman Mike Lowell from the Yankees in a three-for-one swap that cost only unproven pitchers Mark Johnson, Todd Noel, and Ed Yarnall on February 1, 1999.

The year was significant for Florida: Beckett, the 2003 World Series MVP, was drafted on June 2, while Miguel Cabrera, whose power and versatility helped Beckett win the award, signed as a non-drafted free agent exactly a month later. Beckett signed in August, inking a four-year, major league contract worth $7 million, an enormous sum for a frugal-minded team to lavish on an untested player. But Dombrowski, with an eye on the future, decided Beckett would be a sound investment.

Also that summer, Dombrowski pulled off a sleeper swap, sending proven closer Matt Mantei to the Arizona Diamondbacks for Brad Penny, a starting pitcher with potential; reliever Vladimir Nunez; and outfielder Abraham Nunez (no relation). A separate swap with Arizona, a year later, netted all-purpose sub Andy Fox for outfielder Danny Bautista.

There wasn't much to write home about in 2001, a year of ownership transition, but the Marlins did sign free agent Brian Banks, a valuable member of their bench last year.

Two years later, Larry Beinfest was the beneficiary. The visionary general manager, who spent his first 10 years in the game working in the player development department of the Seattle Mariners, made more moves than Suitcase Simpson.

Though forced to live within the confines of a modest budget, he invested wisely.

"When you run a reasonable payroll," he said, emphasizing the last two words, "you cannot afford underperforming contracts. That was the bottom line."

As Florida's chief bean counter, Beinfest insisted that talent was more important than experience. The Marlins entered the postseason with a modest payroll of $52.5 million and an average player age of 29.

Beinfest knew that ballclubs ask not what you've done for them but what you've done for them *lately*.

"You have to use all your resources," he said. "It's not about that trade or that move. It's your next move that counts."

Cabrera and Willis, earning the first-year minimum of $300,000, provided value far greater than their salaries. So did the team's youthful nucleus and some of the veterans signed as free agents in the fleeting months of summer.

Before the first chill, the general manager's preseason prediction had been vindicated more vividly than even he might have imagined.

On March 30, the day before the 2003 season opener, he said, "I'd be disappointed if this team didn't play well, because I expect it will."

Florida's philosophy, from the GM down, focused on player development.

"You have to grow your own," said Dan Jennings, vice president of player personnel for the Marlins since June 2002. "The last two world champions (the Angels and Marlins) show you that. You can make trades, you can get six-year free agents, or Rule 5 guys. There are so many ways to bring guys in. But they all supplement the most important factor, and that factor is growing your own."

The Marlins are marvelous in that department, with three top farm clubs combining to finish 40 games over .500 last summer, capturing two titles and a division crown. That caught the attention of *Baseball America*, which named the Marlins their 2003 Organization of the Year.

"I don't think you ever know you're going to win the World Series," Jennings said, "but we believed we had a chance to be good. I think one of our players summed it up best when he said we shocked the world. He may have been right."

If anyone shocked the world, it was Beinfest. In less than a year, he dumped two starting pitchers, a former league leader in saves, an

All-Star catcher, and two All-Star outfielders, including the only 30/30 man in Marlins history. His return included a starter with a losing record, an outfielder with no power, a few minor-leaguers, and enough of a budget surplus to ink another losing pitcher plus a catcher other clubs considered unhealthy or over the hill.

Other general managers must have thought he was smoking something funny.

"There was a lot of movement," Beinfest conceded. "We had two three-way deals. We had conventional deals. We had player sign-ings. We had a player sale. I don't know if we're big-time traders or big-time free-agent spenders. But I like to think we're creative."

Bienfest benefited from strong support, supplied by assistant GM Michael Hill, scouting director Jim Fleming, international operations director Fred Ferreira, and Jennings, plus a plethora of scouts and cross-checkers (more than 50, including 10 in Venezuela and three in Australia, at one point last year).

"We're efficient," said Fleming, one of many front-office figures who followed Jeffrey Loria to Florida. "We can't survive on free agents, so we have to produce."

The system even produced midseason coaching replacements: Wayne Rosenthal, who had been minor league pitching coordinator, and Doug Davis, the minor league field instructor, joined the big league coaching staff when Beinfest made Jack McKeon manager in May. Jeff Cox, who yielded his seat as bench coach to Davis, became bullpen coach instead.

Rosenthal, who succeeded Brad Arnsberg as Florida pitching coach, had worked closely with virtually all of the team's top pitch-ers, including Dontrelle Willis most recently, and arrived with a pre-arranged comfort zone. But he had never worked with Jack McKeon or even met the man.

Beinfest's best move may have been one he didn't make. With Lowell eligible for off-season arbitration and Cabrera fully capable of playing his position, trade rumors swirled as the July deadline approached. The Marlins had a history of swapping high-salaried veterans that dated back to the dismantling of the 1997 world champions. Trading Lowell, a local hero who had been the regular third baseman for five years, would have reinforced the worst fears of the fans.

Florida's announcement that Lowell was off the market sent a message that the team was serious about winning. And that's exactly what it did.

Marlins GM Larry Beinfest, right, and president David Samson, left, introduce Ivan Rodriguez after his late-January acquisition in 2003.
AP/WWP

MARLINS®

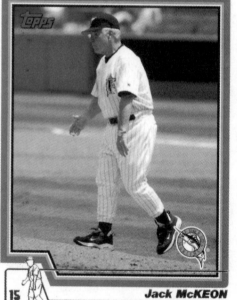

15 Jack McKEON
MANAGER

Chapter 5

THE OLD MAN AND THE SEASON

The only thing he said to me, and I think he may have said my name right the first time, is "Jeff, great to have you. Have fun." And that was basically our first conversation. Go out there and have fun. And he epitomized letting the guys go out there, have fun, and play. I think everyone fed off that. We could all joke with him. He was part of our little in-dugout banter.

You want a guy you can have some dialogue with as your manager. A lot of managers wield the hammer so much that you don't want to talk with them. Because you feel like they're going to slam you or be demeaning to you. Jack's a guy you can joke with, you can cut up with. But when it comes down to it, he's going to tell you what he thinks, and if it's bad, he's going to let you know it's bad. But he forgets it. And the next day you can cut up with him again. It's a great combination of discipline and fun.

—*Jeff Conine*

Broadway hits seldom get such good press clippings.

Asked to pick the probable National League Manager of the Year for 2003, all four *USA Today* writers named Jack McKeon.

"Reversed Florida's fortunes," said Rod Beaton.

"Guided most impressive turnaround in recent memory," wrote Chuck Johnson.

"75-49 record after he arrived was majors' second best," Mel Antonen noted.

Hal Bodley's rationale? "Made sure Cinderella team didn't step out of glass slippers."

McKeon, like the Marlins, roared back to life from relative obscurity. He spent spring training and the first 38 games of the season on his North Carolina farm, watching baseball on a satellite dish and playing with his nine grandchildren. At age 72, he thought his days in the dugout were over.

But that was before Florida traveling secretary Bill Beck, who had served as San Diego's media relations director during McKeon's tenure as general manager in the '80s, quietly mentioned his name to Jeffrey Loria. Though reluctant to fire manager Jeff Torborg, a long-time personal friend, the owner strongly believed his team was underachieving.

He and general manager Larry Beinfest coaxed McKeon down for a lunch meeting at Rascals, a popular South Florida deli. They talked baseball, but McKeon admitted his knowledge of the Marlins was limited to what he remembered from a Cincinnati tenure that ended after the 2000 campaign. Although he watched games on his satellite dish, he seldom saw the Marlins. But he read the papers and followed the fortunes of players he once managed. He also had a sharp eye for analysis and talent evaluation, as well as a track record of turning struggling teams around quickly.

"I didn't go down to meet Mr. Loria thinking I was interviewing," said McKeon months after the fact. "I went down for a B.S. session, to talk about baseball. We had a nice lunch, talking about baseball and philosophy in baseball but never mentioned the manager's job. Two days later, when I got a call, I was almost shocked that they were making a change."

So was Torborg.

"Jeff was a friend of mine and still is a friend of mine," Loria explained. "We had agreed early on that if either of us had an issue, we would sit down and speak with the other, and that's what we did. Jeff's comments to me at the time were, 'If I were in your position, I'd probably be doing the same thing you're doing.' So we made the change."

McKeon's reputation for quick turnarounds clinched the deal.

As a rookie manager in 1973, McKeon's Kansas City Royals, a fifth-year expansion team, finished second in the American League West with an 88-74 record.

In San Diego, where he served as Vice President of Baseball Operations from 1980-90, he added the title of manager on May 28, 1988, with the team in fifth place (16-30). After losing a game, McKeon's men regrouped to go 67-48, second-best in the NL, over the rest of the season. A year later, San Diego finished second in the NL West with 89 wins, most by the Padres since their 1984 NL title campaign. In 1990, however, McKeon resigned as manager in July and lost his GM position in September.

"I like managing much better than being a general manager," he said. "It's so much more competitive. You have to make decisions, with pressurized situations every day, and you have to be strong to make those decisions. I think I am strong enough and tough enough to know that some are going to work and some are not. And some you are going to be criticized for. But I think I've got thick enough skin to handle all of that."

After leaving San Diego, it didn't take McKeon long to hook on with the Cincinnati front office, as senior advisor for player personnel. Halfway through his fifth season on that job, on July 25, 1997, McKeon returned to the dugout, succeeding Ray Knight. At the time, the team was 43-56, fourth in the NL Central, and nine and a half games behind. Its 33-30 record the rest of the way, the best in the division, lifted the Reds to third place.

Two years later, they were second, winning 96 times but missing the playoffs after losing a sudden-death playoff for the wild-card spot. McKeon was named NL Manager of the Year.

His resume also included separate stints, within a two-year span, as manager of the Oakland A's under mercurial owner Charlie Finley. If that wasn't punishment enough, the baseball lifer had spent 17 years managing in the minors. His commitment to the game, and his knowledge of it, were never in doubt.

"I always believed you let the players play and the coaches coach," McKeon told *Sports Illustrated* after the World Series. "You have to give the players the freedom to roam. I don't want robots. I want players who use their imaginations."

During his date with the Florida brass, McKeon gave his opinions on the National League, and especially the teams in the Eastern Division. The meeting concluded with a handshake and a couple of misstated names but no agreement. After two days of mental anguish, Loria decided to make the change.

"It was a very difficult decision," the owner admitted. "It's a very painful moment when you have to put your personal feelings aside. But the team, the city, and the community come first."

Making a change is one thing. But bringing an old man out of retirement?

"Everybody thought we were nuts," the owner admitted. "But I didn't care if he was 72 or 142. He was as sharp as he was 40 years ago."

Beinfest agreed. "Jack is 72, but it takes about three seconds to realize that's not an issue," he told *The Miami Herald* after the World Series. "He is just vibrant, on top of things, enthusiastic. His baseball knowledge is excellent. He makes tough decisions and knows he's doing the right thing. He has a lot of faith."

McKeon proved that age is a matter of mind: if you don't mind, it doesn't matter.

"I've got nine grandkids," said the father of four. "I'm used to dealing with kids a lot younger than myself. I've had great success with young guys. I just have a feeling I can reach a lot of them."

News of the managerial change came as a shock to the players. Though the team was wildly inconsistent, and had a record of 16-22, Torborg was popular in the clubhouse.

When player rep Braden Looper was awakened by *The Miami Herald* with news of the change, the pitcher's first words were, "Who? What's his background?"

Though many of Looper's teammates weren't even born when McKeon started managing, few could question his credentials. The new pilot's 50-year baseball career included service as a minor league catcher, coach, scout, pennant-winning general manager (1984 Padres), and pilot of four major league teams: the Royals, Athletics, Padres, and Reds. He was even NL Manager of the Year in 1999, when Cincinnati came within a whisker of winning the wild card.

That was the closest McKeon had come to reaching the post-season as a manager after compiling a record of 770-733 in a dozen seasons. A guy more comfortable with an alarm clock than a digital watch, he was more than triple the age of his best pitcher. Only two major league managers had worked at an older age: Connie Mack, who spent 50 years in the dugout of the Philadelphia Athletics because he also owned the team, and Casey Stengel, a New York name hired out of retirement to head the fledgling New York Mets in 1962.

To many in the media, McKeon seemed like a caretaker, a guardian who could keep an eye on the young Marlins while they matured. He was perfect fodder for caricature, with the hat, the glasses, the creased forehead, the heavy eyelids, the cigar, and the quizzical, sometimes pained expression of a man who either can't hear his questioner or doesn't like the question. Nicknamed Trader Jack in San Diego because of his penchant for pulling off multi-player swaps, he looked like a riverboat gambler stuffed into a baseball uniform.

When he was called onto the field with his team before Game 1 of the World Series, McKeon scanned the Yankee Stadium throng and realized a lifelong dream had materialized. "The Lord looked down on me and said, 'He's worked hard. Let's give the old man one more chance.'"

Like Jeff Torborg, McKeon has long been a man of faith and family. But unlike his predecessor, he showed a penchant for exposing his players to purple invective and a brand of wrath unknown under Torborg's tenure. He ignored some players, giving them the hated silent treatment, but screamed at others, including rookie Miguel Cabrera after the converted third baseman let a catchable fly ball drop in front of him in left field.

"Too many managers are afraid to confront younger players," said veteran pitcher Rick Helling, a late-season pickup. "They want to be liked. Jack didn't care."

McKeon might have been created by a committee: he plays the bongos, chomps cigars during solitary early-morning walks on outfield warning tracks, and loves to trade stories as well as players. He liked the Trader Jack tag so much he used it on his San Diego radio show. And he laughed when the playful Marlins did Jack McKeon impressions that would have made Rich Little proud.

McKeon calls himself an old goat—or worse—but insists his methods work.

"These young men worked hard," he said during the Division Series against the Giants. "The only thing I've done is tried to encourage them to hard work [through] dedication, staying focused, having fun, and if they did all those things, they could enjoy playing in October. They all believed it."

With McKeon running the Marlins and Felipe Alou, four years his junior, at the helm of the Giants, the 2003 NL Division Series featured the two oldest managers in the game.

"I think it was a real plus for all the senior citizens out there in this world," said McKeon, who insisted he felt 25 years younger than his birth certificate. "I realize that regardless of your age, you can go out there and if you're still capable of working, fight on. Don't give up."

McKeon credits osmosis for fueling his personal fountain of youth.

"Hanging around with young guys and dealing with aggressive, enthusiastic players have made it much easier for me to enjoy life and feel young again," he noted during the first round of the playoffs.

Neither a complicated man nor a simple one, McKeon proved to be the gem of Larry Beinfest's collection of uniformed bodies. The only problem was sneaking him past the commissioner.

By ignoring an April 1999 directive from Bud Selig ordering teams to consider at least two minority candidates before hiring a manager or general manager, the Marlins were risking a seven-figure fine they could scarcely afford. But not signing McKeon would have cost them more.

From day one, the master motivator told his charges to play to win but also play to have fun. His motto was "Winning is fun and fun is winning."

He encouraged the Marlins to laugh, loosen up, and work their way up the ladder in the National League East. The division was dominated by the Atlanta Braves, who leaped to an early lead in their bid for a 12th consecutive division title. But the wild-card spot could be had.

"I'd have been a fool to say we were going to the World Series," he conceded, "but I believed we would turn it around and have a winning record. I told them I was not a miracle worker, but in my mind I believed we could win."

The manager said he remembered sitting in the other dugout, admiring Florida's young starters from afar with Don Gullett, his pitching coach at Cincinnati. Three years later, he said, those same starters needed to realize their potential.

McKeon proved unafraid to speak his mind or make bold moves. He benched slumping leftfielder Todd Hollandsworth, temporarily dropped 10-time All-Star Pudge Rodriguez from third to sixth in the lineup, and got maximum mileage from inexperienced players, especially Double-A call ups Dontrelle Willis and Miguel Cabrera.

When Looper, the year-long closer, endured three straight bad outings in September, McKeon switched him with set-up man Ugueth Urbina, who had closed for previous teams, and watched the veteran save all four opportunities he received in the final week. One of them came in the wild-card clincher.

"He made moves some of us didn't like," Looper admitted, "but in the end, this was a team, and I think that was the difference. We wanted to win as a team."

The manager might have made his toughest decision in refusing to return Mike Lowell to third base at the start of the playoffs because the hot-hitting Cabrera had been playing the position with the poise of a veteran. When Lowell, sidelined in September with a broken hand, proved ready with a game-winning pinch homer against the Cubs, McKeon found a way to add him without losing Cabrera. The rookie simply shifted to left field, where he had played less than half a season, and finally to right, where he had never appeared. He also survived a one-day benching during the Division Series. Hitless in the first two games, Cabrera sat out the third, then collected four hits and three RBIs when restored to the lineup.

McKeon will do that. A big believer in gut instinct over statistics, McKeon used four starters in relief during the postseason, twice pitched ace Josh Beckett on short rest, and even gave a start to Carl Pavano in a potential elimination game—even though Pavano had never made a postseason start.

When Brad Penny balked at being lifted from a June game in the fourth inning, McKeon told the media he would have left Penny in if he could get anybody out. He added that the pending return of injured starter Mark Redman would force another starter to the bullpen and hinted that starter could be Penny.

McKeon also arranged that the radar gun readings not be posted during Penny's starts, feeling the pitcher had become obsessed with the numbers rather than the quality of his pitches. The manager blamed the outages on electrical problems, even though they occurred like clockwork, every fifth day.

Penny got the message: he won 10 of his final 16 regular-season decisions and was the only Marlin to beat the Yankees twice in the World Series.

Josh Beckett said the manager went weeks without talking to players who weren't listening or producing, while Willis reported that McKeon gave him three profanity-laced lectures on the mound that he couldn't repeat but needed to hear.

"I told a few of them, Beckett included, that they have the potential, but when is it going to happen?" McKeon told *USA Today's* Hal Bodley. "I didn't want .500 pitchers. I had to lay it on the line to them. They could have hated my guts, but that's the way it had to be."

Beckett didn't mind.

"He's a fun guy to play for," the pitcher said. "He expects a certain amount out of you and if you don't give it to him, he won't even talk to you. He ignores you. That's his way of motivating you. It gets under your skin, but that's how he is."

Willis was also a quick learner.

"He knew how to push everyone's buttons a certain way," the lefty insisted. "He knew with some guys, he had to get in their face and some other guys he would just have to talk to. Jack was big for all of us."

The manager ignored prevailing strategy about pitch counts, insisting that pitchers got better by pitching more often. If anyone didn't subscribe to that theory, he said, he'd find someone else.

He yelled at the team when he had to, coddled it when it needed coddling.

Seven games into the job, after Florida looked feeble while losing a three-game series in Los Angeles, McKeon closed the clubhouse doors and launched into a tirade that would have made Torborg blush. Under the previous skipper, doors were closed only to announce personnel changes.

Blessed with a sixth sense, McKeon knew when a player needed a pat on the back or a kick in the rear. He confided that he could look a player in the eye and know when he needed a rest or a boost of confidence.

The manager admired versatility. Two of his players, Andy Fox and Mike Mordecai, played all four infield positions and also filled in elsewhere. Mordecai twice ran for Lowell in late-inning situations where it might have been preferable to keep Lowell's bat in the line-up. Mordecai, batting in Lowell's spot, responded with game-winning home runs on both occasions. They were the only two home runs he hit all year.

"He was never afraid to make a move," said batting coach Bill Robinson of his boss. "He has a lot of Old School but because he has kids and grandkids, he's got some New School too. He could talk to these guys. He managed with his head more than his heart, and that's harder to do."

Some people just get lucky, the manager suggested with a wink. Perhaps he was thinking about Hall of Fame pitcher Lefty Gomez, who once said, "I'd rather be lucky than good."

McKeon also got lucky when a Cub fan named Steve Bartman deflected a foul ball that Moises Alou seemed likely to catch during the playoffs. Given another life, the Marlins erupted for an eight-run inning that reversed a 3-0, eighth-inning deficit in NLCS Game 6.

Whether by Lady Luck, McKeon magic, or both, the fact remains that Josh Beckett, working on two days' rest, supplied four innings of strong relief in the NL Championship Series finale and the same pitcher, on three days' rest, blanked the Yankees, 2-0, in the sixth and final game of the World Series. To make the performance even more amazing, both were road games.

Just a few months earlier, the manager had cajoled Beckett and fellow starter Brad Penny to work harder. He told his players to check their egos at the clubhouse door, putting the good of the club above personal goals or other considerations. Apparently, they listened.

A big believer in playing the hot hand, the manager stayed with the same lineup and starting rotation, especially during the second half. He kept the pressure low by convincing the club it could reach the playoffs by improving one game at a time. Over a week-long span, McKeon said, he'd settle for four wins and three losses.

The Marlins gave him more than that. They were three games over .500 at the All-Star break and 20 games over by the end of the season. Their final mark of 91-71 was only one game off the pace of the only other winning team in Florida history, the 1997 World Champions. Under McKeon, the club was 75-49, three games better than the team's record under Jim Leyland in his first 124 games.

The seventh replacement skipper to guide his team to the World Series, McKeon was only the second to win it, joining Bob Lemon of the 1978 New York Yankees.

A native of South Amboy, NJ, McKeon grew up rooting for the New York Giants (before they fled to San Francisco) and the Yankees. He went to his first game at age 11 and once caught a foul ball hit by Phil Rizzuto.

Known locally as "Butts" because he started smoking cigars in high school, McKeon was a tough guy in a tough blue-collar town. A part-time driver for his dad's taxi company, he once punched out a customer who wouldn't pay. His younger sister Marge (whose Hallandale Beach winter home was occupied by McKeon last summer) still lives in South Amboy, a town of 8,000 that produced a previous world championship manager in Tom Kelly (1987 and 1991 Twins). Both he and McKeon are in the St. Mary's High School Hall of Fame. Alumni who played with McKeon included Johnny and Eddie O'Brien, twins who played for the Pirates.

McKeon, who never played in the majors, managed teams that played in Yankee Stadium. But he had never managed anywhere in the postseason before making it with the 2003 Marlins. He was general manager in San Diego when the powerful Detroit Tigers of 1984 routed the Padres in a five-game World Series.

A feisty little guy with a quick quip and, when the occasion warrants, a big mouth, McKeon keeps cigars in his mouth and rosary beads in his back pocket, realizing they might not help but couldn't hurt. After wins, he makes a habit of grabbing the St. Teresa picture in his office and saying, "She was with us tonight."

Maybe the Saint of Miracles really did help: Florida posted 37 come-from-behind victories, 19 of them in its last at-bat, and won 53 games at home, trailing only the Braves and Giants. The Marlins also took at least 10 games from each of their four rivals in the competitive NL East. Florida's 48-28 mark against divisional rivals ranked second in the league to San Francisco's 53-23, and the Marlins led the league against lefthanded starters, finishing at 27-11.

"Whether it's magical or fate or St. Teresa or whatever, it's been the ride of a lifetime," said Beinfest. "But Jack is the kind of guy who doesn't want a lot of credit."

A devout Catholic who attends mass every morning, McKeon speaks the language of the dugout when arguing with umpires or talking to players and coaches. He's not shy about blasting a player in print.

McKeon has a hearing problem and a tough time remembering and pronouncing names. During the four-hour interview that preceding his hiring, he kept referring to Jeffrey Loria as "Jerry." Ugueth Urbina, called Ugie by teammates, was "Yogi" to the manager. And both Mark Redman and Mike Redmond were "Red."

Nobody really cared. McKeon persuaded the team, a mix of veterans and rookies with a heavy Latin contingent but little postseason experience, that it could win under any circumstances. When the pitching staff proved healthy over the second half, the Fish flew past seven rivals in the wild-card race, then won three straight games to overcome early deficits in each of the three playoff rounds.

The result was the NL Manager of the Year award, the second won by McKeon in four seasons and the first ever given to a Florida pilot. He received 116 votes, nearly double the total for runner-up Dusty Baker of the Cubs.

Jeffrey Loria thanked him with a new car, a black SL500 Mercedes convertible.

"I have to go to school to learn how to drive this thing," McKeon cracked. "I'll be strolling the beach in a convertible."

"Jeffrey didn't have to do that. I didn't need the top of the line. He said it was a token of his appreciation for what we accomplished."

McKeon also was the toast of the town in Greater Miami, where fans hoisted "In Jack We Trust" banners, wore "Marry Me, Jack" T-shirts, and even knitted "I Love Jack" sweaters. McKeon even saw his picture plastered on restaurant walls.

According to MLB.com columnist Mychael Urban, a local grandmother said, "I haven't loved a man I don't know this much since I first saw Paul McCartney."

McKeon, a natural comic with a knack for a one-liner, brought a fresh approach when he breezed back into the dugout wars.

"When I got there," the manager remembered, "I didn't think we were a club in chaos. They were just struggling a little bit. It was just a matter of getting them to go out there and try a little harder. They had the talent. I was just wanted to get them to build confidence in themselves."

When McKeon took over, the Marlins had a mark of 16-22 and looked like the last-place squad most pundits had predicted. Florida won its first game under the new boss, then dropped six straight to reach their low point of the season (19-29). But they followed with a six-game winning streak that turned them from Marlins into Flying Fish. McKeon watched his charges go 75-49 during his watch.

"Let the spotlight shine on them," he said. "They're the ones who have done everything. And hats off to Jeffrey Loria for providing the resources and Larry Beinfest for getting the players."

The 51-year baseball veteran, who sometimes called himself "an old fart," managed to get the most out of his men.

"He was ideal for this team because all that was needed was a push," said reliever Chad Fox, a late-summer addition. "Some managers mentally beat down their players. But Jack didn't do that. With him, everything was direct and right to the point."

"We didn't give up," said supersub Mike Mordecai. "A lot of that came from the manager."

Florida manager Jack McKeon signals "V" for victory after the Marlins won their second championship by defeating the Yankees in six games. It was the first trip to the Series for the 72-year-old skipper.

AL BELLO/GETTY IMAGES

Chapter 6

LEADER BY EXAMPLE

It's undisputed. In the postseason, Pudge came through huge in the first two series. To have a guy who can dominate a game behind the plate like he can—literally shut down a running game—gives your pitchers more confidence. He was basically the captain in the field, and he filled that role flawlessly.

—Jeff Conine

For Pudge Rodriguez, the cycle is complete.

Four years after winning a Most Valuable Player award for his work during the regular season, he also was a postseason MVP. He might have won two, but no such honors are given for the Division Series.

The compact Puerto Rican backstop, who has 10 Gold Gloves, also added something his trophy shelf lacked: a World Series ring. It was an unlikely ending to a dream season that began as a winter nightmare. For months, the longtime Texas Rangers star—at the time a free agent—felt like a man without a country. Scared by his salary demands and concerned about his health, general managers passed him over more quickly than a flying traffic reporter at rush hour.

Only the Marlins, seeking a prime-time Latino star who might boost attendance, nibbled. Their offer was a one-year deal worth $10 million, four-fifths of it deferred.

Rodriguez already had a 70-foot yacht and a palatial Miami Beach estate with nine bedrooms, 11 1/2 baths, and a larger-than-life bronze statue of himself in full catcher's gear. What he needed was a team.

For Florida, signing Rodriguez was a surprise.

"We had no idea he'd be receptive, but it was worth a try," said general manager Larry Beinfest. "It wasn't something we had considered. We were at budget and accomplished the things we had wanted to do in the off season. But then I saw he was still available in the middle of January. I picked up the phone and asked Jeffrey (Loria) if he would allow us to make a call. He said yes almost immediately."

At the January 22 news conference announcing his signing, the 10-time All-Star boldly predicted a playoff berth for the Marlins. Veteran newsmen had to suppress their laughter. They apparently didn't realize that I-Rod was healthy again after a spate of nagging injuries. They also didn't realize that Rodriguez is a fierce competitor, even in Monopoly games with home-schooled son Ivan, 10, and daughters Amanda, 7, and Ivanna, 3. Dereck got his own locker, next to his dad's, in the Pro Player Stadium clubhouse.

It was a small concession for a man who became a $10 million bargain.

As former Marlin Gary Sheffield said at the time, "I said the Marlins were a good team in spring training. When they added Pudge, they added a guy with credibility."

After a slow start, perhaps because of unfamiliarity with National League pitchers, Rodriguez ripped the ball with regularity. Playing in 144 games, his highest since matching that figure during the 1999 MVP season, he hit .375 with runners in scoring position, fourth in the NL, and set club records for batting average (.297) and RBI (85) by a catcher.

At his best when it counted most, he hit .323 over the final 98 games and .406 with runners in scoring position in his last 96 contests. He murdered lefties (.376) and excelled in day games (.327) but fell three points short of his eighth straight .300 season.

Florida manager Jack McKeon, a minor-league catcher during his playing days, prodded Rodriguez, urging him to assert himself as the team leader. At age 31, he was the oldest and most experienced player in the Florida lineup. But the 10-time All-Star wasn't producing, despite a home run in his first NL game. He hit .247 over the first two months, dropping from third to sixth in the lineup.

"I knew what Pudge could do," the manager said, "but he had to take charge of this team and particularly the pitching staff."

The rifle-armed Rodriguez, who caught more would-be bases-tealers than any AL catcher for six straight seasons, responded. After hitting .169 in May, when the team lost 16 of 28 games, he turned his game around. Proving more selective at the plate, he had a banner July, with a better batting average (.376) and more RBIs (21) than in any other month. It was no coincidence that the team won 17 of 24 and established itself as a legitimate playoff contender.

"He's back to his All-Star status again," McKeon insisted before the season ended. "He's playing remarkably well. He's been a take-charge guy, a leader of the ballclub."

Mark Redman, who also crossed league lines to join the 2003 Marlins, agreed.

"He brought that strong leadership and his influence of how to play the game," the southpaw starter said. "He called a great game and took pride in calling a good game. He didn't just call the pitch but looked at what the hitter might be doing or the hitter's weakness. He really worked behind the plate, thinking and trying to make it easier for his pitcher."

Dontrelle Willis, whose reliance on Rodriguez paid off with the NL's Rookie of the Year award, added, "I've grown to trust him completely. Whatever he wants me to throw, I'll throw."

Fellow starter Carl Pavano concurred. "We look to him for just about everything," he said.

"A lot of us had to get used to the idea of throwing to Pudge," said Brad Penny. "We knew his reputation and what he had done. But once we all got to know each other, it went very smoothly."

Reliever Chad Fox, released by Boston, blossomed in Florida, partially because of Rodriguez.

"He was our leader, on and off the field," said the pitcher, who joined the Marlins late in August. "Sometimes it wasn't even vocal. He could do it with body language, just the way he looked at you. Whenever I was questioning myself on the mound, I'd look at Pudge and see a stare that said, 'Let's go. Be aggressive.' If he believed in me, I believed in myself."

Wayne Rosenthal, promoted to pitching coach when Jack McKeon became Marlins manager on May 11, also praised the work of the star receiver.

Speaking of Rodriguez late in the season, the coach confided, "He's done a great job with the pitching staff. They've got confidence knowing they can throw any pitch they want and he's going to get in front of it. Pudge is the type of guy you would want on your team forever."

Rosenthal said he hardly talked to Rodriguez during games, preferring to let the Puerto Rican standout serve as the team's general on the field. Rodriguez helped off the field too: when the Marlins played American League teams during the interleague portion of the schedule, Pudge provided plenty of pertinent advice.

He also provided a powerful throwing arm. According to former Cincinnati manager Bob Boone, "You have to respect Pudge's ability to throw. There is no running game against Florida. You go into games saying, 'Well, we can't run today.' He keeps you from getting that extra-step jump at second base or at first because you have to respect his ability to throw behind you."

During his MVP season in 1999, I-Rod nailed a career-best 52.8 per cent of runners who tried to steal against him. That same year, he joined Hall of Famer Mickey Cochrane as the only catchers to score at least 100 runs in more than one season. His numbers weren't as sensational last summer, but his presence provided the lift the Marlins needed.

In addition to his contributions on the diamond, Rodriguez commanded respect in the clubhouse, not only because of his awards but because of his attitude. He even became a ringleader of Florida's Latin Quarter, which eventually included Dominicans Juan Encarnacion and Luis Castillo; Venezuelans Alex Gonzalez and Miguel Cabrera, and Ugueth Urbina; Cuban-born Michael Tejera; and a Puerto Rican contingent consisting of Rodriguez, Ramon Castro, and Mike Lowell.

"What the franchise lacked was a true superstar," pitcher Braden Looper told *Sports Illustrated*. "He was our missing link."

Rodriguez led the world with 17 postseason RBIs, an average of exactly one per game and six more than Yankee outfielder Hideki Matsui, who finished with the next best total. I-Rod had eight extra-base hits, posting a .313 batting average in 67 at-bats. Among his teammates, only Jeff Conine, at .367, had a better postseason average.

I-Rod contributed on both offense and defense. In the third game of the NL Division Series against San Francisco, he ripped a two-run, first-inning homer against Kirk Rueter, then poked a game-inning, two-run single in the last of the 11th to give the Marlins a 4-3 win in the pivotal third game. Florida took another one-run decision, 7-6, the next day, when Rodriguez held Conine's throw during a violent collision with San Francisco's J.T. Snow, carrying the tying run with two outs in the ninth inning. Just an inning earlier, with the tables reversed, Rodriguez had knocked the ball from rookie receiver Yorbit Torrealba, plating the lead run.

That inning had started with a two-out single by Rodriguez. After Derrek Lee was hit by a pitch, Miguel Cabrera singled to right. The two-hop throw from Jose Cruz, Jr. arrived in time, but the compact catcher threw a football-style block that befuddled his counterpart. Seeing the loose ball, Rodriguez reached for the plate with his hand and Lee steamed home with an insurance run.

San Francisco scored one in the ninth, when Ugie Urbina surrendered three hits to earn a shaky save, but couldn't tie it. Not with Rodriguez guarding the plate. The catcher called the game one of the best of his career.

"We held the ball and they didn't," said Jack McKeon after the game. "It was a matter of winning or losing the game."

Rodriguez was even more potent against the Chicago Cubs in the next round. His three-run homer in the Championship Series opener erased a 3-0 deficit in a game the Marlins eventually won. He scored a run and knocked in another with a Game 6 double that came on an 0-2 pitch from Cubs ace Mark Prior. Another double, in the fifth inning of the seventh game, also produced a run scored and an RBI.

The catcher had five RBIs in the opener and five more in the next six games, giving him a record 10 for the Championship Series. He then quieted the raucous winning clubhouse with a brief speech telling teammates that reaching the World Series wasn't enough. He wanted to win it.

Rodriguez took that task upon himself. In the very first inning, he plated a run with a sacrifice fly that followed a surprise bunt by Juan Pierre and a short single to right by Luis Castillo. That was the difference in a 3-2 Florida win that negated New York's much-ballyhooed home-field advantage.

After two Marlin losses in which he contributed a pair of harmless singles, Rodriguez scored the first run of Game 4, again in the first inning. His two-out base-hit to right preceded a Miguel Cabrera home run. Three more singles plated another run, sending Florida to victory, 4-3, in a game eventually ended by an Alex Gonzalez home run in the 12th.

In Game 5, Rodriguez singled and scored in the fifth inning, helping the Marlins build a 6-1 lead in a game they eventually won, 6-4. The catcher didn't contribute with his bat the next day but did a stellar job of game-calling for Josh Beckett, who pitched a five-hit shutout on short rest, just four days after holding the Yankees to three hits in seven-and-two-thirds innings of Game 3.

Before the game, Rodriguez revealed his strategy. "The key for Josh is to make him throw strikes," he explained. "He has to keep the fastball down and use both sides of the plate. He has a great change and breaker. I have to keep talking to him during the game, to calm him down. He's fired up too much sometimes."

After signing with his hometown team, Rodriguez was fired up too.

"I prepared myself to play a great season and thank God I did it," he said. "I was injured for a year and a half but finally was healthy again."

In his last Texas campaign, I-Rod had languished on the disabled list for more than a month with a herniated disc in his lower back. In the wake of previous heel, knee, and back problems, the injury sapped his power and deflated his value in the free agent market. A veteran catcher who had missed 176 games over a three-year span just didn't seem worth the risk—except to Florida.

"We saw his injuries but didn't see them as major," said Marlins general manager Larry Beinfest. "We felt that Pudge could reassert himself. Just his presence alone made the team feel different. Big guys step up in big games, and Pudge was huge."

Rodriguez, whose 35-homer season in 1999 was the best ever produced by an American League catcher, felt the same way, especially after a winter of workouts that ranged from running wind sprints to lifting weights. Rodriguez dropped 30 pounds off his 5'9" frame, slicing his weight to a svelte 203.

"I felt light and flexible with no pain anywhere," he said. "I wanted to show the world that Ivan Rodriguez is healthy and had a lot of years left. I thought it would work out well but never imagined what ended up happening."

In addition to his personal journey from worst with the Rangers to first with the Marlins, Rodriguez was named *Baseball*

Digest's Player of the Year, an honor he also won while with the Rangers in 1999.

Editor John Kuenster explained the choice of Rodriguez: "He excelled on defense, and with his powerful throwing arm neutralized dozens of enemy runners. He guided young Marlin pitchers, not only in conferences on the mound but in the dugout. He hit in the clutch, especially in the playoffs during which he batted .333. He was a workhorse behind the plate, catching in 155 games including all six in the World Series. Without him, the Marlins never would have attained the heights that they did."

Both Pudge Rodriguez and the Florida Marlins took a gamble on each other during the 2002 offseason. It's safe to say that both were satisfied with the results.
CRAIG JONES/GETTY IMAGES

Chapter 7
THE RABBITS

My first experience with Juan Pierre and Luis Castillo was in spring training. We played them so much in the spring, so I got to see them create havoc on the base paths by bunting, slashing, or hitting two-hop choppers they're going to beat out. That puts a lot of pressure on the defense. To be able to have them at the top of the lineup back to back is a weapon few teams have. Having that much speed, plus the ability to make contact, two .300 hitters who run faster than lightning, really makes the middle of the order better. They're on base all the time, so it gives us a lot of opportunities to drive in runs. And a lot of opportunities for them to score runs.

I knew when I first saw them in spring training that they were going to be tough for a lot of teams to handle. And that proved right. Those guys got on base and we won.

—Jeff Conine

Good pitching stops good hitting, but it does not halt speed.

The Florida Marlins, playing half their schedule in a ballpark more beneficial to bunnies than busters, proved the point in 2003. They ranked 11th in the league in home runs. But they scored 751 runs—eighth in the league—because their rabbits ran opponents ragged, leading the majors with 150 stolen bases.

In an era when power is prized, the Fish made it fashionable to run, bunt, and steal. With two speedsters at the top of the batting order, and a sprinkling of speed throughout the order, the Marlins evoked memories of Whitey Herzog's winning formula with the Runnin' Redbirds of the '80s.

Newcomer Juan Pierre, in his first Florida season after a winter trade from Colorado, led the majors with 65 stolen bases. Luis Castillo, whose 48 steals led both leagues in 2002, dropped to the No. 2 spot to accommodate Pierre, led the National League in sacrifice bunts, and hit .300 for the fourth time. He legged out six triples and even connected for a half-dozen homers. In the field, their speed enabled them to make plays others couldn't, resulting in Castillo's first Gold Glove. While reeling off endless doubleplays, he didn't make an error after the All-Star break.

Pierre, Castillo, or both reached base in 145 of the 151 regular-season games they started together. In games both men reached, the team went 76-53.

"Speed is a tremendous asset," said Jack McKeon, who took over as Marlins manager on May 11. "We have two or three or maybe four guys who can steal bases at will. However, we try to steal intelligently. When you talk about speed, the ability to go from first to third, or score from second, is just as important as stealing bases. Sometimes people go overboard on stolen bases. We try to steal in a smart way, when we need it. We don't steal bases just to set records. The biggest thing is being able to get the extra base."

Named after Hall of Fame pitcher Juan Marichal, Pierre possesses the most improbable baseball name since Syd O'Brien (with all due credit to Biff Pocoroba) and certainly the most memorable combination of first and last names since Juan Epstein of *Welcome Back, Kotter*.

But he runs a lot faster.

At age three, Pierre spent eight weeks in a body cast after breaking his hip in a fall at his aunt's house. He later made a practice of waking at 6 a.m. for a half-hour of preschool hitting practice. His target was a whiffle ball perched on a highway cone obtained by his father, a technician for the local phone company.

As salutatorian of his high school graduating class in Alexandria, La, Pierre pointed out that players can make up for their God-given limitations by being the first on the field and the last to leave it. Though he now stands six feet tall and weighs a well-proportioned 180 pounds, the wiry lefthanded hitter is called "Peanut Head" by teammates, because even the smallest cap is too big for him.

Drafted twice by the Seattle Mariners but not signed, Pierre worried when he went undrafted after his second season at Galveston Junior College. After switching to the University of South Alabama, the Rockies reached out, picking Pierre in the 13th round of the 1998 amateur draft. After two-and-a-half years in the minors, he reached the majors to stay.

Castillo grew up poor in San Pedro de Macoris, the Dominican town known for sending skilled shortstops to the major leagues. He helped his parents, who worked in the sugar cane industry, by riding a broken-down bike to the Zona Franca and selling food his mother made. Riding that bike, which had one pedal and no brakes, helped Castillo strengthen his legs for baseball. His eyes were already wide with wonder: he frequented the nearby parking lot of Estadio Tetelo Vargas, home of the Estrellas de Oriente of the Dominican Winter League, to catch a glimpse of the players.

Times have certainly changed: now it is opposing pitchers who try to catch a glimpse of Pierre and Castillo as they measure their leads.

When Castillo struggled in the World Series (.154), Pierre persisted in pestering the Yankees. New York infielders, worried about bunts, played at the edge of the grass whenever the Marlin leadoff man stepped into the batter's box. Pierre still managed seven hits, two of them doubles, in 21 at-bats. In addition to his team-best .333 average (tied with Jeff Conine), the fleet centerfielder scored two runs and knocked in three. He even showed enough patience at the plate to draw five walks, boosting his on-base percentage to a robust .481, best by any of the regular World Series participants last fall.

Florida could not have reached the Fall Classic without their rabbits, whose race through the last three playoff games suggested a hunter might be on their tails. The top-of-the-order guys combined for 10 hits in 28 at-bats, two walks, and four runs scored.

Speed kills, Pierre insisted. "Getting into the pitcher's head, the manager's head, the defensive players' heads, you can't measure that by numbers or statistics," he said. "We played with that style and we got into the World Series. A lot of teams that hit more home runs are sitting at home watching."

Vanquished Cubs manager Dusty Baker delivered a lefthanded compliment to the Marlin roadrunners when he compared them to the old Pixie and Dixie cartoon characters. "I hate meeces to pieces," he said.

Art Howe, manager of the New York Mets last year after seven years in Oakland and five in Houston, agreed. "The two guys at the top of the lineup can make a big difference," he said. "The way they run gives you fits."

It helps that the 26-year-old Pierre bats lefthanded, as he's a step closer to first base. In three-and-a-half seasons, he's hit .307 with 23 triples, 76 doubles, and 165 stolen bases. He's only hit four home runs, one of them near the end of last season, but nobody's complaining.

The Mobile, Ala. native led the National League with 688 at-bats, 168 singles, 45 infield hits, and 29 bunt hits. He also ranked third with 204 hits (the first time a Marlin enjoyed a 200-hit season) and fourth with 60 multi-hit games.

Adding to his reputation as a pest, Pierre proved to be the opposite of predecessor Preston Wilson, a speed-plus-power package with perpetual contact problems. While Wilson whiffed often, Pierre emulated personal hero Tony Gwynn by becoming the most difficult strikeout in the majors. He fanned 35 times in 746 plate appearances last year, an average of once per 21.3 at-bats.

The second Marlin with 60 or more steals, Pierre later became the fourth to score 100 runs in a season, reaching that goal on the final day. His 576 hits since the start of the 2001 season trail only four other hitters: Ichiro Suzuki, Garret Anderson, Albert Pujols, and Todd Helton. In addition, he's only the fifth player in the last 80 years with at least 200 hits and 60 steals in a season (along with Maury Wills, Lou Brock, Willie Wilson, and Kenny Lofton).

Syndicated columnist Anna Quindlen, who rarely writes about baseball, couldn't help but notice. In a Halloween essay about television, she suggested that Pierre steals bases "with the kind of ease Carl Reiner once brought to a comedy script."

To opponents, there's nothing funny about a lithe leadoff man who puts the ball in play, then zips around the bases like the Flash.

Pierre stole 44 bags before the 2003 All-Star break and would have stolen many more if his manager had asked. Though he stole three bases in Jack McKeon's first game on May 11, Pierre and his teammates ran less after the firing of Jeff Torborg, a former teammate of Dodger speed merchant Maury Wills. Pierre, for example, had 14 stolen bases in July but only 13 in the last two months combined.

"Juan Pierre is the catalyst of our ballclub," McKeon said during the playoffs. "He's the guy who makes things happen. When he gets on base, he causes havoc with the pitchers. He can steal with the best of them. He's a workaholic, the guy who's out at the ballpark early every day. He's looking for angles, checking the fields, checking the basepaths. He and Tony Gwynn are the two most workaholic players I've ever been around."

Castillo, plagued by lingering pain from November hip surgery, ran less than usual last year. He wound up stealing 21 bases but was caught trying 19 times. His presence on the base paths was a decoy, a distraction to rivals who thought he might run.

Pierre, on the other hand, finished with five Florida records: hits, multi-hit games, stolen bases, at-bats, and singles.

"He could have a bad day and you would never know it," said Bill Robinson, Florida's hitting coach, of Pierre. "He never swears when he comes back to the dugout. He just puts his bat down and then goes back to work the next day."

There's always a next day for Pierre. With no reason to remove him from the lineup, he played in all 162 games, matching the club record shared by Jeff Conine (1992) and Derrek Lee (2002). After the season, Florida writers named him the club's Most Valuable Player.

Not content to rest on his laurels, Pierre kept the pressure turned up during postseason play. He and Castillo swiped three bases each (one apiece in the World Series), while Derrek Lee netted Florida's two other steals.

In the World Series opener, Pierre reached base on a bunt single to the right side, moved to third on a hit-and-run single by Castillo, and scored the first run on a sacrifice fly. His fifth-inning single than plated two more, all the Marlins needed for a 3-2 victory in front of a disbelieving Yankee Stadium crowd.

"My job is to create a little havoc," he said. "After the bunt, they weren't as comfortable for the rest of the game. Joe Torre kept yelling 'Move up, move up,' but it was already in their head with the bunt. It just opened up the whole field for me."

David Wells, victim of the Pierre bunt in the opener, was on the mound again for Game 5. Though the element of surprise was long gone, the Florida leadoff man bunted again. Wells went after it but stopped, aggravating an existing back injury. He finished the inning, then was finished himself. Florida won the pivotal fifth game, 6-4.

"If you put pressure on the defense and the pitcher, it makes a lot of people uncomfortable," said the outfielder, who consciously copied the slash-and-run style of Gwynn, an eight-time National League batting champion. "You can't measure that by statistics, but you can feel it."

Pierre perfected his bunting prowess while working with Dave Collins, a former base-stealing outfielder who served as a coach for the Colorado Rockies while Pierre was there. Collins taught his eager student the delicate art of deadening the ball and placing it anywhere in the infield. Pierre, the poster child for rigorous and extended workouts, practiced for hours, bunting baseballs by the bucket. Two years later, those lessons paid off in a world championship.

The mere *possibility* of a bunt keeps opposing teams guessing. And sometimes teammates, too.

"We were playing Montreal in my first game here," said Jeff Conine, acquired from Baltimore in an August 31 waiver deal, "and Juan Pierre was leading off. Both corners were in on the grass. He squares around to bunt and I'm thinking, 'What's he doing?'

"In the World Series, the Yankees were playing the infield in with nobody on base when Pierre was up. I can't remember ever seeing a team as adept at bunting as we were."

Aaron Boone, the Yankee third baseman in the 2003 Series, admitted that the threat of a bunt shortened his range. And he acknowledged that threat could come from anywhere in the Florida lineup.

"Derrek Lee, Ivan Rodriguez, and Miguel Cabrera can bunt," he said, "and even Jeff Conine will drop a bunt once in awhile."

Pierre, a perfectionist at the craft, did it twice during the Series. He also hit well under pressure.

Picking up an RBI is not usually part of Pierre's game plan, though producing in the clutch is. He knocked in a surprising seven runs in the 17 postseason games played by the 2003 Marlins.

"I take pride in that," he said. "It's good for me to drive in runs. But Luis and I have the same goal: to get on base and try to steal. It helps the whole lineup. When we're on, they get fastballs and balls up. I can't see a pitcher being comfortable when we're on base."

Pierre was in a special position last year, getting the green light from manager Jack McKeon when other potential base stealers received stop signs.

"He makes us go," McKeon said. "When he reaches, the pitchers keep throwing to first base. They don't know when he's going to go. Even I don't know when he's going to go.

"People overlook what kind of clutch hitter he is. He hasn't gotten many RBIs but he doesn't get that much of a chance (as a lead-off man). He's a remarkable player."

So is Castillo, an inch shorter and 10 pounds heavier than Pierre but blessed with similar quick reflexes. The switch-hitting Dominican started the year in his customary leadoff spot before he and Pierre played their own game of *Trading Places*.

A clubhouse card shark who calls himself "the King," Castillo wasn't quite ready for prime time when the Marlins reached the 1997 World Series. He was in the Opening Day lineup that year but back in the minors by year's end. His game has improved dramatically since then, with a personal peak of a 35-game hitting streak in 2002.

Castillo was just as impressive last year. En route to career peaks in hits (187) and extra-base hits (31), he produced three four-hit games and a 16-game hitting streak, best among the 2003 Marlins. He also topped 20 steals for the fifth consecutive season.

Like a squirrel burying nuts for the winter, Castillo can't always remember where he put his glove between innings. But he knows what to do once he finds it. He's also productive at the plate, where he disrupted San Francisco's strategy by reaching base four times in the pivotal third game of the Division Series. Florida won, 4-3, in 11 innings.

Castillo and Pierre were just two of the five Marlins who finished with double digits in steals last year: Pierre (65) was followed by Castillo and Derek Lee (21 each), Juan Encarnacion (19), and Pudge Rodriguez (10).

"We don't steal bases just to steal bases," said McKeon, doing his best Yogi Berra imitation. "We try to pick important times to run, crucial times in the game."

Opposing managers just *think* Marlin runners are always hot to trot.

"If we can get our rabbits on base, anything can happen," McKeon insisted.

As Luis Castillo, left, and Juan Pierre, right, proved time and time again:
there's no substitute for speed.

Chapter 8

ANCHORS
AT THE CORNERS

I came from the Kansas City Royals organization that built their teams on pitching, speed, and defense. We were as good in the field as anybody. We might not have had the best fielding percentage, but we could get to more balls and make more plays than anybody else. On the corners, with Mike Lowell and Derrek Lee, that same kind of perform- ance showed in the postseason big time.

They are also great people. You can't get more quality—not just in baseball players but in people to hang out with. They're good family guys, they treat the fans well, they're just class acts. If you could make up a team of guys you want to have, those are two of the ones you pick. They're class people who happen to be baseball players.

—Jeff Conine

The men who manned the infield corners for the 2003 Marlins were products of strong baseball bloodlines.

Born in Puerto Rico but raised in Miami, Mike Lowell is the son of a Cuban-born father who starred for the Puerto Rican nation- al team in the '60s and '70s.

Derrek Lee, the Florida first baseman last year, is the nephew of former big-leaguer Leron Lee and the son of Leon Lee, a Triple-A standout who later spent 10 years in the Japanese majors.

Both Lowell and Lee were acquired in four-player trades. Lee came first, in the mid-December deal that sent star pitcher Kevin Brown to San Diego for three prospects in the wake of Florida's 1997 world title. Less than two years later, on February 1, 1999, the Yankees yielded Lowell for Ed Yarnall, Todd Noel, and Mark Johnson, none of whom amounted to anything. Brown helped the Padres win the 1998 NL pennant before moving to Los Angeles as a free agent, but the Marlins got much more mileage out of Lowell and Lee.

Even before donning black and teal, Lowell had a reputation as an extremely intelligent player. While playing on the same youth league team as Alex Rodriguez, he posted a perfect 4.0 grade point average at Coral Gables High and scored more than 1300 on his SAT. He earned a degree in finance from Florida International University, where he was a freshman All-America selection and a three-time all-conference player.

Though he played eight games for the Yankees in 1998, Lowell realized his potential only after coming to the Marlins. He finished last year with career peaks in home runs (32) and RBIs (105), even though he missed the last month after a Hector Almonte pitch broke his left hand on August 30. Lowell still became the first Florida player with a pair of 100 RBI seasons and one of five to enjoy a 30-homer season.

An All-Star for the second straight year, Lowell led the Marlins by example. But his biggest contribution came with an assist from the front office. After months of rumors that a trade was likely, the cost-conscious Marlins announced in early July that their star third baseman was off the market. Convinced that management was serious about winning, the players responded with baseball's best record over the final four months.

That momentum continued into October, with a major assist from Lowell.

Returning for the season finale after missing 26 straight games, the third baseman needed to recapture his batting stroke. It didn't take long. In the opening game of the NL Championship Series against Chicago, his pinch homer in the 11th inning gave the Marlins a 9-8 victory. He connected again in Game 5, giving the team a 2-0 advantage in a game Josh Beckett later won, 4-0.

Lowell continued his comeback with five hits, one of them a double, and two RBIs against the Yankees in the World Series. For the veteran third baseman, coming back from an extended layoff is old hat. His first season with Florida was limited to 97 games after a spring training diagnosis of testicular cancer. Just 18 days after his February 1 trade to Florida for three young pitchers, Lowell had to undergo immediate treatment.

He had another cancer scare last July, when pain in his groin prompted the slugger to seek medical help. Doctors discovered a hollow spot in his right hipbone, gave him crutches, and told him he might need a hip replacement. When the team went to Chicago for a midseason series against the Cubs, Lowell went to Gainesville, Florida for further tests. Those tests revealed fibrous dysplasia, a non-threatening condition that looks like cancer on X-rays.

"I was scared," said Lowell, whose wife Bertica had given birth to daughter Alexis 18 months after doctors discovered his testicular cancer. "I was more scared than the first time I had cancer because I knew what to expect (with a recurrence of cancer). Ignorance is bliss sometimes.

"The most frustrating part of the surgery and radiation treatment I had in 1999 was that it took away my physical ability. It made me realize there are more than just little adjustments in this game, and in that sense it made me stronger. I've made it a goal to come in each spring in better shape than the year before. I try to take steps forward, and I think it shows on the field."

Lowell lost his appetite and his energy during treatment—but not his desire.

"I knew I could work hard enough to succeed," he said, "but there's always that part where you don't know how far your skills will take you."

Lowell also found a sound mental approach critical to the recovery process. In addition to concern over his own condition, Lowell had to worry about his father's surgery for prostate cancer in 2002 and his wife's well-being after removal of a tumor from her right ovary four years earlier. The No. 19 he wears on his uniform is the same one worn by his father, who also served as his first baseball coach.

"I wanted to be a big-leaguer since I was six," he said, "but I was sure it wouldn't be in Miami. Then when we get a team, I'm with the Yankees."

Lowell languished in the minors longer than expected because Scott Brosius blocked his path to the Bronx. When Brosius was World Series MVP in 1998, the Yankees gave him a new three-year contract that sealed Lowell's fate.

"It wasn't easy seeing him go," said Yankee manager Joe Torre during the 2003 World Series. "But we did him a favor sending him someplace he could play."

They also sent him home, to a place he could prosper in front of family and friends. He did just that.

An advocate of weight and flexibility training, Lowell's power production increased in direct proportion to his strength. He hit a dozen homers during his first Florida season, 22 a year later, and finally a career-peak 32 in 130 games last year. He also topped 90 RBI four years in a row.

"I know everybody talks about home runs," he said, "but RBI is what I'm happiest about. I've always felt comfortable with guys on base and just like hitting in those situations."

He proved the point in Fenway Park on June 28. With the Marlins just awakening to the idea that they might make the play-offs, Lowell lifted an 0-2 pitch into orbit with two on and two out in the ninth. The game-winning blast helped ease the sting of Boston's 25-8 bombardment the previous night. Lowell's message to his teammates was clear: we can come back from anything.

According to Florida manager Jack McKeon, "I saw him play when I managed Cincinnati but didn't appreciate it until I saw him play every day. I call him a blue-collar worker, a real professional. He's one of those guys you love to have around."

Lowell played hurt in 2002, when a hip bruise hampered his hitting skills, but managed to appear in a career-best 160 games. Last year, he was on pace to challenge Preston Wilson's club record of 121 RBIs when his injury intervened.

Lowell still hit more home runs in a single season than any Marlin not named Gary Sheffield (42 in 1996) and led all NL third basemen in fielding (.973), making just three errors in his last 66 games.

Mike Lowell reacts after having his left hand broken by a pitch on Aug. 30.
The injury could have proven too costly for the Marlins, but instead they acquired Jeff Conine and added the setback to a long list of overcome obstacles.
AP/WWP

Derrek Lee gave the Fish another potent righthanded bat. En route to his first 20/20 season, the 6'5", 248-pound Californian clouted 31 homers and collected 92 RBIs, both career highs. Florida's career leader in home runs (129) and extra-base hits (306), Lee did his best work when it counted the most. He raised his batting average 20 points in September, hitting .341, his best performance for any month, to finish with a final mark of .271. That eased the sting of the Lowell injury and helped the Marlins win the wild card. In his final 21 games, when the pressure was acute, Lee hit .356 with eight doubles, a triple, five homers, and 19 RBIs.

Prone to hot spells, Lee reached base in nine straight plate appearances, one short of his 2002 club record. The streak came at the expense of the Philadelphia Phillies, Florida's top NL East rival for the wild card, on July 25 and 26.

By the time the regular season ended, Lee owned the club's longest consecutive games playing streak, reaching 315 before a shoulder problem forced him to miss a game on July 29. His was the third longest active streak in the majors, trailing only Miguel Tejada and Alex Rodriguez.

"He's made tremendous progress," said Jack McKeon late last summer. "I think it's a case of being more selective, getting a chance to see pitches better. Derrek is a very intelligent young man. He's worked at his trade, he's studied the pitchers, and now it's starting to pay off."

Lee also contributed in the field. The Sacramento native combined with Luis Castillo to provide airtight defense on the right side of the infield. Both won Rawlings Gold Gloves, with Lee making only five miscues in 155 games, a .996 fielding percentage. Since Lowell led the league's third basemen in fielding and Alex Gonzalez supplied strong defense at short, Florida's infield gave its young pitching staff plenty of support. The team not only posted the second best fielding percentage in the majors but rarely gave opponents extra outs.

"I've never had a first baseman you could call a vacuum cleaner," said Jack McKeon. "There's hardly anything that gets by this guy. He makes all the plays. He's a tremendous defensive player."

Florida infield coach Perry Hill agreed. "I don't think there's anyone better than Derrek Lee," he said late last summer. "He's just such a great athlete. He can get to bunts, he can get to balls over the foul line. I've seen him get to balls halfway to second base, it seems like."

Lee, just .001 of a percentage point behind the league leader at his position, also drew praise from Mike Lowell.

"I've never seen a first baseman as big as he is move around as well," said Lowell of Lee. "He's hands down the best first baseman in the league. And offensively, he can beat you at any time."

The Chicago Cubs learned that lesson in the NL Championship Series, when Lee stroked key hits in the last two games, both on enemy turf at Wrigley Field. The first was a two-run double against Mark Prior that tied the score, 3-3, in the eighth inning—the same inning in which the Marlins staged an improbable eight-run uprising. A day later, Lee's fifth-inning single to right gave the visitors a 6-5 lead they would never relinquish. Florida finished with a 9-6 victory and the NL pennant.

The acrobatic first baseman contributed to Florida's successful World Series run with a walk, five hits, two runs scored, and two runs batted in against the Yankees. He singled home the team's only run in the ninth inning of Game 2, knocked in the final run of Florida's three-run first against Roger Clemens in Game 4, and had a hit and two runs scored as the Marlins took a 6-4 decision in the sixth game.

For all his recent success, Lee didn't develop overnight. After spending much of his childhood in Japan, Derrek moved to California, became a Sacramento Kings fan, and was offered a basketball scholarship by the University of North Carolina. He turned it down to sign with the San Diego Padres, who made him their first pick in the 1994 amateur draft. Lee played only 22 games for the Padres before his trade to the Marlins on December 15, 1997.

Though he showed occasional power, Lee didn't hit with consistency as Florida floundered for two seasons. He and the team gradually showed improvement, starting with a 28-homer campaign by the first baseman in 2000. He knocked in 70 runs that year, then 75, 86, and 92 in succeeding seasons.

"I was just happy to get a chance to play," he said of his shaky start in the majors. "I knew I was coming to a young team and that gave me a chance to get my foot in the door."

Once it was there, it never left. Lee worked his way up the player payroll, earning $4.25 million in 2003, and was in line to get a huge raise through arbitration before the Marlins moved him to the Cubs in a three-player trade that brought Hee Seop Choi, a potential replacement at first base.

Within days of the deal, columnist Dave Barry's assistant at *The Miami Herald* started signing her e-mails, "Judi (I Miss Derrek) Smith." Thousands of other Florida fans felt the same way.

Chapter 9
UNSUNG HEROES

Juan Encarnacion was one of the quietest people I ever played with. But obviously his contributions were big. He had a great year for us and was one of the main reasons we got to the playoffs. And Alex Gonzalez, when you think about the strength of a team being defense up the middle, I had the opportunity to see Alex and Luis Castillo when they were coming up through the minor leagues. I went to the instructional league in '94 to learn how to play third base and that's when I got my first look at Alex and Luis. And seeing those two do what they do on the field and see them turn doubleplays that I've never seen turned before and the range that they possess—they can change the course of a game. And they did that in September and October just by being able to catch the ball and get to stuff that normal people don't get to.

—Jeff Conine

Every team has its share of unsung heroes—major contributors overshadowed by bigger names, bigger numbers, or charismatic newcomers. The 2003 Marlins were no exception.

Alex Gonzalez, in his sixth year with the team, reached career peaks in both home runs (18) and runs batted in (77) but disappeared from the public spotlight until winning a World Series game with an unexpected extra-inning home run.

Prior to that home run, Gonzalez received most of his publicity when writers confused him with the other Alex Gonzalez, also a six-foot, 200-pound shortstop with a good glove and pop in his bat. Since that Gonzalez played for the Chicago Cubs, Florida's opponent in the NL Championship Series, the confusion reached its zenith during the playoffs.

Juan Encarnacion didn't have that problem: on a team dominated by potent pitching, he just wanted to be recognized for his own abilities. In his first full season with Florida, who acquired him from Cincinnati in a midseason swap the previous summer, he fell one short of his second straight 20/20 campaign. The 6'3", 215-pound righthanded hitter had 19 steals and 19 homers, then added two more home runs in the postseason.

Gonzalez, who turned 26 on the eve of spring training, is a year younger than Encarnacion, who turned 27 less than a month later. He's also been an All-Star more often, making the team as a rookie in 1999. Only one other rookie shortstop has made a National League All-Star squad.

Although he's been a Marlin for his entire six-year career, Gonzalez is known to his teammates as Sea Bass. Former teammate Kevin Millar, traded to Boston last spring, first applied the tag because the shortstop's constant frown suggested the expression on the face of the fish.

The Venezuelan infielder, whose father lives in the same town that produced teammate Miguel Cabrera, had little to frown about last summer. His 10 postseason hits—including four doubles and that game-winning homer—knocked in six runs.

The 13th walkoff homer in World Series history came on a 3-2 pitch from Jeff Weaver in the bottom of the 12th inning in Game 4. It gave the Marlins a 4-3 win and tied the World Series at two games apiece. The time was 12:28 a.m., way past the bedtime of almost all East Coast viewers. But Alex Gonzalez, escaping from a five-for-53 skid, didn't care.

"I thought it would hit the wall," the shortstop said in the jubilant clubhouse. "I kept saying, 'Get over, get over.'"

Miraculously for the Marlins, the ball listened. It barely cleared the 330-foot marker in left, just below a sign that said 1997 WORLD CHAMPIONS.

That ended a roller-coaster game in which Florida led, 3-0, let the Yankees tie with two outs in the ninth, and then came within a whisker of blowing the game in the 11th.

While shortstop Alex Gonzalez's walkoff home run in Game 4
of the World Series stole the headlines, his stellar defense throughout
the playoffs proved to be of equal value.
EZRA SHAW/GETTY IMAGES

"This is probably the seventh or eighth time we've done this," said manager Jack McKeon. "We had the lead, lost it, battled out of a tough situation, and cashed in.

"I was happy to see Alex hit the home run because he's been struggling. This is a very interesting team. It doesn't drain on me."

Among NL shortstops last year, only the other Alex Gonzalez hit more home runs (20) and only Edgar Renteria (100) and Orlando Cabrera (80) had more RBIs. Florida's Gonzalez had four homers in three games, April 3-5, and homers in consecutive games on June 18-19 and August 22-23. He produced one personal peak with 57 extra-base hits and tied another one with a five-RBI game at Atlanta on April 5.

His .340 batting average on June 8 ranked fourth in the National League before the Law of Averages started to assert itself. The shortstop stayed above the .300 mark for the first 78 games, through July 2, but finished at .256 when he went 49 for 241 (.203) over his last 72 contests. Gonzalez made up for the slump with his work in the field.

He finished with a .976 fielding percentage, fifth in the league, and was especially tough at the end, with only two errors in his final 53 games. Gonzalez, who once made 37 errors in a season, made only 16 last year, even though he played in a career-high 150 games.

The entire infield made only 40 boots, a remarkably low number. Much of the credit goes to infield coach Perry Hill, whose philosophy of baseball defense may not rival Albert Einstein's theory of relativity, but will place fielders in the right spot at the right time.

"Positioning really helps," said Hill, who starts each series by making marks on the infield and lining them up with outfield markers such as billboards or prominent scoreboard letters. Knowing precisely where each fielder is, he relies on scouting reports to shift players around.

"All these guys are athletes who've played enough to know the hitters," he explained. "My system is a security blanket. It's there if they need it. They've been blessed with a gift. They're quick, they have great first steps, and they take tremendous angles. "

The system, which drew raves when Hill introduced it to Florida in 2002, obviously jelled last year. Florida had the best defensive infield in the National League, with Derrek Lee and Luis Castillo winning Gold Gloves, Mike Lowell leading third basemen in fielding percentage, and Gonzalez supplying game-saving defense at the vital shortstop spot.

"All four of these guys could win Gold Gloves," Jack McKeon said. "They're part of the best infield I've ever been associated with."

The outfield defense wasn't too shabby, either.

Encarnacion, best known for his bat, supplied even stronger defense than Gonzalez, completing the entire season without an error (336 chances). The first Florida outfielder with a perfect 1.000 fielding percentage, Encarnacion finished the season with an errorless streak of 220 games, topped in the majors only by Doug Glanville (223) and Joe McEwing (228). Few runners test his powerful throwing arm.

Playing a career-best 1,355 1/3 innings in right field, third in the NL behind Shawn Green and Bobby Abreu, Encarnacion made his first full season in Florida a good one. Though he missed his second straight 20/20 campaign by one homer and one steal, he made his hits count.

The 6'3", 215-pound righthanded hitter won four games in Florida's final at-bat:

• On April 23, his RBI single in the 12th inning beat the Brewers, 5-4.

• On May 9, he homered in the ninth to deny the Rockies, 5-4.

• On July 11, a ninth-inning RBI single at Montreal won another 5-4 game.

• And on July 25, his bases-loaded walk plated the winning marker against Philadelphia during an eight-run eighth as the Fish won, 11-5.

Still potent in the postseason, Encarnacion contributed one double, two home runs, three singles, three runs scored, and three batted in. His solo homer in the sixth inning of Division Series

Game 2 ignited a three-run sixth that sent the Marlins to a 9-5 win over San Francisco.

His other home run, also with nobody aboard, followed a Miguel Cabrera blast and plated the fifth and final run of a third-inning uprising against Carlos Zambrano of the Cubs in the NLCS opener. Florida won, 9-8, in 11 innings.

Encarnacion, signed out of his native Dominican Republic as a non-drafted free agent in 1992, had spent the first five years of his career with the Detroit Tigers. He then played 83 games for Cincinnati in 2002 before the pitching-starved Reds sent him to Florida, along with infielder Wilton Guerrero and minor-league left-hander Ryan Snare, for former 15-game winner Ryan Dempster on July 11. It turned out to be one of the better trades in the short history of the Marlins.

In a pre-playoff analysis for *USA Today* last fall, former Cincinnati manager Bob Boone said of Encarnacion, "He was always known as a top prospect and a five-tools guy and he's just learning how to play. He has speed and power. He also has the ability to lay off pitches now and that's something he didn't have when he was with Detroit.

"Encarnacion played for me in Cincinnati in 2002 and was probably my most valuable player during the first half of the year. He's a terrific player and he's getting better."

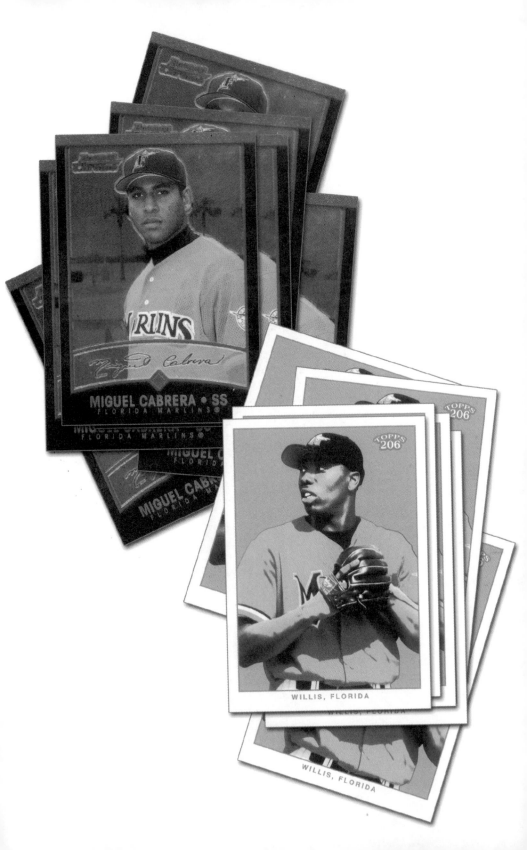

Chapter 10
BOUNTIFUL HARVEST

Miguel Cabrera and Dontrelle Willis brought to the table a naivete and an enthusiasm for the game that is so refreshing nowadays because you just don't see it anymore. You see a lot of guys their age who have been first-round picks come up touted as stars that received tons of money to sign. But, these two guys are all about the game. They're all about baseball, and they're all about having fun.

There weren't too many old guys on the team, but I was one of them. And I fed off the young guys' enthusiasm. I became enthusiastic along with them. It was so refreshing to be able to see baseball in that light again, remembering when you played Little League or high school ball, when you just had a passion for it. These guys have a passion for the game that was infectious down the stretch.

—Jeff Conine

Few teams find one rookie standout in a season. The odds against finding two are astronomical.

But three months into the 2003 season, the Florida Marlins found that lightning can strike twice. Dontrelle Willis surfaced in time to make the All-Star team, while Miguel Cabrera became a key cog in an unlikely world championship season.

"They're a big part of what we accomplished," said Jack McKeon. "It's unique to have two guys like that on one team in the same season. Miguel and Dontrelle possess the mental toughness required to handle their roles and not be intimidated. They've done everything the organization asked of them and more."

On March 27, 2002, the Marlins made a trade. On the surface, it seemed like a salary dump, another in a long line of fire-sale swaps aimed more at the bottom line than the winning percentage.

The swap in question sent Matt Clement, a promising righthanded starter, and Antonio Alfonseca, the team's closer, to the Chicago Cubs for well-traveled pitcher Julian Tavarez and three prospects. Nobody noticed at the time, but one of the three prospects was named Dontrelle Willis.

When the 2003 season started, he was in the minors. But not for long. Summoned to the big leagues on May 9, Willis was a left-hander with a frenetic delivery, high leg kick, resilient arm, and 4-0 record for the Class AA Carolina Mudcats.

Like Vida Blue, an earlier southpaw from Oakland, he broke into the big leagues with a bang. In June, when his 5-0 record and 1.04 ERA earned him simultaneous NL Pitcher of the Month and Rookie of the Month honors, Willis worked a one-hitter against the New York Mets and became the first rookie with back-to-back shutouts since Tampa Bay's Rolando Arrojo in 1998. In July, he beat defending Cy Young Award winner Randy Johnson. In between, Willis won nine of his first ten decisions and made the NL All-Star team.

According to Blue, a former American League MVP and Cy Young Award winner who now works for the Giants, "The sky's the limit for him. He can write his own ticket. I was just a raw guy. I learned the art of pitching after my career was over. I see a bright future for Dontrelle if he keeps his head on straight and doesn't get caught up in what everybody is saying."

A product of the same East Bay high school that produced Willie Stargell and Jimmy Rollins, Willis showed potential early. As a senior, he went 10-1 with a 0.82 ERA, batted .621, hit 12 home runs, and knocked in 49 runs in 28 games to win California sectional player of the year honors. Willis studied the game—opting to be a volunteer batboy for the high school team during his grade school years—watching and learning from others' mistakes.

It's hardly surprising the pitcher had an aptitude for baseball: mom Joyce Harris was not only a union welder who scaled bridges and tall buildings like Catwoman but was also a slugging catcher-first baseman who played competitive softball for 27 years. Joyce roots for the Oakland A's and remembers attending the game where Vida Blue received a blue Cadillac from club owner Charley Finley. She taught Dontrelle how to pitch on the front steps of their family home.

"I remember watching her play," said the pitcher, whose cap has the word JOYCE emblazoned under the bill. "She's a tough woman. She's my inspiration."

Harris taught her son respect and humility, making sure he addressed others with a formal "sir" or "ma'am." He repaid her with a 62-inch television set so she could watch his exploits on television. He likes to laugh and have a good time, but he's unfailingly polite.

"I'm just trying to soak it all in," he said shortly after reaching the majors. "Every day is a blessing to be here. You never want to take that for granted. Once you do, something bad can happen and it's done."

Harold Willis, Dontrelle's dad, left the family when the future pitcher was just two years old. Only last year, at age 21, did Dontrelle meet his dad, a Denver resident who had no idea his son was a big-league pitcher. Dontrelle had no memory of his father.

The emotional visit, arranged by his mom when the Marlins played in Denver, was one of many memorable moments for the young lefthander.

"He's definitely for real," said fellow rookie Jason Phillips, a catcher-first baseman for the Mets. "He's got a good arm, and it seems like he's enjoying himself."

Richie Sexson, now the first baseman for the Arizona Diamondbacks, went even further. "You've got to see him a few times before you can even begin to learn how to hit a guy like that," he said.

After a 7-3 victory against St. Louis on August 6, Willis's record stood at a lofty 11-2. Though he encountered a few bumps in late summer, the strong-armed southpaw still finished with a 14-6 log and 3.30 ERA, more than enough ammunition to become the first Marlin to win the NL Rookie of the Year trophy.

"He blows people away with his sneakiness," said pitching coach Wayne Rosenthal late in the season. "Because of his delivery, the speed of his fastball is deceptive. It may be 90 miles an hour but looks like 94."

Even neutral observers were mesmerized by the lefthander last year.

"Willis pitched back-to-back games against us, and each was as good as you can throw," said Bob Boone, who began last year as Cincinnati's manager. "What a tremendous kid. What exuberance. Even when you're in the other dugout, you love him. He's just a real refreshing personality."

Boone, a former catcher whose sons are American League infielders, suggested the lefty's late slide might have been the result of the heaviest workload of his career.

A fastball/slider pitcher who also throws a sinker and change-up, Willis showed good command of his pitches before the All-Star break. His second-half fade came when the pitcher, banking too heavily on the fastball, tended to fall behind in the count and make mistakes that resulted in runs.

"He was trying to be too fine," said Rosenthal, Florida's minor league pitching coordinator before succeeding Brad Arnsberg as big league pitching coach on May 11. "I think it was more fatigue than anything. Everybody expected him to do something great every time out."

Willis is still working to perfect his changeup. He even carried baseballs with him while walking the streets and practiced his grip. "I knew if I could get it down, it would make me more successful," the pitcher explained.

Willis signed with the Cubs out of Encinal High School after posting mind-boggling numbers as both a pitcher and hitter. Chicago's eighth-round pick in the 2000 amateur draft, Willis went 3-1 in rookie ball, the lowest rung of the minors, and 8-2 in Class A the following summer.

In 2002, his first year in the Florida organization, he was *Sports Weekly's* Minor League Pitcher of the Year after going 10-2 with a league-best 1.82 ERA at Kane County (Midwest League) and 2-0 for Jupiter (Florida State League). Invited to 2003 spring training, he pitched nine impressive innings before his assignment to Double-A Carolina. His perfect record and 1.49 ERA there convinced the injury-ravaged Marlins to bring him up. Incumbent starters A.J. Burnett, Mark Redman, and Josh Beckett were all disabled at the time, and Willis had a 27-6 career record in the minors. The move looked like a no-brainer, save for the inexperience factor.

Blessed with an omnipresent smile and plenty of self-confidence, Willis added energy and spark to the rotation. He made a habit of stopping at the top of the dugout each inning and high-fiving his position players. Opposing hitters shook their heads in disbelief at his ability to hide the ball behind a high-kicking, back-turning delivery that can best be described as funky. Part Luis Tiant. Part Gene Garber. Part Fernando Valenzuela.

"You just can't pick him up," former Marlin Cliff Floyd confessed after the Willis one-hitter against the Mets. "I never knew where the ball was coming from for three at-bats. I haven't been that uncomfortable in a long time."

Willis probably iced the rookie award when his strong September helped Florida win the wild card. He went 3-1 with a 2.89 ERA in five starts, fanning 33 and walking 15 in 37 1/3 innings.

"At whatever level I played, I just wanted to go out there, play good baseball, and enjoy what I was doing," said the pitcher, whose crooked hat and quirky habits suggest he's a black Mark Fidrych. He may not talk to the ball, but he's refreshingly different in an era of sterility.

Willis and Juan Pierre, his driver during spring training, even developed a clubhouse dance routine to celebrate September victories. The night the club clinched the wild card, they went public along with teammate Derrek Lee, dancing with delirious fans under a party tent.

Willis was the instigator. "He helped generate the enthusiasm with the fans in Florida," coach Jeff Cox told *USA Today Sports Weekly*. "He didn't come in here with an ego, but he's one of the liveliest guys in the clubhouse."

In a June 30 column for *USA Today*, Ian O'Connor explained the phenomenon of Dontrelle-mania: "Willis is a child playing a child's game with a child's joy. All of baseball is revolving around this *Saturday Evening Post* portrait come to life, this young pitcher throwing his right leg in the air and letting millions of fans hang on the blur of white magic that comes spinning out of his left hand. Watching Willis is watching a sport without brawls, steroids, corked bats, and labor disputes."

Willis worked three times in the World Series without yielding a run, fanning three and walking two in three and two-thirds innings against the Yankees. He was less successful in the Division Series, when he blew a 5-1 lead in the sixth inning of the decisive fourth game. Willis had retired 11 in a row but might have lost steam legging out a triple with two outs and nobody on in the home fifth inning. Third base coach Ozzie Guillen had tried to stop him at second.

The lefty also had a bumpy ride in the NLCS. The starter and loser of Game 4, Willis was a victim of his own wildness. He yielded three hits, five walks, and six earned runs in two and one-third innings as the Marlins fell, 8-3. Working in relief in the sixth game, he yielded a run in his only inning.

The pitcher admitted that the most important thing he learned as a rookie was how to deal with failure.

"You have to stay on top of your game, day in and day out," he said. "If you have adversity, you deal with it head on. You climb out of your struggles. I was able to do that in late September."

Willis is an even-tempered player who never anticipated reaching the majors in 2003, let alone the additional pressure of pitching in postseason play. However, he showed poise beyond his years. He even had the courage to throw his changeup for strikes on hitters' counts.

Rookies Miguel Cabrera, pictured, and Dontrelle Willis brought a fresh perspective and a fiery zeal—not to mention plenty of talent—to the 2003 Marlins.
ELIOT J. SCHECHTER/GETTY IMAGES

According to Rosenthal, "The kid worked hard. He capped off a year that included a World Series, a trip to the All-Star Game, and the Rookie of the Year award. Not bad for a kid who started off in Double-A."

Miguel Cabrera followed a similar path. After starting the season at Carolina, Cabrera was promoted on June 20. At the tender age of 20—a year younger than Dontrelle Willis—the righthanded slugger showed that his skills superseded his inexperience.

Cabrera had grown up with baseball in his blood. His mother Gregoria had a 10-year tenure at shortstop for the Venezuelan national softball team, while two uncles played minor-league ball in the States. In addition, the neighborhood Little League field is in his parents' backyard.

A child prodigy on the diamond, Cabrera began in baseball at age three, playing on the field behind his house. Like his mom, Cabrera was a shortstop. Only 16 when he signed with Florida for $1.8 million, then the highest bonus ever given to a Venezuelan, he turned down more money from the Yankees. The Marlins prevailed in the bidding war after convincing Cabrera that he'd reach the majors more quickly while enjoying the camaraderie of the numerous Latino players in the organization. They delivered on both counts.

He hit .325 for the big club during 2003 spring training but was deemed not ready for prime time by Marlin management. They changed their minds after Cabrera hit .365 with 10 homers, 29 doubles, and a league-leading 59 RBIs in 69 Double A games, convincing Southern League managers to select him as the league's top prospect in a *Baseball America* poll.

Although Cabrera found himself in the majors, he couldn't find his new home ballpark. In his second day with the Marlins, he reported an hour late because he got lost trying to find Pro Player Stadium.

Florida officials might have thought their latest phenom was out celebrating: he had won the previous night's game against Tampa

Bay, 3-1, with a two-run homer against Al Levine in the 11th inning. Only two other players, Bill Parker (Angels) in 1971 and Josh Bard (Indians) in 2002, had ever hit walk-off home runs in their first big-league games.

In Venezuela, the home country of Luis Aparicio, Dave Concepcion, and Andres Galarraga, the Cabrera clout was front-page news.

El Meridiano simply stated the obvious: "Miguel Cabrera debuts with home run."

El Siglo said, "Miguel Cabrera ascending."

But *El Mundo* kept it short and sweet: "Young Power."

Cabrera comes from Maracay, a city of 500,000 not far from Venezuela's Caribbean coast. It's located on the Maracay-Valencia-Miranada corridor, birthplace of many professional players. Dave Concepcion, a former All-Star shortstop for Cincinnati, hails from Maracay, while incumbent Florida shortstop Alex Gonzalez comes from nearby Cagua. New White Sox manager Ozzie Guillen, Florida's third base coach last year, is also a Venezuelan national who played short.

Cabrera's tenure at shortstop was limited. He moved to third base at Single A Jupiter in 2002, to left field last season, and then back to third when veteran Mike Lowell was sidelined with a broken hand. When Lowell returned, Cabrera wasn't left out: he shifted back to left field again. He even acquitted himself well when assigned to right field, another unfamiliar position, during the NL Championship Series.

"The coaches moved me on every pitch," he revealed. "Gerald Williams and Juan Encarnacion showed me a lot."

Milton Jamail, who writes often about baseball in Venezuela, said of Cabrera, "He's something special. He'll hit. I've never heard anyone who has seen him say anything bad about him. Everyone loves him."

Especially the Marlins.

They know he's just a kid, not old enough to buy the champagne for the victory party that followed the 2003 World Series but skilled enough to bat cleanup in all six games against the Yankees. He had four hits in the NL Division Series finale, hit three home runs during the NLCS against the Cubs and one of two Marlin homers in the Fall Classic (a two-run shot against Roger Clemens in the first inning of Game 4). With 10 homers in the minors, 12 in the majors, and four in the postseason, the baby-faced slugger finished 2003 with 26 total round-trippers.

During the World Series, *USA Today Sports Weekly* published a Paul White feature in which Cabrera was compared to Albert Pujols by Andre Dawson and to Manny Ramirez by Ozzie Guillen.

"He's going to be better than Manny," said Guillen. "He's a better defensive player. He runs better. He's a better baseball player. And I say that with unbelievable respect for Manny. But this kid, there's nothing he can't do."

Dawson, a former MVP outfielder who spent last year as a Marlins special assistant, worked with Cabrera to ease his transition to the outfield. The work paid off when the rookie made consecutive highlight film plays against the Cubs in the fifth inning of Championship Series Game 4, thwarting Alex Gonzalez with a diving catch and Damian Miller with a running grab.

"He listens, he works, he makes it easy for me," said Dawson, who emphasized that his Pujols-Cabrera comparison concerned only the hitting end of the game.

Cabrera already swings the bat well enough to win the full confidence of his manager.

"I'd like to get him up every inning if I could," Jack McKeon said during the World Series. "He's very tough under pressure, and he's been a big-game player for us. I didn't have any qualms about sticking him in the fourth slot. When he's up there, something good happens."

Perhaps Cabrera was inspired by a pre-game visit to Monument Park at Yankee Stadium. He knew about Babe Ruth, and other highlights of Yankee history, from watching baseball on television in Venezuela. Cabrera collected three RBIs during the Series, tied with Pierre for most among the Marlins, and added his fourth postseason homer.

Florida expects more from Cabrera as he adjusts to NL pitchers and tempers a tendency toward hot-and-cold streaks. After hitting in five of his first six games, the kid finished June in a funk, going without a safety on the last four days of the month. Both McKeon and hitting coach Bill Robinson assured Cabrera he hadn't lost their confidence.

On July 1, the short-lived slump ended with a vengeance. Cabrera collected two doubles, two homers, four runs scored, and four RBIs in a 20-1 win over Atlanta, launching a month of production that would produce a .318 batting average. A month after Dontrelle Willis was named the NL's Rookie of the Month, Cabrera won the same honor.

Another slump struck in September, when the Marlins were making their move in a seven-team scramble for the wild-card spot. Over a span of 33 at-bats, Cabrera hit safely only once.

Like a Florida tornado that exits as quickly as it appears, Cabrera's bad karma lifted quickly. In the final 23 games, he hit .333 with three homers and 20 RBIs, then carried his momentum into postseason play.

"He doesn't get intimidated," said McKeon of Cabrera, who dodged a high-and-tight pitch from Clemens before ripping the home run that gave Florida a 3-0 lead in a game they would win by one run, 4-3. "He's strong and mentally tough. He was 0-for-4 in his first game with us when he came up in the 11th inning and hit that home run. He's getting better every day."

Derrek Lee, Florida's first baseman last year, thinks Cabrera will blossom into a superstar.

"He's a natural," said Lee, who was traded to the Cubs in November. "Nothing bothers the guy. He made an impression the very first day and he's been doing it since."

Chapter 11
ARMED
AND DANGEROUS

Scary. That's the word I used to describe A.J. Burnett, Josh Beckett, Brad Penny, and Carl Pavano when I faced them in spring training. They are all guys who have above-average stuff. Having to face them night in and night out, for an opposing team, it's crazy. When I'd get to first and talk to the other first baseman about Beckett or Penny, he'd say, "With you guys, everyone throws 100." If you can put a doubt in a hitter's mind about his confidence or his ability to hit against a pitcher, you're one step ahead of him. If you're not confident as a hitter, you're not going to do very well. And our pitching staff is all about instilling fear in batters with their aggressiveness and the way they throw.

—Jeff Conine

Taking their cue from the Atlanta Braves, who parlayed pitching prowess into a string of 12 straight division titles, the Florida Marlins won a world title last year on the strength of their young arms.

Although the rotation membership was altered when injuries intervened, the Fish flew through the postseason because their pitching was better than anyone else's.

No Marlins pitcher won more than 14 games, the level reached by Brad Penny, Mark Redman, and rookie lefthander Dontrelle Willis, who joined the Marlins from the minors in May. But, since Carl Pavano produced a dozen wins, the team had four double-digit winners for the first time.

Josh Beckett wasn't one of them. Sidelined almost two months with tendinitis, he returned in time to roar through the postseason as the ace of the staff, winning two critical games and the World Series MVP award. In a strange twist of irony, though, Beckett also lost twice, giving him a .500 winning percentage that matched his 17-17 career record for the regular season.

Entering the season, the Marlins believed that A.J. Burnett would top the rotation. At 26, the 6'4", 229-pound righthander was coming off a 12-9 season that included five shutouts. He had thrown a 3-0 no-hitter against San Diego the year before, on May 12, 2001. But the 2003 season, supposed to be so promising, went sour early: After going 0-2 in four starts, Burnett went on the disabled list for the third time. His elbow needed Tommy John ligament replacement surgery, and he missed the rest of the season.

Just days after Burnett's bubble burst, the injury wave hit Redman, a first-year Marlin who had been acquired from Detroit on January 13 in a trade that involved five pitchers: Redman and Jerrod Fuell to Florida and Gary Knotts, Rob Henkel, and Nate Robertson to the Tigers. The lone lefty in the rotation suffered a fractured left thumb on April 30 while trying to bunt at Bank One Ballpark. He won that game against Arizona but missed the next month due to the injury.

Proving that bad things happen in threes, Beckett was also idled in early May. Disabled with a right elbow sprain on May 8, he didn't return until July 1. But the Marlins didn't miss him as much as they had anticipated: a red-hot rookie named Dontrelle Willis took his spot.

While the Fish found help from unexpected sources, including career minor league lefthander Tommy Phelps, Willis proved to be a *wunderkind* of historic significance. Acquired from the Chicago Cubs in a trade that cost the cost-conscious Marlins starter Matt Clement and closer Antonio Alfonseca, the effervescent Willis won nine of his first 10 starts, pitched a one-hitter, and was a late replacement on the NL All-Star team for the injured Kevin Brown, ace of the Marlins team that won the 1997 World Series.

Though Willis suffered a second-half slump before righting his ship in September, he managed to stay healthy, a feat duplicated only by Penny and Pavano among Florida's starting pitchers last year.

Jack McKeon, who succeeded Jeff Torborg as Marlins manager on May 11, juggled furiously in an effort to keep his rotation intact. Phelps, who had spent more than 10 years in the minors, made seven starts and 20 relief appearances after taking Burnett's roster spot on April 28. Fellow lefty Michael Tejera, otherwise used as a relief pitcher, made six starts before the All-Star break. Even Justin Wayne, whose career consisted of eight years in the minors and five starts for the Marlins, managed to start two games.

Fortunately for Florida and its frazzled manager, the rotation returned to stability after the All-Star break. Needing just five starters the rest of the way, McKeon got 14 starts each from the left-handed Redman and Willis plus 13 each from the righthanded Beckett, Pavano, and Penny.

Not surprisingly, the team's push up the wild-card standings started in July, the same month the walking wounded returned to action. With Burnett out for the year, and perhaps longer, Beckett inherited the mantle of staff ace.

A towering Texan with a fastball to match, the 23-year-old Beckett was brilliant down the stretch, going 6-4 with a 2.55 ERA and 93 strikeouts in 88 1/3 innings. Pavano, 27, and Penny, 25, also won six times each, while Redman, at 29 the old man of the rotation, topped the staff with seven wins over the second half. Willis, just 21, had five post-All-Star wins, three of them in September.

Redman, a 6'3", 245-pound Californian who had begun his big-league career in the Minnesota bullpen five years before, struggled through the spring as Brad Arnsberg, then the team's pitching coach, tried to change his delivery. Just before camp broke, the southpaw reverted to his former style, then proceeded to win nine of his first 13 decisions. He finished the year with a 2.88 ERA at home, sixth best in the National League, and topped the team with three complete games. Redman ended the season with a three-game winning streak.

Penny also finished strong, winning his last three and six of his last eight to move within two wins of Ryan Dempster's team record (42). Especially effective at night, he posted a .765 nighttime winning percentage, tied for fourth in the NL, while winning 13 of 17 evening decisions. He also poked two homers, a feat matched by only six other pitchers last year, and collected a career-high eight RBIs.

Compared to many of his Marlin teammates, Penny was an elder statesman. Arizona's fifth-round pick in the June 1996 free agent draft, he never pitched for the Diamondbacks. Instead, they packaged him with the unrelated Vladimir Nunez and Abraham Nunez in a July 9, 1999 swap for closer Matt Mantei.

Pavano was traded twice. A 13th-round pick in the 1994 amateur draft, he left the Boston farm system on November 18, 1997 when the Sox shipped him to Montreal with fellow pitcher Tony Armas, Jr. for Pedro Martinez. Elbow problems hampered his progress, convincing the Expos to move him again. On July 11, 2002, Pavano, Graeme Lloyd, Mike Mordecai, Justin Wayne, and Don Levinski went from Montreal to Florida for Cliff Floyd, Wilton Guerrero, and Claudio Vargas.

Although the Montreal-to-Florida shuttle had already made Marlins of owner Jeffrey Loria, team president David Samson, general manager Larry Beinfest, and manager Jeff Torborg, the deal for Pavano—initially derided as a salary dump by South Florida media outlets—turned out to be one of the best.

The 6'5", 235-pound pitcher, used mostly in relief the year before, thrived as a full-time starter in 2003. A control artist who yielded 2.19 walks per nine innings, Pavano topped the team with 21 quality starts, nine home wins, and 201 innings pitched. He also was the starting and winning pitcher for the Marlins on September 26, when they clinched the wild card with a 4-3 victory over the Mets.

"Carl is a pitcher who likes to throw balls in the corners," said catcher Pudge Rodriguez during the World Series. "He's a pitcher with a 91 mile-an-hour fastball. He needs to hit the corners."

Beckett, the only Florida starter who did not arrive by trade, turned pro after the Marlins made him their top pick in the June 1999 amateur draft. Certain of his future stardom, the team gave him a four-year, major-league contract plus a $3.625 million signing bonus. Two seasons later, he was not only named the nation's No. 1 high school player by *USA Today* and *Baseball America,* but made his big league bow with four solid starts, spanning 24 innings, for the Marlins. He went 2-2 with a 1.50 ERA and averaged a strikeout per inning.

By 2003, Beckett had blossomed into Florida's top starter. He started both the Grapefruit League and regular-season openers plus the first games of both the Division Series and Championship Series. But it was his last game that counted more than his first: his complete-game, five-hit shutout in the sixth game of the 2003 World Series made the Marlins world champions for the second time.

For Beckett, who had not finished any of the 48 regular-season starts in his short career, the performance punctuated a perfect finish, for himself and his team. His other complete game, also in the postseason, had been a two-hit, 4-0 shutout of the Cubs in NLCS Game 5.

"I'm not content to just pitch well in the playoffs," he said later. "I need a year with 200 innings. I need to come out strong next spring."

Beckett wasn't bothered by the crowds, monuments, or myths at Yankee Stadium.

"We weren't playing against any of the guys on the plaques," he said. "We ain't playing against ghosts. Babe Ruth ain't here. He ain't in the lineup."

That attitude, as much as his powerful right arm, helped. A combination of momentum, adrenaline, and the adulation of his admirers gave Beckett the boost he needed to fit the glass slipper onto his Cinderella team.

"I've had a lot of young players," said Jack McKeon of Beckett, "but believe me, that guy is the most outstanding young man I've had as far as mental toughness.

"He's a great kid. We agitate each other once in a while, but there's one thing about him: he may talk a lot but he also walks the walk."

During the 2003 regular season, the native of Spring, Texas fanned 152 hitters in 142 innings, an average of 9.63 whiffs per nine innings, and held hitters to a .246 batting average. He was especially tough during the second half of the season and at Pro Player Stadium, where hitters managed a feeble .233 mark against him.

Saving his best work for the end, Beckett went 3-1 with a 2.16 ERA and .213 opposing average over his last six starts. Seven of his last eight, dating back to August 17, were quality starts.

Bedeviled by recurring blister problems in 2002, when he served three separate stints on the disabled list, Beckett was bothered by a right elbow sprain last year. The injury kept him idled for seven weeks but could have been much worse: the Marlins had Birmingham orthopedist James Andrews make sure it didn't require the same "Tommy John" ligament transplant surgery Burnett received.

"God gave me another chance," Beckett said at the time. "I'm trying to make the most of it."

Changing his delivery helped. Wayne Rosenthal, promoted from minor league pitching coordinator to major league pitching coach the same day McKeon became manager, slowed the pitcher's windup, convinced him to rely more on his legs, and told him to aim his left hip at home plate. The coach used tapes of Curt Schilling, co-MVP of the 2001 World Series, to illustrate.

Apparently, the message got through.

Even though he missed nearly eight weeks, Beckett threw 142 innings, by far the heaviest workload of his three-year career, plus another 42 2/3 in the postseason. His lone regret was not having a face-to-face matchup with boyhood hero Roger Clemens, another tall Texan from the Houston area. Beckett's brother Jesse is a taxidermist who's worked for Clemens and his dad John worked with Richard Clemens, the pitcher's brother, in the oil industry. When Beckett was 12, his father brought home an autographed ball from The Rocket.

"I've probably got a whole binder full of his baseball cards," Beckett revealed. "I'm going to have him sign them all and then sell them when he goes into the Hall of Fame."

If he stays healthy, Joshua Patrick Beckett could follow him. The pitcher, whose high school nickname was Kid Heat, had the word "phenom" stitched into the letter jacket he wore as a senior. Big-league scouts wouldn't disagree.

Neither would opponents who played the Marlins last season. When their pitchers didn't leave enemy batsmen flailing at thin air, they made them hit balls directly at the club's sure-handed fielders.

"We've got the best defensive club all around in the major leagues," McKeon said during the postseason. "I managed a number of years in the big leagues and never had a defensive club as good as this one. That in itself helps the pitching.

"When you've got young pitchers like we have, developing and maturing, we tell them, 'Put the ball over the plate, let the guys hit the ball, don't try to strike them out. With the infield and outfield you got, hey, they will make the plays for you.'"

The combination of potent pitching and airtight defense made Florida a more formidable foe as the season reached its climax. That allowed the Marlins to survive the eight-team scramble for the wild card as well as deficits of at least one game in all three rounds of the playoffs.

Chapter 12

LATE-INNING LIGHTNING

Everybody stepped up. Chad Fox, cast off from organization after organization, came in and threw 97-98 miles an hour with a nasty slider. He came up as big as anybody for us, especially the last two weeks of the season. Urbina joined the team and brought one of the best change-ups in baseball. And Looper came in throwing 98 mph.

—*Jeff Conine*

Suddenly last summer, the Florida Marlins realized they could reach the playoffs by rebuilding their relief corps. The cowpen that had lost 22 games and blown 11 save chances the previous year just wasn't playoff caliber. It needed lots more bull.

Scouring the midseason trade mart, Florida found a formidable force floundering in Texas. Ugueth Urtain Urbina, the most famous U-named person since U Thant headed the U.N., or maybe since Ulysses S. Grant served as President of the United States, was leading the American League with 26 saves. But his team was going to finish last anyway.

With the Rangers going nowhere and the need for rebuilding reaching critical mass, Texas found a bevy of suitors singing "I Can't Take My Eyes Off U." Just as a trade to a big-market club seemed imminent, the Fish found a way to fry their fellow bidders.

Florida offered first baseman Adrian Gonzalez, outfielder Will Smith, and lefthanded pitcher Ryan Snare, all blue-chip prospects, for the 29-year-old Urbina. With both Urbina and Rafael Palmeiro, the aging incumbent first baseman, eligible for free agency after the season, the July 11 swap was a no-brainer from the Texas point of view.

The Marlins felt the same way.

The hard-throwing Venezuelan had led the National League in saves with 41 when he worked for the Montreal Expos in 1999. He also had at least 30 saves in three other seasons. But the Marlins wanted him to serve as chief set-up man for rubber-armed righthander Braden Looper, in his first full season as closer. Though some veterans would consider that assignment a demotion, Urbina didn't complain. In fact, he rallied the troops around him, offering the pitching staff the veteran presence it lacked.

As Looper's set-up man, he posted a career-high 11 holds, then switched places with his fellow righthander on September 22 after the incumbent started to struggle. In a familiar role, Urbina converted all four save opportunities he attempted in the final week. He was on the mound, saving a 4-3 win for Carl Pavano against the Mets, when the Marlins clinched the wild-card on September 26, with only two games remaining on the schedule.

"He was great for this team, and especially for the young guys," said Dontrelle Willis, eventual winner of the NL's Rookie of the Year award. "Right away we started talking to him about hitters, about situations. He was great in the clubhouse."

Urbina was also great on the field. In 33 games for the Fish, he went 3-0 with six saves and a 1.41 ERA. He retired 19 of the last 20 batters he faced in the Championship Series against the Cubs, then saved the first and fifth games of the World Series against the Yankees. He even brought some Latin passion, celebrating his saves by kissing catcher Ivan Rodriguez.

Sure, he had a few tough outings: he yielded a Sammy Sosa homer that tied NLCS Game 1 and blew a two-run lead in the ninth inning of World Series Game 4. Closers have to cope with occasional failures. In Urbina's case, the key word is occasional.

During his nine-year career, the 6-foot, 205-pound flamethrower has saved 206 games in 243 chances. Working a career-high 72 times last year, his combined 2.81 ERA lowered his lifetime mark to 3.32.

"Getting him was the best move we made all year," said Marlins manager Jack McKeon. "He solidified the bullpen and turned the club around."

Urbina also proved to be a missing link in the Marlin clubhouse. Shortly after his mid-July arrival, he made it a nightly practice to stroll across the clubhouse to the side-by-side stalls of fellow Latins Luis Castillo and Alex Gonzalez. There, the veteran from Venezuela would talk baseball with countrymen Ozzie Guillen, a long-time shortstop turned third base coach, and Miguel Cabrera, a 20-year-old whose Marlin career began just three weeks before Urbina's. Gonzalez also comes from Venezuela, while Castillo is Dominican.

Ivan Rodriguez, the star catcher from Puerto Rico, and Cuban-born special assistant Tony Perez often joined the group, perched in the corner of the clubhouse near the door.

"We call it *la esquina caliente*, the hot corner," Cabrera revealed late in the season. "That's where we talk about baseball, about life, about everything. We're like a family. Nobody bothers us. It's great. I think that's a big reason why we're able to go out on the field with confidence and play well."

According to Guillen, now managing the White Sox, "Uggie and I sat there and talked about baseball and all kinds of stuff. Whatever came to mind. We talked about the game, what we did right, and what we did wrong. We talked about other teams, and we talked about the next game we were going to play."

Such shared experiences melded the Marlins into a close-knit team and proved particularly beneficial to the younger players.

"They talked a lot about [their] careers," said Cabrera of the after-hours clubhouse confabs. "The little things they told us helped a lot. It created a spirit to go out on the field with confidence and work hard."

His part in the sessions made Urbina far more valuable to the Marlins than a typical one-inning performer.

But he wasn't the only reliever who provided a breath of fresh air in midseason. Chad Fox, released by the Red Sox after a ragged showing, made a miraculous recovery after Florida signed him on August 8. The 33-year-old set-up man, used only 17 times by the Bosox, had been 1-2 with three saves in five chances and a 4.50 ERA. With the Marlins, he worked 21 times while posting a 2-1 mark, seven holds, and a 2.13 earned run average. The only member of the Florida relief corps with more strikeouts (27) than innings pitched (25 1/3), he was especially effective against lefthanded hitters, holding them to a .205 batting average.

"He was our biggest surprise," said coach Jeff Cox of Fox. "He kept coming through in crucial times. We weren't sure exactly what we were getting but found he was ready to go every day, he didn't take long to get loose, and he had the nerves of a burglar."

His success against lefties was especially important, since the Fish had entered the fray without a proven southpaw in the pen. Fortunately for Florida, there was enough righthanded talent to compensate.

Despite his struggles late in the season, Looper posted career peaks with six wins and 28 saves. He also won the Charlie Hough "Good Guy" award, given to the player who best fosters positive relationships with the South Florida media.

Looper wasn't such a good guy to rival hitters. He appeared 74 times, the fifth straight season he has topped 70 appearances, and was especially effective during the first half, with a 2.28 ERA before the All-Star break. The 6'3", 220-pound righthander yielded only one home run during that stretch.

Starting in 1999, his first Florida season after a trade from the Cardinals, he has become the club's career leader with 368 games pitched, trailing only Steve Kline (397) and Scott Sullivan (373) in the majors over the same span.

Urbina, Looper, and Fox combined to hold National League MVP Barry Bonds to one hit and four walks in 12 tries. They also received strong support from Armando Almanza, who worked 51 times before landing on the disabled list prior to the postseason, and Michael Tejera, who made 50 appearances and picked up the only two Marlin saves not recorded by Urbina or Looper.

Two other set-up men, Rick Helling and Nate Bump, combined for a 5-0 record and worked well during the September stretch. Helling, who had opened the season in Baltimore's starting rotation, posted a 0.55 ERA in 11 relief appearances for Florida, and held hitters to a .192 batting average. Bump, a rookie who spent six years in the minors, did his best work on the road, posting a 1.80 ERA in 10 games away from home between August 22 and September 21.

After watching their rotation average only six and one-third innings per start during the regular season, the Marlins realized air-tight relief work would be crucial to their chances in the playoffs.

Once postseason play opened, Jack McKeon masterfully moved his pitchers around as if maneuvering chess pieces in a game against Bobby Fischer. With Tejera the lone lefty in the pen, Dontrelle Willis added southpaw support. But fellow starters Josh Beckett, Brad Penny, and Carl Pavano also pitched in relief.

Urbina, working a staff-high 10 times in the team's 17 October games, saved four of them, with Looper adding the only other save the Marlins recorded.

The team got its best relief outing of the three championship rounds when erstwhile starter Josh Beckett surfaced in the fifth inning of NLCS Game 7 and threw bullets for four innings. The only hit he surrendered was a pinch-hit solo home run by Troy O'Leary in the seventh.

Just three days removed from a complete-game shutout win in Game 5, Beckett fanned three and walked none. When he entered the game, Florida was nursing a 6-5 lead. When he turned the ball over to Urbina in the ninth, the Marlins held a more comfortable 9-6 advantage. Urbina fanned two of the three hitters he faced, bringing the NL pennant to the land of the butterfly ballot.

Facing the Yankees in his first World Series appearance, the 29-year-old Urbina came on in the eighth inning of the opener and got the final four outs, fanning two and walking two, as the Marlins won, 3-2.

After two Florida defeats, the Venezuelan righthander was given another chance in Game 4. Pavano had retired 15 of 16 batters through the eighth, but McKeon decided not to repeat the mistake of Al Gore, who had a proven closer in Bill Clinton but neglected to use him.

"You're damned if you do, and damned if you don't," McKeon said later. "We thought he was running out of gas."

Urbina coaxed Jason Giambi to fly out to left but Bernie Williams singled to center. Hideki Matsui walked, moving Williams to second, before Jorge Posada hit into a fielder's choice. With runners at the corners, pinch-hitter Ruben Sierra took Urbina to a 3-2 count, then fouled off two pitches. The switch-hitting outfielder then laced a drive to right, scoring both runners and tying the game, 3-3. Aaron Boone then grounded out to end the inning but the damage had been done.

Fortunately for Florida, the bullpen brigade had not used up its supply of late-inning lightning. Fox and Looper, neither of whom had pitched well in previous Series games, held the Yankees scoreless for three more innings. Facing 14 batters, they allowed three hits and two walks but escaped further trouble each time.

After pitching a perfect 11th for New York, Jeff Weaver faced only one more batter. Alex Gonzalez, pulling a perfect imitation of Yankee hero Jim Leyritz, homered to left, just over the wall and barely fair.

"We've got tough character," said Looper, the winning pitcher in a 4-3 game. "We're a good team that shows it."

McKeon chimed in too. "If we get good pitching," he said, "we're going to figure out a way to beat you."

Proving the manager's point, the relief corps rode to the rescue again the next night. Instead of Looper bailing out Urbina, the sequence would be reversed.

With the World Series tied at two games each, Brad Penny pitched seven strong innings, allowing the Fish to take a 6-2 lead. Willis worked a scoreless eighth, but Looper, starting the ninth, retired only first batter Aaron Boone.

Jason Giambi homered, Derek Jeter singled, and Enrique Wilson smacked a run-scoring double. Urbina relieved and retired Bernie Williams, who flied out to right, and Hideki Matsui, who grounded out to first. Florida won, 6-4, and took a 3-2 advantage back to New York in the best-of-seven set.

Two nights later, the team won the World Series. It wouldn't have completed the task without its bullpen.

Before the first victory parade, when players were measured for their championship rings, Urbina pulled his last surprise as a Marlin.

"Everybody put out their ring finger," revealed Jeffrey Loria, whose team lost the closer to free agency. "Ugie put out his thumb. He was the only player being measured for a World Series ring who wanted to wear it on his thumb.

"I knew him in Montreal and I knew the charisma that he brought to the table. It was tough to let him go. But it's part of the economy of the game and you have to make decisions."

Looper left too, leaving future ninth-inning chores in the hands of free agent signee Armando Benitez, who pitched for three teams last season. The Marlins are hoping more McKeon magic rubs off on the Dominican righthander.

Chapter 13

COMPLETING THE CYCLE

Jeff Conine is a real pro. He knows how to play the game. And I think he brings that fire and determination to the club. I think we already had a great deal of it but he added a little more to it.

Being a veteran player, the young players go out and watch him play. The way he plays the game, he leads by example.

—Jack McKeon

He won the first game in the history of the Florida Marlins. He took his black and teal uniform to two All-Star Games. He earned a World Series ring.

To Florida fans, he's the prodigal son, the man they called Mr. Marlin even during a five-year exile. But he roared back—oh did he ever—like the Lone Ranger finding Tonto after years of separation.

The only man to play for both Florida world champions, Jeff Conine shared first base with Darren Daulton in 1997 but spent the 2003 postseason in left field.

Traded away in the salary purge that followed the first world title, Conine returned last August 31 after team home run leader Mike Lowell was idled with a fractured hand. The rebuilding Orioles asked only for pitching prospects Don Levinski and Denny Bautista.

"You can't pack it in because you lose Mike Lowell," said Derrek Lee, Florida's first baseman, at the time. "We've got guys here that can get it done and we're going to fight for it."

Conine proved to be the perfect replacement for Lowell. Capable of playing the infield and outfield corners, he was a pro with a presence, a man respected by teammates, worshipped by fans, and appreciated by his manager.

During the World Series, Jack McKeon said of Conine, "He's certainly a big factor in making it easier for the young guys, making them realize what the postseason is all about. He adds a lot to the clubhouse. The confidence, the example he shows, the way he approaches the game. He's always mentally prepared."

Conine also has a personal investment in the South Florida community. He and his wife Cindy, who live in suburban Weston, are not only parents of three young children but co-founders of the Conine All-Star Classic, an annual golf tournament that raises money for the Joe DiMaggio Children's Hospital in Hollywood, Florida. The Conines also happen to be racquetball enthusiasts who won the 25-and-over mixed doubles championship as recently as 1999.

Probably the best all-around athlete on the team, Conine inherited his skills: his dad was an Olympic wrestler and world-class handball player.

When the 2003 baseball season opened, the man teammates call "Niner" was still wearing the black and orange livery of the Baltimore Orioles. The 6'1", 220-pound righthanded hitter, in his fifth year with the team, hit 15 homers in 124 games before the hurry-up waiver deal, finalized just before postseason eligibility rosters were frozen, sent him across league lines.

Florida was hardly unfamiliar territory for Conine, who got a shot at daily duty after the Marlins made him a first-round pick in the 1992 expansion draft. The first leftfielder in Marlins history, he played the entire 162-game schedule in 1993 and collected 39 extra-base hits. In that bleak first year of expansion, when the last-place

Marlins drew more than three million fans to Pro Player Stadium, the one thing spectators could count on was that Jeff Conine's name would appear in the lineup.

His home run total went up each of the next three years, peaking at 26 in 1996. He also reached career peaks with a .319 average in 1994, when he made the All-Star team for the first time, and 105 RBIs in 1995, when his solo home run in his first All-Star at-bat won the game and the MVP trophy.

That was heady territory for a player whose professional start almost seemed like an afterthought. A pitcher at UCLA, Conine wasn't selected until the 58th round of the amateur free-agent draft on June 2, 1987. Three years later, as a first baseman, he was Most Valuable Player of the Southern League and a definite big-league prospect. But he played only 37 games, spread over two seasons, with the parent Kansas City Royals before the Marlins made him the 11th man chosen in the expansion draft that followed the 1992 season.

Five years later, Conine was a seasoned veteran who helped the Marlins win the National League's wild-card berth. Heavy underdogs against the Giants in the Division Series, the Fish surprised with a three-game sweep fueled in part by Conine. Playing in all three games, he went four for 11 (.364) with a double, a walk, and three runs scored.

Platooned with the lefty-hitting Daulton in the NLCS and World Series, Conine hit five singles, knocked in three runs, and scored two.

Older and wiser, Conine was up to his old tricks in the 2003 postseason, finishing with almost exactly the same batting average (.367) that he had in the 1997 NLDS. Appearing in all 17 games Florida played, he went 22 for 60 with 10 runs scored, two doubles, a triple, a home run, five RBIs, and a memorable throw that ended the 2003 Division Series.

"The first time, I got my starts against lefties and when left-handed pitchers came in," said the Tacoma native, who played high school and college ball in California. "It was much more gratifying to be in there the whole time. I had a bigger role in helping us get there [this year] than in 1997.

"I like to get in there all the time and get my timing down. I'm not as good when I don't do that. You definitely learn to respect the good bench players when you're not in there all the time."

Though Conine spent only the last month of the regular season with the Marlins, he supplied strong defense in left field and did his best work with the bat against Philadelphia in pivotal games of the wild-card race. Conine even contributed some power, hitting five regular-season homers in September for Florida to give him a sea-

Jeff Conine—whose return to the Marlins couldn't have come at a better time—salutes the crowd at a rally held in downtown Miami to honor the World Series champions.
AP/WWP

son's total of 20 homers, his highest total since his career-best 26 in 1996. He also had 95 RBIs, a figure he last reached in '96. Conine has knocked in more runs only twice, with 97 in 2001 and 105 in '95.

"He was a man on a mission," Marlins coach Jeff Cox told Paul White of *USA Today Sports Weekly*. "You talk about dedicated. You talk about intense. You talk about drive. Some people got on him because he didn't hit right away but he got some of the biggest hits at the end for us. And the defense, we sure didn't expect that...

"When Jeff rejoined the (Marlins), he came in and said to the club, 'I've been to the playoffs one time in 12 years. And we're going back.'"

Conine, stepping in where Lowell left off, helped the Marlins sizzle in September, sewing up the wild card by a four-game margin over the Houston Astros. Playing almost exclusively in head-to-head games against determined NL East rivals, Florida's 18-8 mark during the month was four games better than division-winning Atlanta's.

It didn't matter whether the Marlins were playing at home or away. On September 7, Conine's RBI single in the sixth helped the Marlins win two out of three from the Expos in San Juan. Two days later, his homer completed a three-game sweep of the Mets at Shea Stadium.

"Nobody expected anything out of this team," Conine confessed. "South Florida has been much more enthusiastic this time around. A lot more fans are recognizing everybody now and they get fired up when they see us. It was so unexpected.

"The 1997 team was built to win. When they put that team together, they expected it to be good, and good enough to go to the playoffs and World Series."

Conine hit his 100th homer as a Marlin on September 17 against the Phils, then connected in consecutive games against Philadelphia on September 23 and 24. He twice knocked in three runs in a single game, including the September 17 contest at Veterans Stadium.

The September 17 game was especially significant. Conine's two-out, two-run double in the first and solo home run in the fourth helped the Marlins build a 6-4 lead. In the fifth inning, with a Philadelphia runner on first, Conine caught up with a long Jim Thome smash, snared it with his back to the plate, and recovered in time to complete a double play, nailing Mike Lieberthal. An inning later, he converted a medium-depth fly ball into a one-hop throw home, wiping out fleet Jimmy Rollins.

"If you're going to script it," Conine said later, "that's as good as it's going to get."

He called the catch the best of his career. "You live to make plays like that," he told *The Miami Herald*. "I was going to make that catch no matter what, even if I had to run through the wall."

Six days later, at Pro Player Stadium, Philadelphia's Kevin Millwood, author of a no-hitter earlier in the season, threw blanks for six innings before Conine crushed a three-run homer, part of a five-run seventh-inning explosion. His homer the next night gave Florida a 6-0 lead it needed, since the Phils scored five in the eighth.

Florida's elder statesman, who turned 37 in June, showed surprising stamina, hitting in five of his last six games (eight for 21) with three home runs and eight runs batted in. He was the perfect example of a player who got hot at the right time.

Conine collected one of three Marlin hits in the NLDS opener against the Giants, went two-for-five in Game 2, and collected another hit in the third game. Leading off the 11th inning of that game, Conine hit a lazy fly ball to right. Jose Cruz, Jr. circled under the ball, planted himself, and then dropped it. That was the opportunity the Marlins needed.

With Conine at first, Tim Worrell walked Alex Gonzalez, then watched slugger Miguel Cabrera bunt the runners to second and third. Juan Pierre was walked intentionally, setting up a potential double play. Luis Castillo grounded to Worrell, who went home to nail Conine for the second out, but Ivan Rodriguez spoiled San Francisco's strategy by poking a 2-2 pitch to right. Two runs scored, giving the Marlins a 4-3 win.

"We took it from the jaws of defeat today," said Conine, who earlier robbed Rich Aurilia of a home run with a leaping grab against the wall in the seventh. "We were down to our last strike. You can't script it any better."

Conine contributed again the next day, knocking in a run without a hit, as the Marlins eked out a 7-6 win that eliminated the Giants. But his throw will be remembered long after that RBI is forgotten.

With one run home and the potential tying run at second with two outs, Jeffrey Hammonds hit a single into left field. Conine, who was charging, picked up the ball and threw a strike to Rodriguez. J.T. Snow, trying to score the tying run, slammed into the Florida receiver, knocking off his mask but failing to jar the ball loose. The game and the series were over.

On the other hand, Jeff Conine's bat was just warming up. He had a hit and an RBI in Florida's 9-8 win in the first game of the Championship Series. He followed with a three for three performance in Game 2, added another hit in Game 3, and went one for four with an RBI in the fourth game. Conine hit a solo homer in Game 5, helping Josh Beckett to a 4-0 victory, and had another hit and RBI in Game 6. Conine saved his best for last, going three for three with two runs scored in Florida's 9-6 win.

In the World Series opener, Conine served as the designated hitter. He had a hit, a walk, and a run scored while inexperienced rookie Miguel Cabrera, stationed in left field, misjudged a fly ball that led to a Yankee run. Conine scored the go-ahead run in the fifth en route to a 3-2 Marlin victory.

Held hitless by Andy Pettitte in Game 2, Conine recaptured his stroke in the third game with a two for four showing. He had three hits and scored a run in the fourth game, another one-run win by the Marlins, and a hit and run scored in Game 5.

The outfielder got the collar in the tight sixth game but, reaching on a rare error by Derek Jeter, still managed to score one of Florida's two runs, giving Josh Beckett the insurance he needed for a 2-0 victory.

It was poetic justice that Jeff Conine, the old and new Marlin, scored the final run of the storybook season. The former racquetball champion, with a reputation for limiting his emotional displays to occasional thrown helmets, found the noise and enthusiasm of the young Fish engaging. In his opinion, it was attitude as well as ability that made the Marlins champions again.

"They were the most enthusiastic and vocal bunch of guys I've ever played with," he said. "They were almost like a Little League team."

The only difference was the size and weight of the World Championship trophy. Part of that trophy belongs to Jeff Conine.

Chapter 14
THEY ALSO PLAYED

Jack McKeon managed us like an American League team. We didn't do a lot of double-switching. So the bench guys weren't getting a whole lot of playing time. But I think they played just as big a role as every starter who was out there every day. Nobody griped. Nobody complained. They were all enthusiastic. They kept the energy level on the bench higher than I've ever seen on any other team I've been on. They kept it light in the clubhouse. They were great guys to be around and everybody knew it. It was almost like they contributed two different ways. And one was as equal as the other. When they did play, they came through huge for us. When you can create that kind of energy from your bench guys, you've got one heck of a situation.

—Jeff Conine

Mike Redmond won't wear plaid. But naked batting practice is fine.

So is wearing name tags on the bench, wearing vintage football or basketball jerseys, or poking fun at the 72-year-old manager.

The 2003 Florida Marlins not only had a bunch of valuable subs but a barbershop quartet of comedy, a group that kept teammates laughing even when the pressure was greatest.

"I spent my first three innings here laughing uncontrollably," said Jeff Conine, who returned to the team in an August 31 trade after a five-and-a-half-year absence. "It was like a Little League team, the most enthusiastic and vocal bunch of guys I've ever played with."

Conine, who launched his 13-year career with the 1990 Kansas City Royals, has seen a lot, both in his own and visiting dugouts. But he's never seen anything like the stunts pulled by bench players Redmond, Andy Fox, Todd Hollandsworth, and Brian Banks.

It was Redmond, a catcher whose claim to fame is serving as Tom Glavine's personal nemesis, who decided to shake up his teammates (not to mention his own body parts) by taking batting practice nude in Pittsburgh and Cincinnati. Early arrivals at the ballpark were not witnesses; Redmond confined his bodacious displays to private indoor batting cages close to the confines of the clubhouse. But he got the results he wanted.

So did Fox, who came up with a seating chart for the reserves and pasted name tags for subs and coaches on the Pro Player Stadium dugout wall.

He also insisted that bench players untuck their shirt tails before running to congratulate teammates after wins. Fox also created Throwback Fridays, when players wore vintage football or basketball jerseys to the ballpark.

"We started the throwback thing in honor of Juan Pierre because he's into throwbacks and is such a throwback-type player," Fox said. "We just wanted to have a day for him.

"It's good team stuff. Like the name tags on the bench. These things are playful, a reminder that everybody on this team knows his place.

"We have a job to do on the bench, to stay in the game and keep the guys playing in front of us rolling. It's a fun thing but also symbolic."

That attitude helped the Marlins come from behind in seven of their 11 postseason victories.

According to manager Jack McKeon, who told players from Day 1 to play hard and have fun, "I have never had a ballclub like this. I've never had so many unselfish, dedicated players who are interested in one thing: winning. I can't say enough about the guys and what great attitudes they have. They're unbelievable.

"I sometimes have to apologize to them. They should be playing more and I feel bad for them. To a man, every one of them came up to me and said, 'Don't worry about me, Skip. As long as we win, we're fine. Just keep doing what you're doing.'"

McKeon's decision to use a set lineup after he became manager in May severely limited the playing time for Banks, who had just 149 at-bats, and Redmond, who batted 43 times after July 2. Though he played all four infield spots, pinch-hit 37 times, and entered five games as a pinch-runner, Fox had just 108 at-bats in 70 games.

Hollandsworth, the 1996 National League Rookie of the Year with Los Angeles, was a regular when McKeon arrived but lost his job five weeks later when hot-hitting Miguel Cabrera was promoted from Double A. Instead of sulking, he became the team's top pinch-hitter, batting .350 off the bench during the season and four-for-eight with three runs scored and two RBIs in postseason play.

"Maybe (comedy) is our way of contributing, knowing that when guys come off the field, we'll be there to pump them up if they made a good play or maybe a not-so-good play," said Redmond, during the World Series. "Anyone who comes into this clubhouse knows that we have fun through stressful times.

"...Ask anyone who's been in the Series and he'll tell you one of the major things is chemistry. This is the best clubhouse I've ever been in, and I'm a firm believer that's why we're here."

Never nervous, at least on the surface, the Marlins boarded the bus to Game 6 at Yankee Stadium knowing they needed to win only one of the final two games. But they weren't worried about foul-mouthed fans, rowdies in the bleachers, or the legendary Yankee mystique.

In fact, they made light of it. During their police-escorted bus ride from Manhattan to the Bronx, they made bets on what street would be the first to produce a fan offering half a peace-sign. Fox picked 101st Street but Banks, who bet on 77th, wound up the winner. Watching the streets like hawks, players found the first fan with his middle finger extended at 66th.

"You've got to find what you can do to help the team," said Banks, a 6'3" switch-hitter who played a dozen or more games at first base and left field, 10 in right, and pinch hit 53 times.

All four bench players were veterans with at least 10 years in professional baseball. That experience helped them accept their roles.

Banks, Fox, and Mike Mordecai also remained ready to provide relief in the field.

"We have chances to change a game and keep the wheel rolling," Mordecai said in a prophetic statement during spring training. "You figure if your five bench guys can account for two wins each, it's 10 wins per season. In a pennant race, that's a lot."

Mordecai delivered, just as he had during previous races with other clubs.

"He's a special player," said McKeon of Mordecai. "He sits there and doesn't complain. He studies the game. He's a kid I think with an outstanding future as a manager. He's always interested in learning a little bit about the game. He's like a secret weapon. You put him in a defensive role or a pinch-hitting role, he stays in the game, and he hits a home run to win the game for you. He did that twice during the season. He's a gamer. All those guys are."

Throughout the Marlins' march to the pennant, the reserves stayed ready.

According to infield coach Perry Hill, "These guys work hard when they take ground balls. Nobody just goes out there and flies by night. We spend a lot of time on fielding position and footwork, just making sure that they maintain that through the course of a long season.

"If you watch these guys take their ground balls during batting practice, they're constantly working on that. You never see them go out there and catch balls the wrong way. All of them work at what they do."

Staying sharp, at bat and in the field, is critical for players who don't get into every game but can be inserted at any time. As a group, Florida pinch hitters produced 49 hits in 196 at-bats, a .250 average that ranked fifth in the National League. And the team ranked second, trailing only Colorado, with a .332 on-base percentage by pinch hitters.

Although the Marlins did not produce a pinch hit during the World Series, the team wouldn't have gotten that far without key contributions from bench players during the playoffs.

Consider the National League Championship Series against the Cubs. With the opener tied 6-6 in the ninth, Hollandsworth led off with a pinch double and Juan Pierre walked. When Mark Grudzielanek failed to tag Pierre on Luis Castillo's grounder, the bases were loaded. Pudge Rodriguez then singled home two runs, putting Florida up 8-6 before a Sammy Sosa homer tied the game again.

That set the stage for an even bigger pinch hit by the Marlins. Mike Lowell, batting for Ugueth Urbina in the 11th inning, homered against Mark Guthrie to give the Marlins a 9-8 win and eliminate Chicago's home-field advantage. The veteran Lowell, whose 32 regular-season homers led the Marlins, had lost his job to Cabrera when he missed September with a broken hand. Two days before his pinch homer, the All-Star third baseman told reporters he did not consider himself a bench player.

A less likely extra-base hit came in the eighth inning of the sixth game, also at Wrigley Field. Mordecai, inserted earlier in a double-switch, doubled to left center, clearing the bases to increase the Florida lead to 7-3. The eight-run eighth gave the Fish an 8-3 win and tied the series, which the Marlins won the following night.

Mordecai, who rarely started, made his two regular-season homers count: they won extra-inning games. The first came on July 23 against Atlanta righthander Trey Hodges in the 12th inning, with the second an 11th-inning blow against Victor Alvarez of Los Angeles on August 13. Both times, the versatile infielder had been inserted as a pinch-runner for Lowell.

Before Jeff Conine returned, the 35-year-old Mordecai was the oldest Marlin and the shortest position player. He was also the least likely to hit a home run.

His second shot, which came on a 2-2 changeup, allowed the Marlins to keep their half-game lead over Philadelphia in the National League's wild-card chase.

"You can't win the wild card right now," he told teammates in the jubilant clubhouse. "But you can lose it."

Mordecai, one of the few Marlins who had tasted a World Series atmosphere (with the 1995-96 Braves), knew the road ahead would be long and difficult.

His first homer ended a personal streak of 164 games (298 at-bats) without a home run, while his second gave the Marlins consecutive extra-inning walkoff homers for the first time in team history (Ramon Castro's 13th-inning homer on August 12 also beat the Dodgers).

Winning back-to-back games with extra-inning homers doesn't happen often: the last team to do it before the 2003 Marlins was the Los Angeles Dodgers on April 5-6, 1999.

Like Fox, Mordecai played every infield position last year, pinch-hit 25 times, and pinch ran 11 more. Lefty-hitting Lenny Harris, who leads the lifetime list with 181 pinch hits, went four for eight with two walks in his first 11 Marlin games, all in pinch-hitting roles. Signed for the stretch drive after the Cubs released him, the versatile Harris also contributed a pinch single in Game 2 of the NL Division Series against San Francisco.

Florida's most successful pinch-hitter was Castro, who hit .346 (nine-for-26) with two homers in the role. He led the National League with a .654 slugging percentage in the pinch and was one of 18 major-leaguers with multiple pinch-homers last year. Those home runs, both in the seventh inning, came in consecutive appearances by Castro, on August 28 and September 6. The 6'3" Puerto Rican played in 40 games, 27 of them as a pinch hitter, and made two starts behind the plate, catching 65 2/3 innings in 18 games.

Like the rest of the bench brigade, he was ready when called upon and ready to help with a smile when he wasn't.

The Marlins prepare for a whirlwind of a season during spring training in Jupiter, Florida.
ELIOT J. SCHECHTER/GETTY IMAGES

Chapter 15
DATELINE JUPITER

When Baltimore played Florida in spring training, we had an inkling that the Marlins were a special talent. You saw the raw talent, the speed, the arms on the pitching side. The power. Everybody could run real well. Great defense. At that point, they were considered by us to be a very dangerous team. They could beat anybody on any night with the talent they threw out there. If they could do it consistently, you knew they would have something. And the Marlins ended up doing that.

—Jeff Conine

Great Expectations was the title of a Charles Dickens novel. It was not the atmosphere surrounding the 2003 spring training camp of the Florida Marlins.

Other than the arrival of Pudge Rodriguez, a veteran catcher coming off an injury-riddled season with the Texas Rangers, and the promise of an up-and-coming starting rotation, the biggest thing to be excited about was the team's new training facility.

Roger Dean Stadium, opened in 1998, was not only the newest and nicest complex in the Grapefruit League but also much closer to the Marlins' regular-season home, Pro Player Stadium, than their previous spring headquarters in Viera. Located in Jupiter, just north of the Palm Beaches, the driving time between the two fields was little over an hour, depending upon I-95 traffic conditions.

The Marlins had won the right to migrate south as part of the February 2002 ownership shuffle that enabled the team's previous owner, John Henry, to buy the Boston Red Sox and Montreal Expos owner Jeffrey Loria to buy the Marlins while selling the troubled Expos to Major League Baseball.

In their inaugural season, 1993, the Marlins trained at Cocoa Expo Center in Cocoa Beach. Then they spent nine years at out-of-the-way Space Coast Stadium in Viera.

Compared to those two outposts, Roger Dean represented civilization.

The $28 million, state-of-the-art complex opened on February 28, 1998 as the shared spring training home of the Expos, who moved a few miles north from decaying West Palm Beach Municipal Stadium, and the St. Louis Cardinals, who abandoned an even older facility in St. Petersburg.

The 110-acre complex, which includes ample practice fields, is located within the Abacoa Community, a development consisting of shops, restaurants, golf courses, and living quarters a quarter-mile east of I-95. The ballpark seats 6,700 in luxury skyboxes, field and loge boxes, and bleachers. Another 300 can spread blankets on the grassy berm in the front of the party deck in right field.

Unlike most baseball fields, where the dugouts are attached to the clubhouses via walkways under the stands, denizens of Roger Dean are required to walk to the field from lavish clubhouses located behind the outfield stands and scoreboard. Each team's facilities, including media relations offices, are separate.

It's a good thing the Marlins' PR office is far from the press box: the 2003 Marlins lost five of their first seven exhibition games against big-league opponents. Slow starts in Grapefruit League play usually seem less significant than hanging chads, but Florida fans had hoped the mix of new players, new facilities, and optimistic predictions from team officials would ignite the team immediately.

The comments came from every direction, starting at the top.

"We did what we wanted to do in the off season," said owner Jeffrey Loria before spring training ended. "We couldn't be more excited with the product on the field.

"In my professional art career, I've always tried to be associated with high quality and to piece together great collections, pieces that complement one another. It's no different than baseball."

Realizing the need to revitalize fan interest, the New York art dealer delivered a message to prospective patrons pushed away by the team's track record of selling talented players.

"We're committed to reconnect with South Florida and let them love baseball again," he said. "We're here for the long haul and recognize what it takes. We're going to take the time and we've got the patience."

Loria's stepson, team president David Samson, not only predicted a 91-win season but delivered his own valentine to Florida fans. "We look for big things in year two," he said on February 14, just as pitchers and catchers were shaking off their winter cobwebs. "The fruits of our labor will be shown in wins and losses."

Less than a month later, vice president of player development Jim Fleming dropped a hint of things to come when he said that the young Marlins might become even younger.

"You want to push these kinds of guys along," he said of the team's talented but inexperienced core. "At the same time, you don't want to push them too fast, because the goal is to keep them going forward."

Jeff Torborg, Florida's manager at the time, was asked specifically about one of the newcomers, a third baseman named Miguel Cabrera.

"He's got a nice arm and a beautiful swing," said Torborg, who previously piloted the Cleveland Indians, Chicago White Sox, New York Mets, and Montrel Expos. "All indications are he's got a heck of a future. I wouldn't rule out calling him up in September."

Cabrera, a 20-year-old slugger who had never played above Class A, hit .325 during the spring but wasn't about to unseat Mike Lowell, the incumbent at his position. Instead, he started the season at Double-A Carolina, the same destination assigned to a wiry left-handed pitcher named Dontrelle Willis.

Knowing quality kids were on the horizon, Lowell looked forward to ending Florida's reputation as a losing team.

"If we stay healthy, I'd be disappointed if we didn't finish at .500," he said before exhibition play began. "The talent is there. I think it's time for the whole team to not be 'the young team and let's see what we're going to be.' It's time to let the talent catch up to all the expectations."

Florida finished its Grapefruit League schedule by beating the St. Louis Cardinals, 8-1, and Montreal Expos, 8-4. But the team still went home with a 15-17 spring record.

There were signs of better things to come, however. Rodriguez, a quality catcher who signed as a free agent on January 22, topped the team with a .382 exhibition batting average and 18 runs batted in. The former MVP, whose 35-homer season in 1999 was the best ever produced by an American League catcher, brought veteran presence, commanded respect, and was anointed as the man who would lead the Marlins to their second winning season. Not necessarily the World Series or even the playoffs, just a season in which Florida won more games than it lost.

Other Marlins also thrived in the spring.

Derrek Lee hit .349, utilityman Brian Banks hit .340 with a team-best four home runs, and newly-acquired centerfielder Juan Pierre batted .325. Juan Encarnacion, starting his first full season in a Florida uniform, knocked in 15 runs, second to Rodriguez during Grapefruit League play.

The pitchers also indicated they were ready: Josh Beckett went 2-0 with a 2.14 ERA, A.J. Burnett was 2-1 and 3.09, and closer Braden Looper pitched 11 scoreless innings in 10 outings.

Brad Penny, a starter hoping to be worth a lot more than his surname suggested, made sure March came in like a lion for the Marlins. "I'm definitely coming out to have a great year," he insisted on March 1. "An 8-7 record is all right, but I don't want to be all right. I want to win 15 games."

In two of three previous seasons, Penny had won eight and lost seven. Only once, in 2001, did he win as many as 10 games. Beckett also represented unrefined talent. Prior to last season, he had made 25 starts in two years while posting an 8-9 record. Even Burnett, a 12-game winner in 2002, had a lifetime record with more losses (32) than wins (30). So did Carl Pavano, who was once part of a trade for Pedro Martinez. Still, scouts from other clubs drooled over the potential of the front four, not to mention Mark Redman, a 29-year-old lefthander inexplicably dispatched by the Detroit Tigers on January 11. And that was *before* Willis squeezed into the picture.

None of the probable starters had reached his 30th birthday.

When spring training ended, baseball insiders believed the Marlins would have strong starting pitching, exceptional speed, and a questionable offense—probably not enough for the club to compete against the high-spending Braves, Phillies, and Mets in the National League East.

But Lee would have none of that.

"It's the best feeling I ever had going into a season," the first baseman said. "Nobody knows what we can do because we haven't done it yet."

Yogi Berra couldn't have said it any better.

Manager Jeff Torborg, left, was well-liked by everyone on the Marlins,
including owner Jeffrey Loria, right. Loria found the decision to fire
Torborg difficult yet necessary.
AP/WWP

Chapter 16

CHANGE AT THE TOP

Talking with the guys and conversing with him myself, I found Jeff Torborg was much admired by everyone. Everybody loved Jeff Torborg. Loved playing for him, loved him as a person. As a player, when they decide to make a change and get rid of someone like that, you almost take it personally. Because you know if you had done your job better or if the team had done its job better, he would still have his job. It's all about wins.

Jack brought a no-nonsense approach to the game that I think a lot of the young guys needed. When he had to put his foot down and yell at guys, he would do it. Middle of the game, whenever. He would let you know when you did something wrong. But he would let you play.

And if you played well and played right, you would never hear from Jack. He was an easy guy to play for, a comfortable guy to play for.

—*Jeff Conine*

Ten minutes after the Florida Marlins' seventh loss in eight games, Jeff Torborg stood behind the small desk in the manager's office at Pro Player Stadium, ran his hand over a shock of rapidly graying hair, and began talking about tomorrow.

"We've just got to keep playing," he was saying. "You get breaks in this game over the long haul. You've just got to make your own."

Only tomorrow would never come for Torborg. Two hours later, just minutes after midnight on May 11, 2003, he would be fired by team owner Jeffrey Loria, one of his closest friends in baseball. The Mother's Day massacre would also claim pitching coach Brad Arnsberg and Torborg's son Dale, a former minor league first baseman and professional wrestler known as The Demon who served as the Marlins' strength and conditioning coach.

The firings came as a surprise to no one, though the timing seemed odd. The season was just 38 games old and, despite missing three of his five starting pitchers with injuries, Torborg had his team at .500 until it was swept in back-to-back series by the Giants and Astros—not a bad start for a franchise that had just one winning season in its history. But expectations were higher this season, especially after team president David Samson predicted the Marlins would win 91 games. And they weren't going to get there as inconsistently as the team was playing.

On their first roadtrip of the season, the Marlins scored 17 runs to beat Atlanta ace Greg Maddux, then scored just four runs on 13 hits in the final two games of the series. A week later they scored 12 runs to beat eventual 21-game winner Russ Ortiz, then scored just three times in their next two games. And in the week preceding Torborg's dismissal, the Marlins had lost three times in their opponents' last or next-to-last at-bat.

Clearly something had to give. And that something turned out to be Torborg.

"This is a better team than we've [shown]," said frustrated general manager Larry Beinfest, who called the firing the toughest decision he's had to make as a GM. "There was no one certain thing that we point to. It was the overall underperformance of the ball club that really pushed this decision.

"I just felt that change was necessary and total."

In Torborg's place Beinfest hired 72-year-old Jack McKeon, a former National League Manager of the Year who had been fired four times previously and who hadn't gotten closer to major league baseball than his television set in more than two seasons—though that wasn't by choice, he stressed in his first press conference.

"I didn't retire," McKeon, baseball's oldest manager, said. "I was just unemployed for a while."

McKeon, a baseball lifer and a former minor-league catcher who made $215 a month from his first baseball job, has managed in either the minors or majors in six decades, stopping in more small towns than Greyhound. But his biggest baseball regret is that he never appeared in a big-league game as a player. As a result, he has little patience with players who seem to take their place in the major leagues for granted—and he wasn't shy about letting them know of his displeasure either.

In that way, McKeon and Torborg, another former catcher who spent 10 seasons in the majors, playing on two World Series teams, couldn't have been more different. The ever-patient Torborg would never criticize a player in public, and rarely did so in private, while McKeon would call players out in the press, in the dugout and on the mound when he saw something he didn't like.

Where Torborg knew the names of his players' wives and kids, McKeon had trouble remembering the names of the guys he wrote into the lineup every day. Where Torborg allowed players to retreat to the cool of the Marlins clubhouse during humid South Florida nights to watch the games on television, McKeon had the clubhouse door locked, insisting his players watch the games from the bench.

"I'm not running a babysitting service here," said McKeon, who jokingly admitted he accepted the Marlins offer to get away from his nine grandkids for the summer. "I don't need this job."

Still the change wasn't so much one of style as it was one of substance, with Torborg eventually falling on the sword rather than allowing management to dictate how he would run the club.

Rumors began surfacing in spring training that management was unhappy with pitching coach Brad Arnsberg. In fact, the friction dated back to the summer of 2002, when the Marlins' top four starters had all spent considerable time on the disabled list. So when staff ace A.J. Burnett went down with elbow problems and the newly acquired Mark Redman struggled mightily with a new delivery mandated by Arnsberg midway through spring training in 2003, the front office renewed calls for the pitching coach's head.

Torborg, however, stood by Arnsberg again, insisting the pitching coach wouldn't go unless the manager went first. The battle lines were drawn.

A former first-round draft pick of the New York Yankees, Arnsberg was the Yankees' minor league pitcher of the year in 1985 when he went 14-2 with a 1.59 ERA for Double A Albany. He made his big-league debut the following September but blew out his elbow a year later, eventually undergoing Tommy John surgery. With a reconstructed arm, Arnsberg reconstructed his career as a reliever, appearing in 70 games for Texas and Cleveland—earning the save in Nolan Ryan's 300th career win—between 1990-92.

The experience inspired Arnsberg to reconstruct his plans for the future as well, so at the age of 29, when most pitchers are just entering their prime, Arnsberg left the mound to become a coach.

"The reason I got into becoming a pitching coach was for that reason: the protection of arms," Arnsberg said. "The way I was used was ludicrous. And I didn't ever want to see that happen. I don't care if he's your 11th man or your first man or your middle or whatever he is. I never wanted to see that happen under my tutelage."

But it wasn't the injury as much as the year-long rehabilitation that opened his eyes, because it was during that process that he met pitcher-turned-pitching-guru Tom House, the Timothy Leary of the hardball set, whose sometimes bizarre theories on the physiology of throwing have inspired much derision—and success.

And it was Loria and Samson who gave him his first chance to try out his theories on the big-league level, promoting him from bullpen to pitching coach in Montreal seven months after taking over the franchise. Two years later they brought him to Florida when they bought that franchise, but the honeymoon ended as the Marlins' injuries mounted, with critics charging both Arnsberg and Torborg with overusing their young pitchers.

The evidence gives lie to the criticism, however. Although Burnett's 111 pitches per start was the second highest pitch count in the majors in his first season under Arnsberg, he also set career bests for wins (12), ERA (3.30), innings pitched (204.1) and strikeouts (203) while leading the majors in shutouts with five. And Josh Beckett threw more than 100 pitches in just 10 of his 29 starts under Arnsberg—a figure he topped 14 times in 20 starts under McKeon and new pitching coach Wayne Rosenthal while winning the World Series MVP award.

"I would rather lose a game, I would rather lose a season, I'd rather lose a job. But I'm not losing a kid's career," Torborg would say later, explaining his approach to his young pitchers.

Sometimes perception is more important than reality, however, so when Burnett went down in spring training the season after Arnsberg's staff lost more than 170 days to injury, the front office made it clear it wanted a change. Torborg refused, so when the team got off to a slow start, the manager's days appeared numbered as well.

Less than three weeks into the season, reports surfaced that a member of the front office had been asked to compile a list of managerial candidates—reports that general manager Larry Beinfest refused to deny, leaving Torborg to twist in the wind. A week later Burnett, in an effort to show his support for Torborg and Arnsberg, accused management of withholding information about his fragile arm from the coaching staff. Although there was no evidence to support Burnett's claims, the soap opera surrounding Arnsberg was becoming too big a distraction to ignore. So when the Marlins went on a six-game losing streak the day Burnett's comments were made public, Beinfest invited McKeon to South Florida for a two-hour lunch meeting.

Four days later Beinfest called back and offered McKeon the manager's job. All that was left now was to tell the manager and his pitching coach. After conferring with Loria, Beinfest drove to Torborg's condo and told him of the change.

"There's no blame here. It's a matter of numbers," Loria said hours later.

For Torborg, a close friend of the owner for nearly 20 years, the news brought more relief than bitterness.

"I'm not bitter. How can you be bitter?" he said. "Frustrated? Yeah. I would have liked to have been there with those guys. Sure. …It was almost a miracle what they pulled off. And yet from Day One in spring training, I really felt the ballclub could win."

But the ballclub McKeon won with was different than the one management gave Torborg to play with. Rookie Miguel Cabrera was still in the minors when Torborg was fired and relievers Chad Fox and Ugueth Urbina and outfielder Jeff Conine were still in the American League. When Torborg left, the Marlins were missing three members of their starting rotation, and rookie phenom Dontrelle Willis, who would go on to win the rookie of the year award, had just joined the team. But Willis's callup, which Torborg had been clamoring for since spring training, would be the manager's last victory—as well as his legacy, since Torborg's judgment proved right when the 21-year-old lefthander won nine of his first 10 starts, sparking the Marlins' turnaround as much as anything McKeon did.

In fact, Torborg, who remains friendly with Loria, told his old boss in September that he had studied the other playoff teams on television and was convinced the Marlins were the best. Then he did his part to make sure they fulfilled that promise, watching the team's run through the postseason on TV wearing a good-luck t-shirt bearing the slogan "Little Things Win Rings" he had made up for the team.

"I'm still superstitious," he said. "I wore that darn thing right through the playoffs. It was a very enjoyable time for me, watching them be so successful. Because that's what we had thought they would be. In fact, I thought we'd do that the year before."

Arnsberg wasn't as accepting. After leaving Torborg's condo, Beinfest reached the coach by phone at a nearby bar and asked to meet him back at Arnsberg's apartment. The brief meeting started poorly, then got worse, ending with Loria and Beinfest hustling to their car as Arnsberg shouted profanities at them.

The next morning Beinfest called security at Pro Player Stadium and ordered them to deny Arnsberg access to the clubhouse and players' parking lot, setting up a surreal scene in which fans, arriving for the Mother's Day game unaware of the drama that had played out hours earlier, found Arnsberg standing outside his truck in the public parking lot being embraced by many of his former pitchers.

Inside, McKeon was meeting his players and the media for the first time. "I thought he was a new assistant," said first baseman Derrek Lee.

After addressing his new team, McKeon stepped into the locker room normally used by the NFL's Miami Dolphins for his first press conference as manager of the Florida Marlins.

"I feel very confident that we can make progress with this club. I wouldn't have taken the job if I thought we didn't have a chance," he said. "But I'm not a miracle worker."

Five months later, there would be few in baseball who would agree with that last statement.

Mike Mordecai, center, is mobbed by teammates after connecting for his second
home run of the season, a game-winner that beat the Dodgers on Aug. 13.
AP/WWP

Chapter 17
TEN GAMES
TO REMEMBER

The (Jim) Thome game in Philadelphia was definitely one to remember. With the magnitude of the race and everything that the game meant, it was probably the biggest game of my career. Coming through like I did in that game, it was just one of those nights where you had the opportunity to do things and ended up doing them right. Everything happened to be hit my way and I had guys on base when I was at the plate. It was a turning point for me in the season as far as my confidence and my being able to feel good about making a contribution to a play-off push.

Another game against Philadelphia, I hit a home run against Kevin Millwood in the sixth inning to tie it up. There were so many big games down the stretch and so many guys came up big. They almost all kind of run together because every night was a big win. Every win means so much in September and October.

—Jeff Conine

Before the start of the 2003 season, David Samson predicted the Marlins would win 91 games. It was a bold boast by a man with a vested interest, but the Florida team president must have known something.

Logic suggested less successful results: the Fish had floundered for five straight seasons since their 1997 World Championship team was dismantled and had finished on the sunny side of .500 only once in the franchise's history, in the world title campaign. Moreover, the Marlins were coming off a fourth-place finish in the five-team NL East, where their record for 2002 was 79-83, 23 games from the top.

Early in the year, it looked like Samson's suggestion would turn out to be little more than a pipe dream. But things changed after Jack McKeon jumped out of retirement and into the Florida dugout in May.

By the time the dust cleared, the Marlins had their 91 wins, with 20 of them coming in the team's final at-bat. They won six of their 10 extra-inning games and 30 of their 53 one-run games. But, according to *The Miami Herald*, all of their 10 most memorable games occurred after McKeon supplanted Jeff Torborg. Here's the list:

1. June 28, Fenway Park, Boston. Marlins 10, Red Sox 9. One night after a devastating 25-8 loss that included a 14-run first for the Red Sox, the Marlins rallied from a 9-2 eighth-inning deficit to win in the ninth on Mike Lowell's two-out, two-strike home run with two men on. That victory convinced the club it could rebound from any setback. It also moved the season's winning percentage to .500.

Florida's in-game comeback followed a seven-run explosion by the Red Sox in the bottom of the sixth. The Marlins struck for four in the eighth, thanks mainly to Juan Encarnacion's three-run homer against knuckleballer Tim Wakefield, and another four-spot in the ninth, with Lowell's blast against Brandon Lyon the big blow. It was the biggest comeback win in Marlin history.

The ninth inning started innocently enough. Brian Banks and Pierre poked one-out singles, but Luis Castillo bounced into a fielder's choice. That's when Lyon entered the den. Pudge Rodriguez ripped an RBI single, narrowing Boston's bulge to 9-7, and up stepped Mike Lowell. The third baseman had been zero for four against Boston starter Wakefield, who was lifted in the eighth.

Two quick fastballs lowered the count on Lowell to 0-2. But he connected with the third pitch, sending it into the Boston bullpen in right field for an opposite-field gamer. As former Red Sox pitcher Waite Hoyt once said, "the pitcher was chagrined." So was a packed house of 34,804 Fenway faithful.

"We went from one of the worst games I've ever been associated with to one of the best games I've ever been associated with," said Juan Pierre, who went four-for-four with a walk and scored twice. Pudge Rodriguez produced too, with two hits, two runs scored, and three batted in.

Pierre punctuated his performance with a diving shoestring catch in the ninth. With one out, Jason Varitek was on second with the potential tying run. But Pierre snagged Johnny Damon's sinking liner, bounced to his feet, and threw to second, catching Varitek in a double-play to end the game. The catcher, who thought Damon's drive would fall, had headed for third when he saw the trajectory of the ball.

"I was either going to make the catch or it was going to be an inside-the-park home run," Pierre said later.

2. August 13, Pro Player Park, Miami. Marlins 5, Dodgers 4. Mike Mordecai, inserted into the game as a pinch runner in the ninth inning after the Marlins blew a 1-0 lead, won it in the 11th with his second home run of the season. It was the second consecutive game that the Marlins won on an extra-inning homer by a bench player, with Ramon Castro contributing against the Dodgers in a 5-4, 13-inning win the previous night, and the second time Mordecai connected.

All the elements of drama were there: two outs, two strikes, extra innings, and a paint-scraping home run that barely cleared the left field wall at Pro Player Stadium. Mordecai had entered the game with the fewest hits (11) of any Marlin who wasn't a pitcher.

"If he had thrown me a fastball," he said of Dodger southpaw Victor Alvarez, "I don't know if I would have gotten any wood on it."

The 35-year-old infielder, the old man of the roster before Jeff Conine arrived two weeks later, inspired teammates to stage an impromptu early New Year's Eve celebration in the dugout. They didn't have sparklers, but they did find nicknames for the 5'10" Mordecai, calling him "Big Mo" and "Mordi the Magnificent."

It was the third straight win of a seven-game homestand in which there was only one loss.

3. July 23, Turner Field, Atlanta. Marlins 5, Braves 4. According to Jack McKeon, this was the game that turned the season around. Florida squandered a three-run lead in the ninth, then came back to win in the 12th on Mordecai's first home run in nearly two seasons.

Mark Redman started for Florida, yielding one run on four hits in seven-and-two-thirds innings, but the Braves blasted Braden Looper for a three-spot in the ninth, thanks to a two-run triple by Julio Franco and an RBI single by Robert Fick. Rookie Nate Bump retired all six batters he faced in the 11th and 12th to pick up his third win without a loss. But the real hero was Mordecai.

His home run handed Atlanta reliever Trey Hodges his first loss in four decisions and reinforced Florida's confidence that it could reach the playoffs.

Four days later, after Pierre's ninth-inning single beat the Phillies, 7-6, Philadelphia pitcher Kevin Millwood made a prophetic statement: "If we forget about those guys, then they'll come back and get us. We just have to make sure we don't take our eyes off anybody."

4. June 20, Pro Player Stadium. Marlins 3, Devil Rays 1. Miguel Cabrera, not only making his big-league bow at age 20 but also playing an unfamiliar position, poked a two-run, 11th-inning homer to center that won the game.

Duplicating the instant success of Dontrelle Willis, who won his May 9 debut after promotion from the same Double-A club, Cabrera connected against Al Levine with Alex Gonzalez on second base.

To be sure the rookie was wide awake, Josh Beckett hit him in the face with a shaving-cream pie just after he touched home plate. "I'm not sleepy at all," said Cabrera, who left Tennessee at 6 a.m. and arrived in Florida at 3:30.

His 419-foot homer followed four hitless at-bats, including a strikeout and an inning-ending double play. The Tampa Bay trio of Robbie Bell, Jesus Colome, and Travis Harper had held the Marlins to four hits before Gonzalez and Cabrera solved Levine in the final frame.

"When I hit it, I didn't think it was out," said Cabrera, the third man in major league history whose first hit was a game-winning homer. "I thought maybe it would be a double, but that it would still score a run."

Cabrera feasted on a fastball, a pitch he had been expecting. Tampa Bay kept feeding him hard stuff all night.

"I wasn't trying to do too much," he said. "I was just trying to do my job."

Because he did, the Marlins went on to sweep the series from the Devil Rays and extend their winning streak to five by winning the June 24 opener of a three-game set at Shea Stadium against the Mets. The team ended the month at .500 with a 42-42 record, 11 games behind Atlanta in the NL East and five and a half games from the top of the wild-card race. Six teams stood in front of them, including the streaking Phillies (six straight) and Diamondbacks (12 straight).

5. July 6, Veterans Stadium, Philadelphia. Marlins 6, Phillies 3. Two seasons earlier, Florida's bid to climb back into the divisional title chase crashed when they were swept in a four-game July series in Philadelphia. This time, the Marlins did the sweeping, taking all three games from the Phils even though they were outhit. The win pushed the Fish three games over .500.

"It was a big series for us," said Juan Pierre, whose three-for-three night pushed to his average above .300 for the first time since June 1. "You're going to the park actually looking at other teams, looking at the race and knowing that you're in it."

The Fish scored first, plating three in the opening inning against Randy Wolf, the Phils' top lefthander. Juan Encarnacion and Jim Thome traded two-run homers in the first, leaving the Marlins with a slim 3-2 lead. But Mark Redman held on, yielding only one more run in a 140-pitch, complete-game performance.

Florida completed its scoring with a three-run third that featured RBI doubles by Luis Castillo and Pudge Rodriguez and a sacrifice fly from Encarnacion. Pierre, proving himself the perfect lead-off man, was on base four times, with a walk, a single, two doubles, and two runs scored.

"We're putting things together," said Redman, who survived 90-degree Sunday afternoon heat and humidity that almost matched. "When you have a team that plays small ball and gets guys into scoring position to let the next guy get him in, and the pitchers suck it up like we have been, it's a big testimony to the Florida Marlins and what we have."

The win, No. 800 in the managerial career of Jack McKeon, left the Marlins with a 43-40 mark, 10 games behind the Braves and fourth in the NL East. But the wild-card race was tightening.

"I'll probably get a button from the AARP," the manager quipped. "Maybe Man of the Year. It's nice to be able to say you managed 800 wins in the big leagues. It's quite an accomplishment to think you've been around that long."

6. May 23, Great American Ballpark, Cincinnati. Marlins 8, Reds 4. The Marlins came to town with a six-game losing streak and seven losses in eight games under new manager Jack McKeon. The team, sagging a season-low 10 games under .500, endured another setback when Brad Penny, scheduled to start that night, became violently ill minutes before the game. His replacement, minor-league journeyman Tommy Phelps, rose to the occasion with five and one-third innings of one-hit ball, launching the Marlins on the streak that would lead to the playoffs (72-42, best in baseball from that date to the end of the season).

Entering the series, it was obvious that something had to give: Florida had no offense but Cincinnati had no pitching.

The Reds handed the ball to Jeff Austin, a 26-year-old righthander with no decisions during a two-year tenure in the Kansas City bullpen. Cincy would have been better off with Steve Austin, the Six-Million-Dollar Man.

In seven games last year, all of them starts, Austin posted an 8.58 earned run average and threw nine home run balls in 28 1/3 innings. The May 23 game was typical.

He yielded five runs in the first without getting an out, with the big blow an RBI double by Rodriguez. The catcher added another double later, while Lowell walked twice, doubled, homered, scored twice, and knocked in two more. Brian Banks also went deep for the Fish.

For Phelps, who had spent more than 10 years in the minors without so much as a cup of coffee in the majors, it was the start of an amazing week. He not only held the heavy-hitting Reds to a single run but came back to beat the Expos five days later, also with an outing of five and one-third innings.

His only other win would come June 19, when he threw seven shutout innings against the Mets. He proved to be only a small cog in the Little Teal Machine, but an important one nonetheless.

Two days later, Dontrelle Willis worked eight scoreless innings as the Marlins won a 6-2 verdict to sweep the Cincinnati series. For McKeon, fired by the Reds in 2000, it was sweet justice.

"Pretty nice return," said the manager, whose three-day stay in the Queen City included a visit to his favorite cigar shop and chats with local fans who hadn't forgotten him.

"The reception I got just made me feel appreciated," he said. "They were saying, 'Come back, we miss you, we need you back here.' And some of them said, 'Beat 'em.' It was so gratifying. We were struggling, and to win three made it a little sweeter."

The Cincinnati sweep started the Marlins on a six-game winning streak that neutralized the losing streak Florida had imported to Cincinnati. After a faltering start, McKeon had his men moving in the right direction.

7. June 16, Pro Player Stadium. Marlins 1, Mets 0. At the apex of Dontrellemania, the rookie lefthander one-hit the Mets for his fifth straight win and sixth in seven decisions. A fourth-inning homer by Pudge Rodriguez was the only run Willis needed.

The game began as a battle of lefthanders, the old (Tom Glavine) versus the new (Willis).

Glavine, in his first year with the last-place Mets after 11 straight title seasons in Atlanta, threw his best game of the year in a losing cause. But he had trouble with Rodriguez, who also doubled and walked, and Derrek Lee, whose night included two hits, a walk, and a stolen base.

Only fellow freshman Ty Wigginton, who walked in the first and singled in the fourth, could touch Willis. The Vida Blue clone finished his eight-strikeout effort by retiring the last 17 Mets.

"He's all arms and legs but with a head on his shoulders," said New York cleanup man Cliff Floyd, who fanned all three times he faced Willis. "He looks very confident."

Though the win left the Marlins 13 games behind the Braves with a 34-37 record, fourth in the five-team division, Willis continued to whip opponents with relative ease. His performances made believers out of both teammates and rivals.

"There's no question this guy is going to be here for a long time," said Jack McKeon, who briefly considered lifting the pitcher for a pinch hitter in the seventh. Instead, he resorted to prayer in the dugout.

The third 1-0 complete-game victory in Marlin history was also the fifth one-hitter by a Florida pitcher. By pitching his one-hitter at such an early age (21), Willis showed the potential to join a Marlin No-Hit Club occupied only by Kevin Brown, Al Leiter, and A.J. Burnett.

8. July 1, Pro Player Stadium. Marlins 20, Braves 1. Josh Beckett, back from the disabled list, yielded three hits and an unearned run in six innings while enjoying the biggest margin of victory in club history. Though he pitched for Atlanta, losing pitcher Mike Hampton was being paid by Florida in the wake of a complicated three-team trade that also involved Colorado.

Pounding the Braves was a source of pride for the Marlins. Atlanta was en route to its 12th straight division crown, a professional sports record, and represented the standard of excellence in the league. Not on that dreadful Tuesday, however.

Scoring in seven of the first eight innings, and not needing to play the ninth, Florida finished with club records for runs, hits, extra-base hits, and margin of victory. The 25-hit attack featured a two-homer game by Cabrera, a home run by backup catcher Ramon Castro, and two doubles apiece for Cabrera and Lowell. Cabrera's first homer, which launched a six-run second, carried 440 feet to center.

Castillo and Rodriguez both went four-for-five and scored three times each. Cabrera, ending a zero-for-17 skid by moving closer to the plate, collected four runs and four RBI to go with his four hits, while Lowell was consistent with three hits, three runs, and three RBI.

Adding insult to injury, Josh Beckett pitched his first game since returning from the disabled list with a sprained elbow. The eight-week layoff didn't make a dent in the pitcher's armor, as the Texas fireballer yielded only three hits and an unearned run. Beckett fanned seven and walked two in his six-inning stint.

"There was room for error," the pitcher said later. "It's a lot easier to pitch when you've got 10 runs on the board."

The lopsided win not only pushed the Marlins over .500 for the first time, but made them believe they could beat anybody. After all, they had just manhandled the league's most successful team.

9. May 11, Pro Player Stadium. Marlins 7, Rockies 2. Juan Pierre stole three bases and Luis Castillo collected four hits as the Marlins won Jack McKeon's first game as manager. Florida trotted out every weapon at its disposal, including potent pitching from Carl Pavano, two home runs, and four stolen bases.

Castillo and Lowell, who went deep that Sunday afternoon, combined for seven hits in nine at-bats, while Pierre parlayed three walks, a single, and three stolen bases into four runs scored. All of Florida's eight hits came from the top three batters in the lineup: Pierre, Castillo, and Lowell.

Pavano did his part, scattering 12 hits in seven innings. Working with runners on base in every inning but the fifth, he yielded only two runs because he refused to walk anybody.

McKeon's postgame reaction? "We know we've got speed. We know we've got defense. But what really impressed me is the way Pavano worked out of all those jams."

10. September 20, Turner Field. Marlins 6, Braves 5. The Marlins took over the wild-card lead for good, winning on Miguel Cabrera's leadoff homer in the 11th inning. Cabrera's 12th homer erased the bad taste of a blown four-run lead in the eighth.

Brad Penny, pitching for the first time since leaving a September 12 start with a hyperextended elbow, supplied his own offense with a bases-clearing double in the second. He worked seven innings, yielding only a Marcus Giles home run with no one on, and felt relatively comfortable turning a 5-1 lead over to the bullpen. But no relief was in sight.

In a rare double meltdown, Ugie Urbina and Braden Looper threw late gopherballs to Gary Sheffield and Javy Lopez, allowing the Braves to score twice each in the eighth and ninth.

Cabrera's solo shot off Will Cunnane untied the game and gave the win to erstwhile starter Rick Helling, who hurled an-inning-and-a-third of scoreless relief.

Lady Luck also played a part in the victory. In the fifth inning, Florida scored when a ground ball by Encarnacion nicked Rodriguez, who was headed toward third. Instead of a twin-killing that would have ended the frame, the freak occurrence cost Florida only one out. Jeff Conine walked, loading the bases, and Cabrera came through with an infield single, scoring Derrek Lee with Florida's fourth run.

Though too far back to catch the Braves for the NL East crown, the Marlins managed to seize the wild-card lead they had sought for so long. Their record was 85-69, second best in the division but 10 1/2 games off Atlanta's pace. Without the wild card, the win would have been meaningless.

A loss could have been catastrophic. McKeon, who told players in a pregame meeting that he expected to go to the playoffs, admitted afterward that a defeat would have put the Marlins at a psychological disadvantage.

The team's owner agreed.

"Fish have nine lives too," Jeffrey Loria told *The Miami Herald* after the game.

Once the "D-Train", Dontrelle Willis, started rolling on May 9,
the Marlins hopped on board and rode a wave of momentum all the way
to the World Series title.

Chapter 18

TURNING POINTS

When we swept the Phillies, I think that put us, confidence-wise, on another level. They were our nemesis. That's who we were battling the whole time. To be able to sweep them when it came down to meaning the most of any games all year, I think that's what put us over the top confidence-wise and gave us the boost we needed to take into the postseason.

—Jeff Conine

Like the Yellow Brick Road, the path to the *Miracle Over Miami* had many turning points. The signing of Pudge Rodriguez. The hiring of Jack McKeon. The promotions of Double A prospects Dontrelle Willis and Miguel Cabrera. The acquisition of Ugueth Urbina. And especially the decision *not* to trade Mike Lowell.

According to McKeon, "I took this job with the idea that I could turn the club around and make a winner. I didn't have any idea we would win the wild card or the playoffs. I had no idea we would get to the World Series. And I certainly had no idea we would win the World Series.

"But being with these guys and seeing their attitude and determination, their desire, I knew we were on a mission. We were on that mission since the Philadelphia series, when we were trying to qualify for the wild-card. From that day on, we believed we could go to the World Series."

For a team that rebounded from 10 games under .500 to a world championship in the same season, the turning points were many. But these turned out to be the most significant:

1. May 9. After placing righthanded starter Josh Beckett on the disabled list, the Marlins called up Double-A southpaw Dontrelle Willis to take his spot in the rotation. Willis proceeds to win nine of his first 10, make the All-Star team, and give the sagging, under-achieving team new energy.

2. May 11. Manager Jeff Torborg and pitching coach Brad Arnsberg are fired and replaced by Jack McKeon and Wayne Rosenthal, respectively. Bench coach Jeff Cox is moved to the bullpen and minor-league field coordinator Doug Davis becomes McKeon's bench coach.

3. July 1. After weeks of trade rumors, the Marlins tell All-Star third baseman Mike Lowell they are committed to keeping him through the end of the season.

4. July 11. Florida acquires veteran closer Ugueth Urbina from Texas.

5. August 31. Hours after losing Lowell with a broken bone in his hand, the Marlins again prove they're serious about chasing a playoff berth by trading a pair of promising minor-league pitchers to the Baltimore Orioles for former Marlin Jeff Conine.

Take away any of the turning points and there wouldn't have been a season worth remembering.

Consider Dontrelle Willis, the high-kicking lefthander who had opened the 2003 campaign pitching for Florida's Double-A affiliate in Zebulon, North Carolina. At 21, Willis needed experience: he had split the 2002 season between two Class A clubs and had only a month in Double-A before injuries to the Marlin rotation accelerated his timetable.

With the season little more than a month old, the Marlins looked like a mirror image of earlier editions. Lots of potential, little production, and too many injuries.

On May 9, with Beckett joining A.J. Burnett and Mark Redman on the DL, Willis was summoned. There had been talk of him making the Opening Day roster before cooler heads prevailed. But the rationale for rushing the kid evaporated when he opened the season with a 4-0 mark and 1.49 ERA at Carolina.

In his big-league bow, the lanky lefty with the kooky windup yielded seven hits and three runs in six innings, fanning seven and walking two, in a 5-4 win over the Rockies.

"He had good stuff," said former Florida catcher Charles Johnson, who went to Colorado with Preston Wilson in the winter deal that made Juan Pierre a Marlin. "I thought maybe he would get hyped up and let his emotions get in the way. But he made pitches to get out of jams."

Willis was even more sensational in subsequent starts, compiling a 9-1 record by midseason. He cooled off—who wouldn't?—but not before he made the NL's All-Star squad. It was heady stuff for an Oakland native who was drafted out of high school by the Chicago Cubs three years earlier.

"I never thought at this age I would get an opportunity like this," said the pitcher. "It's unreal. This is something I've been dreaming of."

Jeff Torborg, the beneficiary of the first Willis start, never got to manage a second. A catcher-turned-broadcaster who had managed four other clubs before joining Jeffrey Loria's shuttle from Montreal to Miami, he was popular with both players and press. But the club sputtered under his command, winning by a big margin one day and failing to generate any offense the next, while the young pitchers were more often hurt than helpful.

Burnett, the projected ace of the staff, was sidelined for the season in April with elbow woes that required surgery. Beckett's elbow acted up. And Redman broke his hand.

With three-fifths of his rotation gone, even the arrival of Willis wasn't enough to save Torborg's job. He and pitching coach Brad Arnsberg got the ax on the night of May 10 after Florida had lost 22 of its first 38 games.

"We knew we needed to get our stuff together," Beckett said in retrospect. "We were better than that (16-22) and that's a tribute to my teammates for knowing they were better than that. We've got a bunch of guys on our team who truly believed in themselves. We just stuck it out."

McKeon, who thought his managerial career had ended three years earlier, was rushed into the fray with the fanfare of an old tea kettle fire truck rounding the corner with a thick plume of black smoke trailing behind. McKeon's monumental project was two-fold: to put out the bad fire consuming the franchise and to light a new, motivational flame under players striving to reach their potential. By stretching them to the limit, McKeon reasoned, they just might be able to grab that elusive brass ring.

The manager succeeded through a combination of craftiness, good humor, and guts, plus healthy doses of help from the front office and more than his share of good luck.

"I knew a little bit about the players because I had managed against them in 2000," he said. "I also did a lot of television watching when I was between jobs. So I had a pretty good idea of what they had.

"I knew the players talent-wise but really didn't know them personally. When you live with players, you get to know the ins and outs of all the guys. But I did know enough about their talent that I thought this was a club that had a lot of ability and could win a lot of ballgames. I knew we would win, but I didn't know how many games. I knew we'd be over .500. But I'd be lying if I said I knew we were going to be in the World Series."

McKeon got the players to improve their work habits, including their concentration, but also to relax, loosen up, and enjoy themselves.

"The main thing is they went out and had fun," the manager said. "They were unselfish and had dedication and desire. I've never seen a club that had 25 guys that are just like a family."

McKeon won his first two games, split his next two, dropped six straight, and brought the team into Cincinnati with its tail dragging. Wanting to remind the Reds they made a mistake letting him go, McKeon lit into his charges in a pregame clubhouse tirade. It might have been the turning point of the Jack McKeon era.

For whatever reason, the Marlins responded, recording the best record in the game for the final four months.

Keeping Lowell was critical to that success. It sent a message that reverberated through the clubhouse. All of a sudden, the players knew management was serious about winning.

Lowell, raised and schooled in Miami, remembers when the Marlins were created and how they suffered through their early years. He was a third-year pro, playing in the Yankee farm system, when the team won its first world title. Two years later, with the team stripped of its stars, he came home as part of the rebuilding process. The 2003 campaign was his best.

"He's the backbone of the team," coach Jeff Cox told Paul White of *USA Today Sports Weekly*. "Management made a commitment to Lowell that was extremely important in the clubhouse. That was the first sign the players got that they knew management was going to try to do whatever it could to win."

An even bigger turning point, according to Cox, was the arrival of Urbina.

"The turning point of our season came when (he) walked through the (clubhouse) door in Montreal," said Cox, who has served the Marlins as bench coach and bullpen coach. "He had a couple of days to report after the trade, but he was there the next day. It was like we got a shot, the way the aura of that clubhouse changed.

"Making the commitment to Lowell was one thing. But when they went out and brought in Urbina, people sure sat up and noticed."

The entire baseball world knew the Texas Rangers, dead last in the American League West, were going to dump Urbina's hefty contract. The question was where. Eyebrows everywhere were raised when the destination turned out to be Florida.

On July 11, few fans and fewer baseball insiders anticipated a playoff spot for the Marlins. But the team's front office had other ideas.

According to Jack McKeon, "When the trading deadline came and all these players were available, Jeffrey Loria, Larry Beinfest, Mike Hill, and I sat down, talked about where we were going to go, and what chances we had to advance. And if we had a chance, how we would go about it.

"A lot of players were available. In fairness to the ownership and management, they decided, 'Hey, we've got a chance to get into the playoffs. Let's shoot the works.'

"I think Larry Beinfest went out as a general manager and did a spectacular job in acquiring Urbina, Chad Fox, Lenny Harris, and Jeff Conine. It made a big difference in our ballclub. At that time, getting Urbina was the biggest move anybody in the game could have made. He was the premium guy out there. Larry just out-hustled everybody else to get him.

"When he joined us, it lifted our players tremendously. The same thing applied to the organization's decision to keep Mike Lowell. Everybody was trying to get him but we were not trying to move him. To ease his mind and the players' minds and to give them a psychological edge, we decided he wasn't going anywhere."

Beinfest hit another psychological home run, the manager said, when he obtained Conine to replace the injured Lowell on August 31.

"Of all the moves that were made at the trading deadline, the moves Larry Beinfest did were the best moves made by any club in the National League or the major leagues, for that matter. They helped our club get where we wanted to get," McKeon concluded.

The return of Mr. Marlin was a surprise, not only because it happened, but because it happened so quickly. Almost immediately after Lowell's injury on August 30, Beinfest began working the phones. After 24 hours of casting, the GM shocked the baseball world by reeling in his biggest catch: Mr. Marlin.

Jeff Conine was a seasoned veteran whose potent righthanded bat made him an ideal replacement for Lowell. At age 37, he was well on his way toward finishing with at least 95 runs batted in for the fourth time in his career.

Though his best position was first base, Conine could also play third base or the outfield corners without embarrassing himself. And he was nothing short of sensational in the locker room.

"He was a big factor in making it easier for the young guys," McKeon told *USA Today Sports Weekly* during the World Series. "He added a lot to the clubhouse. The confidence, the example he shows, the way he approaches the game. He's always mentally prepared. He's a very intense player, and he really came through with a lot of key defensive plays and big hits."

Since the Marlins had a Gold Glove first baseman in Derrek Lee, they placed Conine in left field and moved rookie Miguel Cabrera back to third base, where he had started the season.

The moves must have worked, since the Marlins played nine straight games without an error from September 7-17.

Conine contributed an RBI single to beat the Expos, 3-1, on September 7, a homer two days later that helped the Fish sweep the Mets, and home runs in back-to-back, one-run wins over the Phillies on September 23-24. Conine capped his performance against the Phils on September 25. His two-run single solidified Florida's 8-4 win, gave the team a three-run edge in the wild-card standings, and made Conine the club's career RBI leader. The next night, a Friday two days removed from the end of the schedule, the Fish clinched the wild card with a 4-3 win over the Mets.

The club's record for September was 18-8, leaving it with a 91-71 record that was one short of the 1997 team's 92-70 mark. Last in the wild-card race in April, May, and June, the Marlins had worked their way up to second, a game-and-a-half behind Philadelphia, by finishing July with a six-game winning streak. At the end of August, the two clubs were tied, with four others within three games of the wild-card lead.

The six-game homestand that finished the season made the difference; Florida won all but one, winning the wild card by four games over the fast fading Houston Astros. Philadelphia finished five out, one game ahead of the Dodgers and Cardinals and two ahead of Arizona.

Lesser teams might have limped into the postseason after such a grueling race. But not the young Marlins. Buoyed by the return of Mike Lowell, who left the disabled list in time to play the last game of the season, Florida was fired up to play in October for the first time in six seasons. Cinderella still wanted her glass slipper.

Pudge Rodriguez was the recipient of both "the throw" and J.T. Snow's shoulder blade. Rodriguez held onto the ball despite the violent collision to ensure the Marlins would advance to the NLCS.

AP/WWP

Chapter 19

NLDS: THE THROW

What a series! We wound up reeling off three wins in a row against a team that won 100 games. And we neutralized their best player. Barry Bonds didn't hurt us the whole series.

As far as the throw I made to end the series, they had a guy at second so I expected him to go home on a base hit. Jeffrey Hammonds was at the plate. I saw contact with the ball and just broke in as fast as I could. I didn't think I was going to be able to catch it on a dive—it's amazing how quickly your mind works in those few short seconds of an experience—but if I did dive, the ball would probably squirt away and Hammonds would get to second with the go-ahead run.

If I got it on a short hop, maybe I would have a play at the plate. I didn't think we were going to have a play there because of the way he hit the ball. It was slow, just a bloop hit. When I was running up on it, I just wanted to get rid of it as fast as I could. Just before I let it go, I remember thinking, "Okay, I'll make a throw just to make a throw." But when I saw (J.T. Snow's) position coming around third base, I'm like, "Oh, man, I think we got him!"

Luckily, it was a nice high hop to Pudge. In that instance, I was just sitting out there with 65,000 people. It was like a vacuum had just sucked all the breath out of me. I was just waiting.

I saw the umpire's arm go up and down and then all bedlam broke loose.

You see the highlights of all the other teams and you're thinking, "They just thought it was routine." The Yankees shook everybody's hand going through the line at the end of the game. We dog-piled, we threw each other into the air, we sprayed champagne. We had enthusiasm. We wanted it worse than the others. That's another reason why we won.

—Jeff Conine

Barry Bonds has been Most Valuable Player in the National League six times, including the last three years in a row. No one else has won more than three MVPs and no one had ever won three in a row before Bonds did it in 2003. He holds the single-season record for home runs (73) and has a better than even shot, according to sabermetrics guru Bill James, of topping Hank Aaron's record of 755.

With Bonds in their back pocket, the San Francisco Giants figured the Florida Marlins for a pushover. In the major leagues, only the Atlanta Braves and New York Yankees won more games than the 2003 Giants, who finished with an even 100 after deciding to skip a makeup game that could have given them home-field advantage throughout the playoffs. That advantage went to the Braves, whose 101 wins tied the Yankees for most in the majors.

Florida, with 91 wins, finished 10 games behind the Braves in the NL East title chase but posted the best winning percentage (.562) among the three second-place teams. More importantly, they were hotter than the Florida weather in September.

That momentum would carry into the playoffs—even with Barry Bonds in the other dugout.

To be sure, Marlins manager Jack McKeon was wary of the San Francisco slugger.

"This guy doesn't miss," he said. "You don't see him hitting little dribblers. He either hits a bullet or a line drive somewhere out of the park. Do you walk him and put the tying or winning run on base? Or do you pitch to him and hope for the best?"

McKeon may have worried for nothing. Good pitching usually stops good hitting, and the Marlins refused to let the Giants cash in their Bonds.

After dropping the opener, 2-0, on a two-hitter by San Francisco's Jason Schmidt, Florida simply refused to lose. A big reason was leadoff man Juan Pierre. Told he was swinging too hard by veteran teammate Lenny Harris, Pierre prepared for Game 2 by trying to calm his nerves and concentrating on producing better swings. He succeeded.

"It felt good to get that first hit out of the way in my first at-bat," he said. "From there, I continued to roll."

The Marlins took Game 2, also at Pac Bell Park, when Pierre went four-for-five, knocked in three runs, and stole a base. The bullpen sparkled, holding the hard-hitting Giants to one run in five innings, as the Florida hitters overcame an early 4-1 deficit with a 14-hit barrage. That 9-5 win evened the series and sent it back to Florida, where the Marlins won consecutive one-run games, 4-3 and 7-6, on their home turf.

Pudge Rodriguez, who hit .353 with six RBI in the four-game set, plated the winning runs in Game 3 with a two-run single to right in the last of the 11th inning after the Giants had taken a 3-2 lead in the top of the frame.

Rodriguez, whose two-run homer in the first had given the Marlins an early lead, knocked in all four Florida runs, the last two coming with two strikes against him. The Giants helped when Jose Cruz, Jr. dropped a routine fly ball hit by Jeff Conine near the right-field line.

"That was the key," said Rodriguez, who had finished on the wrong end of three postseason series during his 12-year tenure with Texas. "We've got to take advantage."

After Conine, the first man to bat in the 11th, reached on the error, Alex Gonzalez walked, Miguel Cabrera bunted the runners to second and third, and Pierre drew an intentional pass.

Luis Castillo hit into a force at the plate, bringing I-Rod to bat with the bases still loaded.

"I knew I had the game in my hands," said the catcher, who prolonged his at-bat with a foul tip on an 0-2 count against San Francisco closer Tim Worrell. The next pitch was a fastball on the outside part of the plate. Rodriguez, a skilled opposite-field hitter, served it into right field.

"The last inning felt like it took three hours," said Giants short-stop Rich Aurilia, who had scored the lead run in the top of the 11th. "The Marlins are a feisty club and play like they have nothing to lose."

Losing on the big-league level was indeed unfamiliar territory for Marlins like Cabrera. He had opened the year in Zebulon, North Carolina, home of bad lights, long bus rides, and little media pressure. Promoted in June, he had only a half season in the big leagues on his resume. When his turn to bat came in the home eighth inning of the fourth Division Series game, he was loose.

Batting in a 5-5 tie, Cabrera connected for his fourth hit of the game, a single that scored Rodriguez and Conine. His four for five night included two singles, two doubles, three runs batted in, and one run scored.

"The guy is something special," said McKeon of Cabrera, back in the lineup after a one-game benching. "I felt he was pressing a lit-tle bit yesterday and the day before. I felt like he was feeling he had to carry the club. I could see that in his eyes. The kid was playing pretty good baseball, but I also wanted to get him a breather. I knew we did that before with him, gave him a day off periodically when it looked like he was in a little bit of a rut or a little funk, and he came back with a vengeance. So when I came out this morning, I made up my mind I was going to go with Cabrera again."

Cabrera would have been the hero of Game 4 if San Francisco had failed to rally in the ninth. But the Giants lived up to their nick-name, pushing across a run and threatening to add more.

With Ugie Urbina undergoing an uncharacteristic roughing up on the mound, the Marlins needed one more miracle. They got it from an unexpected source: the arm of leftfielder Jeff Conine, the oldest player on the team.

Conine, who turned 37 in June, had more RBIs than any man in Marlins history. But he'd spent most of the previous five years in Baltimore, returning on August 31 in an 11th-hour waiver deal made after Lowell broke his hand. Had they not already called him "Mr. Marlin," Conine might have earned the tag with his desperate but deadly accurate throw on October 4, 2003.

J.T. Snow, carrying the potential tying run, was at second with two outs when Jeffrey Hammonds slapped an Urbina pitch into left field. Conine, realizing he could catch the speed-challenged runner, charged and threw to the plate. Pudge Rodriguez not only caught the ball and tagged the runner but survived a grueling collision. A loose ball would have meant a tie game.

The first postseason series to end with a play at the plate belonged to the Marlins.

Conine, primarily a first baseman before returning to Florida, had played only six games in left field for the Orioles. But he spent September preparing for October. Just in case.

"When I got here, we were either one game up or tied for the wild card," he said. "We had a lot of baseball to play. We were playing the teams ahead of us that we needed to beat and we ended up doing it."

When the situation required it, Conine uncorked the throw of his life.

"I came in a little bit, knowing Hammonds has pretty good power," said the soft-spoken veteran. "I didn't want to have too much room behind me and have something get over my head. But at the same time, I wanted to be able to make a good throw to the plate in case something came my way.

"When it first left the bat, I thought I had a chance to catch it. I didn't want to dive right at the end and miss it, have the run score easily. So I stopped short and made a good transfer from my glove to my hand."

Conine had his own cheering section on the Florida bench.

As McKeon told reporters later, "I kept hollering in the dugout, 'Come on, Jeff,' 'Come on, Jeff,' 'Come on, Jeff.' When I saw him get it on the first hop, knowing what kind of outfielder he is, I just figured we had a chance at the plate. I didn't realize it was going to be that easy, as good a throw as he made. And you have to give Pudge credit because he made a tremendous block to keep the ball in his hands."

Just one inning earlier, Rodriguez had been on the other end of a home-plate collision. He reached base with a two-out single, moved to second when Derrek Lee was hit by a pitch from Felix Rodriguez, and raced for home on a single to right by Cabrera. The throw home from Jose Cruz, Jr. took two hops before it reached catcher Yorbit Torrealba. Rodriguez arrived at the same time, ran into the rookie backstop, and jarred the ball loose. Lee, spotting the loose ball near the Florida dugout, raced home with another run, which proved to be the eventual margin of victory.

No MVP award is given for Division Series play, but Rodriguez would have been a lock. The Puerto Rican catcher not only pounded the ball and produced when it counted, he also took a personal beating behind the plate. He provided steady and sound guidance for his young pitching staff, too.

"I got the ball in the glove and wasn't getting rid of it," said Rodriguez after the clincher. "Jeff made a great throw and I put my eyes on the ball and squeezed it close. I knew Snow was coming and made the tag."

It wasn't easy: Snow, the son of former Los Angeles Rams star Jack Snow, threw a football tackle at the compact backstop.

"I don't think an 18-wheeler would have knocked that ball out of his hand," said Chad Fox, a Florida pitcher with a clear view of the action.

The hard-fought win eased McKeon's fears that Florida would fritter away numerous early chances. The team had a 5-1 lead, with runners on second and third and nobody out. Then it had the bases loaded with no one out. Both innings ended without a tally.

"It looked awful bad out there when you saw all those golden opportunities go down the drain, especially in the early innings when you could have put them away right quick," McKeon said.

Starting pitcher Dontrelle Willis, whose three for three night at the plate included a fifth-inning triple with two outs, coughed up the lead in the sixth when the Giants hit him for a four-spot.

"I wish he would have stopped at second," said McKeon afterward. "But what are you gonna do with a youngster who's got so much emotion? He's a very determined young man. He only had 71 pitches going into that inning and we felt like we could get six strong innings out of him. We didn't even have time to get someone warmed up. It went bang, bang, bang. But fortunately we were able to come back and get the win, so that takes care of everything."

Although Florida relievers fared better than their starters during the Division Series, the Marlin young guns dropped hints of better things to come.

Carl Pavano, usually a starter, made three relief outings, winning the second and fourth games. Josh Beckett worked a solid opener in a losing effort and Dontrelle Willis pitched well before a sudden sixth-inning implosion in the final game. All three, along with Brad Penny, would make more significant contributions during the next two rounds of postseason play.

Manager Jack McKeon puffs on a victory cigar while accepting congratulations after the Marlins came back to beat the Cubs on their home turf and clinch the NL pennant.

Chapter 20
NLCS: COMEBACK CITY

Playing a playoff series at Wrigley Field is second to none. Their 39,000 fans were as loud as our 65,000. You've got Mark Prior dominating. You've got five outs left to go. And we got breaks. When Steve Bartman made that pseudo try for that ball in the stands, everybody in the dugout, the whole comical corps, started screaming, 'Let's make this guy famous.' And sure enough, we made him really famous.

Not to take away from what we did. We still had to hit the ball regardless of the mistakes they made. We came through with big hits. Afterward we went up to the locker room and we're like, "What happened here? Did we just score eight runs in the eighth inning to beat them?"

Next night, Kerry Wood hits a three-run homer. I've never heard any place as loud as that place right then when he hit that home run. And the next inning (Moises) Alou goes deep for a 5-3 lead with Wood on the mound. But we, like every other time, shook it off, kept battling, and ending up scoring a bunch of runs to win, 9-6.

That was just a tiresome series. It was so close, so up and down, so much offense. Emotionally that was really draining. But I thought if we won Game 6, we would win the series."

—Jeff Conine

The Marlins knew they weren't going to sweep the Chicago Cubs, an opponent that not only had celebrated young studs in the starting rotation but also the home-field advantage in the best-of-seven series. In a boisterous ballpark like Wrigley Field, the smallest but loudest in the National League, that advantage could be considerable.

Florida entered the fray knowing that only three teams (the 1995 Braves and the 1988 and 1990 A's) had swept a championship series since the format switched from best-of-five to the seven-game format in 1985. Only once, when Cincinnati's Big Red Machine was running on overdrive in 1976, had a team swept both the LCS and the World Series.

The 2003 Marlins, all but exhausted from the wild scramble for the wild-card spot, weren't likely to sweep anything. In fact, Las Vegas oddsmakers listed them as decided underdogs against the Chicago Cubs, champions of the Central Division, in the NL Championship Series. But Florida, also favored to flop in the Division Series, liked its chances against the Central Division champions.

Both teams realized the series could run the full length, as it had 16 times since the 1969 advent of divisional play.

The Cubs, trying to reach their first World Series since 1945, had blown a sizable midseason lead (1969) and failed in three previous playoffs, against the Padres in 1984, the Giants in 1989, and the Braves in 1998. They also faced the Goat Curse of Wrigley Field, placed by local tavern owner William Sianis, whose pet goat was denied admission to the 1945 World Series even though it had its own ticket. According to the hex, the Cubs would never again reach the Fall Classic.

On the eve of the 2003 pennant playoffs, the sentimental favorites to reach the World Series were the Cubs, without a world championship since 1908, and the Boston Red Sox, ringless since 1918. The 58-year-old Cub absence from the Fall Classic, plus its ridiculously long run without winning one, represented the longest droughts among the original 16 teams.

Like the Cubs, the Red Sox hoped to reverse a hex of their own. Tradition dictates that Boston has suffered from the Curse of the Bambino since owner Harry Frazee, anxious to fund his production of *No, No Nanette*, sold budding superstar Babe Ruth to the New York Yankees on January 3, 1920. The Yankees won their first pennant in 1921 and a record 38 more since, while the Red Sox, dominant early in the 20th century, failed to win any of their four World Series appearances following the ill-advised sale of their best player.

The Marlins, virtual bambinos themselves, didn't concern themselves with curses, though they might have had second thoughts after a Cub fan deflected a foul ball to fuel an unlikely eight-run uprising in the eighth inning of the sixth game.

Chicago's vaunted young starters, fresh from paralyzing the heavy-hitting Atlanta Braves in a five-game Division Series, were not only the talk of the town but the darlings of the media. Kerry Wood had led the majors with 266 strikeouts, while Mark Prior placed second to Wood with 245.

Though little bothered the Marlins on the surface, the hoopla hefted onto the Cubs had to sting.

"We're right there with them," said Josh Beckett, Florida's best pitcher down the stretch. "I'd put Brad Penny up against any of those guys. I'd put Dontrelle Willis up against any of those guys. We're just going to try and hang in there."

That's just what the Marlins did.

Florida took the first game, 9-8, when Mike Lowell parlayed a Mark Guthrie pitch into a pinch homer in the top of the 11th inning. Earlier home runs by Pudge Rodriguez, Miguel Cabrera, and Juan Encarnacion had turned a 4-0 deficit into a 5-4 Florida lead but Chicago rallied for a 6-6 tie. Rodriguez plated a pair with a ninth-inning single, putting the Marlins up again, but the Cubs got the runs back when Sammy Sosa reached Ugueth Urbina for a two-run homer in the home half.

Then came Lowell, who answered two innings later with the one that decided the game.

"It couldn't happen to a greater guy," said McKeon in a postgame interview. "Mike has been hurt. Cabrera came in and did an outstanding job offensively and defensively. Mike handled it like a pro. He's a team player. He understands the situation. I was very happy to see him deliver the winning hit. It made him feel like he's part of this thing, too."

Lowell got a lift from the weather: with the wind whipping toward Lake Michigan, the clubs combined for 17 extra-base hits, including seven home runs. His happened to be the last.

"The conditions were favorable," he said after the game, the third in a row that Florida won in the ninth inning or later.

"Whomever is writing scripts for these games is just learning baseball," quipped ebullient Marlins owner Jeffrey Loria.

The boss may have spoken too soon: Marlin magic evaporated into the crisp Chicago night in the first inning of the next game. The Cubs scored two in the first, three in the second, three more in the third, and never looked back.

Sosa's second homer, plus a pair by Alex Gonzalez, staked Mark Prior to an 11-0 lead. The 12-3 Cub victory was also the biggest beating ever absorbed by the Marlins during postseason play.

Game 3, the first played in Florida, should have looked familiar to fans: the lead kept switching back and forth in the late innings. The Cubs took a 4-3 lead on Randall Simon's two-run homer in the eighth, but Todd Hollandsworth tied it with a single in the ninth. That's how it stayed until the 11th, when Doug Glanville tripled to score Kenny Lofton and give the Cubs the victory.

Fueled by two homers, including a grand slam, from midseason acquisition Aramis Ramirez, former Florida righthander Matt Clement mastered the Marlins, 8-3, in the fourth game. That gave Chicago a three-games-to-one lead that looked insurmountable, especially with aces Mark Prior and Kerry Wood, who had not lost consecutive games all season, scheduled to pitch the last two games at Wrigley Field.

Although the Marlins seemed hooked, they never let the Cubs reel them in.

Beckett, backed by the home run bats of Lowell, Rodriguez, and Jeff Conine, picked Game 5 for the best performance of his short career. The 23-year-old Texan, hit hard in his only regular-season outing against Chicago, not only posted the first complete game of his career but yielded just two hits and no runs while fanning 11. It was the first time the Cubs had suffered a shutout in the playoffs since Babe Ruth pitched one for the Boston Red Sox in 1918.

Beckett punctuated his performance by throwing high, inside heat not far from Sammy Sosa's chin in the fourth inning. When the Chicago slugger showed obvious displeasure, the brash righthander responded with a curve that broke over the plate for strike three. Beckett, who later said Sosa was overreacting, sent the Cub slugger home wearing an 0-for-4 collar.

"That was probably the best pitching performance against us this year," said Chicago first baseman Eric Karros. Little did he know he had not seen the last of the Florida flamethrower.

Dusty Baker didn't figure on seeing Beckett again, either.

"These guys are extremely tough to beat in this park," he said of the Marlins. "They're a good team. We wanted to win all three here, but I'm satisfied with two out of three. Now we're going home to our fans. It's going to be exciting when we get back."

The Chicago manager was right on the money with that remark.

Needing to win one of the last two games, both scheduled for the usually friendly confines of Wrigley Field, the Cubs had their top guns ready. Mark Prior was scheduled to pitch Game 6 and Kerry Wood, if needed, would work Game 7.

Prior was doing his best to duplicate Beckett's Game 5 shutout when the roof fell in. Leading 3-0 in the eighth, he needed only five outs to nail down the first Cub pennant since the Goat Curse. He never got them.

Although Juan Pierre stood on second after a one-out double (Florida's third hit of the game), the Wrigley Field faithful were wild with anticipation when Luis Castillo lifted a foul ball down the left field line. Then a 26-year-old Cub fan named Steve Bartman did what any fan would do: he tried to catch a ball headed in his direction.

With his eyes on the ball, Bartman didn't notice leftfielder Moises Alou coming over to make the catch. The fan reached for the ball, deflecting it out of Alou's reach, and Castillo received new life at the plate. The next pitch from Mark Prior was not only ball four but a wild pitch, leaving runners at the corners and bringing Rodriguez to the plate. His single to left scored Florida's first run of the night.

The rally looked dead when rookie Miguel Cabrera grounded to short. But Alex Gonzalez, the usually sure-handed Chicago shortstop, booted a likely double-play ball, prolonging the inning. With the bases loaded, Derrek Lee delivered a two-run double. Jeff Conine then put the Marlins ahead with a sacrifice fly before light-hitting Mike Mordecai pounded a bases-clearing double to complete an outburst not topped in postseason play since 1968, when the Detroit Tigers scored 10 runs in the third inning of Game 6 against the St. Louis Cardinals. According to Jack McKeon, the key play of the inning was not in left field but at shortstop.

"Give us an opening and we'll come through," McKeon said during a postgame interview. "Taking nothing away from their shortstop, who's a fine fielder, but someone is going to boot one now and then. When you get into the postseason, everything is magnified."

The eight-run eighth was a repeat of a rally Florida had staged against Philadelphia on July 25. Same inning, same number of runs. But the significance of that game paled in comparison to the importance of the October 14 contest.

Five outs from elimination, the Marlins sent 12 men to the plate, turning a 3-0 deficit into an 8-3 victory.

"We got a break," said Mike Lowell, stating the obvious. "I watched the replay and I thought Moises had a bead on it. I feel bad for the fan because he's going to take the blame. But a lot of things had to happen in the inning. That play was a start."

Mordecai agreed. "The fan probably cost them one out," he said, "and then the funny hop at shortstop gave us two extra outs. When you give our club those extra outs, we usually take advantage of them."

According to Mordecai, something similar happened in the 1996 AL Championship Series opener at Yankee Stadium. As Baltimore rightfielder Tony Tarasco waited under a fly ball, a 12-year-old fan named Jeffrey Maier deflected it into the stands. Umpire Rich Garcia ruled it a game-tying home run. The Yankees won the game and the series.

"Alou had a chance to catch that ball," Mordecai said. "I don't know if it was Jeffrey Maier out there, but it was the same situation."

Alou was angry. He pounded his glove against his knees and pointed to the fan but got no sympathy from umpire Mike Everitt. The arbiter argued that the ball had left the field of play, even though the leftfielder swore later he could have caught it.

Asked about Alou, Chicago manager Dusty Baker told the media, "He said he had it perfectly timed and the ball was just about to enter his glove, then all of a sudden it was gone. We couldn't see it from the dugout. After that, I saw the fans jumping up and down and making noise.

"It had nothing to do with the curse. It had to do with fan interference and the uncharacteristic error by Gonzo, because he doesn't miss anything. Then they just started hitting."

Whether it was a combination of the Goat Curse, McKeon Magic, or the worst bad luck since the Supreme Court stopped the Florida vote count, the Fish caught the Cubs instead of the other way around. The Championship Series was tied, three games apiece, and the race for the pennant was down to a single game.

For Florida, maybe momentum was a factor, or maybe not. The Marlins wasted no time proving they could splinter Wood. A Cabrera home run gave the visitors a 3-0 lead in the very first inning, although Cub homers by Moises Alou and Kerry Wood gave Chicago a momentary 5-3 advantage after three innings. Then the never-say-die Marlins staged yet another comeback.

In the top of the fifth, a two-run double from Florida's Alex Gonzalez was the big blow, but Lee also had an RBI hit. That gave the Fish a 6-5 lead they would never relinquish.

"Every night somebody else comes to the plate, somebody else makes a big pitch, somebody else makes a big play," Conine told Paul White of *USA Today Sports Weekly.* "If you look at numbers on paper, you probably say this team won't stack up to 1997. But if you look at intangibles like heart and stick-to-itiveness, you won't find a team as tenacious as this one when we're down."

No one was more tenacious than the table setters at the top of the Florida lineup. Pierre and Castillo, who struggled early in the NLCS, came alive in the last three games, fueling the Florida victories with 10 hits, four runs scored, and two walks. Their combined batting average was .357.

McKeon contributed too by showing a stroke of genius when he used Beckett in relief in Game 7. Pitching only three days after throwing 115 pitches in his 4-0 shutout, the hard-throwing Texan tossed four fine innings, yielding only a solo home run to pinch hitter Troy O'Leary, while helping to ice the 9-6 win that gave Florida the flag.

"He turned the series around," the manager said of his new-found ace. "He shut them down Sunday and was determined to pitch again."

Without Beckett, there might have been no tomorrow for the Marlins. Scheduled to throw in the bullpen anyway, he threw his 45 pitches from the mound.

Beckett yielded just 11 hits in his three appearances while fanning 19 in 19 1/3 innings. Urbina, the closer, was even more intimidating, fanning 10 and walking none while yielding two hits in seven innings. Neither was the MVP of the series, however.

That honor went to I-Rod, the stocky catcher who also deserved the honor in the NLDS (where no award is given). Against Chicago pitching, which was much tougher than San Francisco's, he hit .321 with two homers and an NLCS-record 10 RBI. Cabrera knocked in six and became the first rookie with three homers in a postseason since Charlie Keller in 1939. Lowell homered twice, and Conine contributed a .458 batting average. Even Todd Hollandsworth, who had lost his regular job during the season, was a factor. He reached base in all four of his appearances, going three-for-three with a walk.

"I've waited 12 years for this," said Rodriguez during the Florida victory party. "I'm going to the World Series with a team that nobody expected to be in the playoffs."

The catcher called time-out during the clubhouse celebration to beckon Jack McKeon to the center of the room. "You have what you want," he said. "You're going to the World Series. And we're going to win the World Series for you."

Rodriguez said the team started to jell right after the All-Star break.

"I know we started the season struggling," he said. "But we never gave up. I remember I had a meeting in Cincinnati after the All-Star break and I tell my teammates to believe in ourselves, play the game, take one day at a time, and do the best that you can in the field. Since that day that I tell them, we start playing the game and do the little things that we need to do.

"Our team can do everything. We have some power hitters, we have guys that can steal bases. We have good pitching. I knew from the All-Star break we started winning games and we win a lot coming back late in the game. That's a great feeling.

"We have to play 27 hard outs. When you do that, you can do a lot of things. We've been doing it all year and we're going to do the same thing in the World Series."

Only three teams had recovered from a deficit of three games to one to win a Championship Series and only one, the 1985 Kansas City Royals, did it by winning its final two games on the road. Before the 2003 Marlins came along, the only NL team to mount such a comeback was the Atlanta Braves in 1996.

Disappointed Cub skipper Dusty Baker, both a winner and loser in previous Championship Series, tipped his cap to the Marlins: "Sometimes you've got to look back and say, 'Hey, at the end, were they better than us?' They might have been better and more well-rounded. They refused to be put away."

For McKeon, it was not the first time he had witnessed a Cub collapse. He was general manager of the 1984 San Diego Padres when the Cubs, needing only one win to clinch the best-of-five NLCS, dropped three straight, blowing a 3-0 lead in the finale on a sixth-inning error. A year later—too late for the Cubs—the Championship Series format became best of seven.

"The Cubs were always America's favorite, but we're the darlings of the baseball world now," McKeon said after the 2003 series. "I think we'll have all those people rooting for us because they're seeing an exciting team."

The veteran manager didn't realize it at the time, but the level of excitement was about to reach a crescendo neither he nor any of his youthful charges had ever experienced.

Miguel Cabrera drops to his knees in celebration of the Marlins 2-0 victory
over the Yankees, which gave the Fish their second championship
in just their second winning season.

Chapter 21

THE WORLD SERIES: A SERIES FOR SNOWBIRDS

For me, the 2003 World Series has to rank above the 1997 Series because of the fact that we won on the most hallowed grounds of all of baseball—Yankee Stadium. To take two out of three in that place as inexperienced as we were was another one of the legendary things that will go down in history for that series. I think Josh Beckett summed it up so eloquently in the first round of the playoffs. Somebody asked him how do you think your team will do because there's so much youth and inexperience. He said, "With inexperience comes stupidity and we might just be stupid enough to win this thing." That was pretty prophetic.

Beckett's performance in Game 6 was legendary. To shut out the Yankees at Yankee Stadium in the sixth game of the World Series will go down in history as one of the best-pitched games ever.

—Jeff Conine

The Florida Marlins weren't supposed to win the World Series. They weren't even supposed to be in it.

When the playoffs started, the sentimental favorites for the final round were the Chicago Cubs and Boston Red Sox, lovable losers afflicted by long playoff winless streaks and rumors of curses. The Cubs, with no world championships since 1908, had not reached the World Series since 1945 and were trying to surmount the Goat

Curse of Wrigley Field. The Red Sox, not world champs since Babe Ruth pitched them to the title in 1918, were trying to overcome The Curse of the Bambino. Since selling Ruth to the rival Yankees, the Sox lost all four of their World Series appearances.

If the fans couldn't have a Cubs-Red Sox match, they would have settled for Giants-Yankees, the first such matchup since 1962, or Braves-Yankees, reviving memories of 1957, 1958, 1996, and 1999. Even Cubs-Yankees, not seen in the World Series since 1938, would have worked because of the intense rivalry between the two cities.

Other potential matchups also provided intriguing possibilities. Twins-Braves would have been a rerun of the Worst-to-First World Series of 1991, A's-Giants would have been a rematch of the 1989 Earthquake Series, and Twins-Cubs would have stirred a Midwest regional rivalry. Even Braves-Red Sox would have worked, matching two clubs that used to play in the same city, or A's-Cubs, reprising the 1929 World Series turned around by a 10-run inning in the fourth game.

But Florida?

Even though the 2002 World Series had paired two wild-card winners for the first time, no one gave the 2003 wild-card entry much of a chance.

With a $54 million payroll, a plethora of unproven players, and the oldest manager in World Series history, the Fish were widely considered bait for the pinstriped whale that had swallowed the world championship so many times. Yankee history showed 26 world championships in 38 tries, a record of success far superior to any other team's. Entering the 2003 World Series, the Bronx Bombers had won four of their last five appearances and six of their last eight, dating back to 1977. While piling up 17 more world championships than any other franchise (St. Louis ranks second with nine), the Yankees had recorded a .604 winning percentage (128-84) in the World Series.

The Yankees were *expected* to win. The tunnel leading from their clubhouse to the dugout at Yankee Stadium even had a framed poster containing Douglas MacArthur's quote, "There's no substitute for victory." Every Yankee saw it whenever he went from the locker room to the field.

Florida didn't bother with signs. Entering the 2003 World Series, the team had just two winning seasons, one world title, and no division crowns. Though named for a fish, the Marlins were decided underdogs.

Like Cujo, those underdogs proved to have strong jaws. Given a chance, the Marlins grabbed hold of their enemy and held on.

Errors and passed balls by playoff opponents permitted the Marlins to score 14 unearned runs, enabling them to win the third game of the NL Division Series and the sixth game of the Championship Series. "We live on extra outs," said Jeff Conine.

Jack McKeon agreed. At 72, he was not only the oldest manager in World Series history but the first to reach the Fall Classic without major-league playing experience since Jim Leyland, also with the Marlins, in 1997. Maybe history was repeating itself.

"Nobody gave us a chance to make it to the wild card but we did that," said McKeon. "No one said we could beat the Giants. We did that. Then they said we didn't have a chance against the Cubs with Kerry Wood and Mark Prior. We accomplished that feat too. Now we're at the next level. Let the pressure be on somebody else."

The Marlins were hoping to emulate the no-name politician who comes out of obscurity to oust a favored incumbent (see Bill Clinton in 1992). But they knew it wouldn't be easy.

Because of a new rule granting home-field advantage to the league that wins the All-Star Game, the Series started at Yankee Stadium, where McKeon once attended games as a boy. The 100th anniversary World Series would also be the first Series for Snowbirds, pitting the winter home of many New Yorkers (Florida) against their summer residence.

The World Series was almost an afterthought for the Yankees, whose pinstriped presence is almost a given every October. On the National League side, however, variety has been the spice of life, with six different entrants in the six seasons since Florida won it last: San Diego in 1998, Atlanta in 1999, New York Mets in 2000, Arizona in 2001, San Francisco in 2002, and the Marlins in 2003.

Florida drew first blood, scoring in the first on a bunt hit by Juan Pierre, a soft single to right by Luis Castillo, and a sacrifice fly by Pudge Rodriguez. The Yankees tied it, 1-1, in the third on an RBI single by Derek Jeter. The shortstop got his chance after Karim Garcia, leading off the inning, reached second on a shallow fly ball misjudged by Miguel Cabrera, who had moved from right field to left so that Conine could DH. Two outs later, Nick Johnson walked and moved to third on Jeter's game-tying single. When Johnson strayed too far down the line, Pudge Rodriguez picked him off with a perfect peg, ending the Yankee threat. New York's only other run of the night came on a solo sixth-inning homer from Bernie Williams.

By then, Florida had a 3-1 lead, thanks to a two-run burst in the top of the fifth. In that inning, Conine walked and Juan Encarnacion singled him to second. Alex Gonzalez dropped a sacrifice bunt, advancing the runners. Pierre lashed a liner past Jeter at short to plate both, though third baseman Aaron Boone might have had a play at the plate if he hadn't cut off Hideki Matsui's throw from left field. He said later he didn't want the fleet Pierre to get to second.

It wouldn't matter. Florida, with four innings of shutout relief from Dontrelle Willis and Ugueth Urbina, won the opener, 3-2.

"I'm tired of people asking why we aren't afraid of the Yankees," Josh Beckett told Dan LeBatard of *ESPN The Magazine.* "We're a good team, that's why. We didn't get here because of any goat. We didn't get here because of a curse or a fan. We got here because we're good."

The pitcher added that he wasn't intimidated by the Yankee mystique, personified by the Babe Ruth, Lou Gehrig, and Joe DiMaggio plaques in Monument Park. "Why should I be?" he said. "I'm not facing *those* guys."

Even after Andy Pettitte evened the score for the Yankees in Game 2, Florida wasn't flustered.

Pettitte, a lefty with lots of postseason experience, limited the Marlins to six hits and an unearned run in 8 2/3 innings before Jose Contreras got the last out. Blanked until the ninth, the Marlins ruined the shutout when Castillo singled, Cabrera was safe on an Aaron Boone error, and Lee singled a run home. The final score was 6-1.

With the series shifted to Florida for Game 3, pitching was again the name of the game. After the Marlins scored in the first on a Pierre double and Cabrera single, playoff hero Josh Beckett held the Yankees to two hits and one run until the top of the eighth. The hard-throwing Texan got leadoff man Alfono Soriano for his 10th strikeout, then yielded a double to Jeter. That was the last man he faced.

Beckett, who fanned 10 and walked three, was charged with another run when Jeter advanced to third on a fly ball and scored on a Matsui single against Willis. Although the score was only 2-1, it didn't stay that way long. In a rare Florida bullpen failure, Chad Fox and Braden Looper combined to throw gopher balls to Boone and Williams in the ninth. That increased the score to 6-1, a repeat of the previous night's final.

Florida would not lose again, though few viewers figured the Fish could win three games in a row for the third consecutive postseason series. Down 1-0 in the NL Division Series, they had rallied to beat San Francisco, three games to one. Against the Chicago Cubs in the Championship round, they rebounded from a 3-1 deficit in the best-of-seven match, not only winning three straight but taking two of them on enemy territory against their rival's best pitchers.

The Yankees were no ordinary opponent. They had won the World Series in 1996, 1998, 1999, and 2000, lost in 2001, and failed to survive the playoffs in 1997 and 2002. That record, impressive enough for normal human beings, was not sufficient for George Steinbrenner, who not only owned the Yankees but a temper that made him an absolute tyrant when irritated. An admirer of General George S. Patton, Steinbrenner regarded losing as aberrant behavior.

With more resources than any other owner, the Yankee boss lavished vast sums on players, creating a virtual All-Star team of free agents and veteran stars other clubs couldn't afford. The 2003 Yankee payroll tipped the scales at $180 million, more than triple the payroll of the Florida franchise. But the veteran-heavy Yankees lacked the youthful enthusiasm of the high-spirited Marlins. Nor could the power-dependent Yankees match the speed, defense, or pitching of their National League opponents.

That became apparent over the next three games, as Florida starters combined to hold New York hitters to two earned runs—that's right, two—in 25 innings.

In the first inning of Game 4, the Fish borrowed a page from the Yankee gamebook. The Yankees sent to the mound Roger Clemens, a 310-game winner who—at the time—was making what was believed to be the final start of his storied career at the age of 41. The Marlins parlayed a Rodriguez single and Cabrera homer into two quick runs against the Rocket. When Conine, Lowell, and Lee followed with successive singles, Florida had a 3-0 lead.

Facing Carl Pavano, the Yanks regrouped quickly, scoring on a second-inning single by Williams, successive infield hits by Matsui and Jorge Posada, and a one-out sacrifice fly by Boone. After escaping the bases-loaded, no-outs situation, Pavano was almost perfect. He yielded seven hits and no walks in his eight-inning stint, retiring 15 of the last 16 men he faced.

But Pavano had thrown 115 pitches, convincing Jack McKeon it was Urbina time. The closer had been perfect down the stretch and was on the mound, saving a game for Pavano, when the wild card was clinched. But October 23 was not his night.

Maybe the stars were not properly aligned. Maybe the moon was full. Maybe the baseball gods didn't want to make the march of the Marlins too easy.

For whatever reason, Urbina didn't have his best stuff. He retired Jason Giambi, the first man he faced, but yielded a single to right-center by Williams. After a walk to Matsui, Posada hit into a fielder's choice, forcing out Matsui at second. With Williams at third and pinch-runner David Dellucci at first, pinch-hitter Ruben Sierra, batting for Karim Garcia, worked Urbina to a 3-2 count, then fouled off two pitches. He followed with a rocket into the right field corner, plating two runs to tie the game. Boone grounded out to end the inning.

The Yankees had another chance in the 11th. They loaded the bases with one out before Braden Looper fanned Boone and got John Flaherty to pop out. In his only World Series appearance, erstwhile starter Jeff Weaver was perfect in the bottom of the 11th. But he faced only one man in the 12th.

Slumping shortstop Alex Gonzalez, deep in the throes of a five-for-53 slump, sent a 3-2 pitch into the seats, barely clearing the left field wall 330 feet away. It was only the 13th time a home run had ended a World Series game. The score was 4-3 in 12 innings, giving Gonzalez a share of the mark for latest home run in Fall Classic history (see Carlton Fisk, 1975).

"I can't hang my head," said the shortstop, whose postseason batting average had been .094 when he hit his game-winning homer. "I just go out there and do the best I can. In the postseason, you can win a game with your defense. I feel so excited. I hit a home run in the World Series!"

Gonzalez continued his revival the next night. He combined with Lowell and Lee, fellow infielders also fighting slumps, for four hits, four runs, and three RBI. Coupled with solid starting pitching from Game 1 winner Brad Penny, it was more than enough to win the last scheduled game at Pro Player Stadium.

"I don't know what it is," Lowell said of McKeon's decision to stick with the same infielders. "It's experience blended with intuition and instincts, I guess. Look at how, when guys are struggling, he keeps sending them back out there. That shows he hasn't lost faith in them."

Penny yielded an unearned run in the first when Jeter singled, Enrique Wilson reached on a surprise bunt hit, and Jeter sped to third on a rare error by Lee. A sac fly by Williams gave the Yanks an early 1-0 lead. It wouldn't last long.

With Yankee starter David Wells out of the game after an inning because of back spasms, Cuban defector Jose Contreras came out of the bullpen. After getting two quick outs, he walked Lowell and Lee. Gonzalez followed with a ground-rule double to right center, scoring Lowell, and Penny, a good-hitting pitcher, singled to score Lee and Gonzalez. Florida never trailed again.

Florida got one in the fourth when Lee singled, Penny bunted him to second, and Pierre doubled to right center. The Fish added a pair an inning later, with ex-Marlin Chris Hammond on the mound.

Rodriguez singled and, one out later, Conine grounded into a fielder's choice. Rodriguez reached third and Conine second when Wilson, the second baseman, made a bad throw. Lowell then drove them both in with a single to right center.

Though he yielded a seventh-inning run on singles by Nick Johnson, Garcia, and Jeter, Penny picked up the win with seven solid innings. He yielded eight hits and two walks while fanning four.

Braden Looper gave up two runs in the ninth on a Giambi homer, Jeter single, and Wilson double but Urbina saved it, retiring Williams on a fly ball and Matsui on a grounder to first.

Game 5 went to Florida by a score of 6-4. By beating the Yankees more than once in a single World Series, Penny joined an elite fraternity occupied only by Sandy Koufax, Bob Gibson, and Randy Johnson. He also became a World Series MVP contender with a 2-0 record and 2.19 ERA, not a bad showing for someone who was ineffective in the Championship Series.

"I went from the lowest I could possibly be to being at the highest I could possibly be," the pitcher said. "I'm just glad I had an opportunity to go back out there and throw like I could."

Penny's win set up a good-news, bad-news situation: the Marlins had three wins in the best-of-seven competition but were heading back to Yankee Stadium, normally a den of ill repute for teams without pinstripes. But Florida uniforms had pinstripes too.

Beckett didn't worry about any fashion statement. A Texas-bred fireballer in the mold of Nolan Ryan, Roger Clemens, and Kerry Wood, he looked even larger than his 6'5" frame when standing on a pitcher's mound. And his three-pitch arsenal included a fastball that flirted with triple digits.

After proving during the playoffs he could pitch well on short rest, Beckett decided to test his arm again.

"I told them I wanted to long-toss to see how stiff I was," he told *ESPN The Magazine*. "I felt fine and told them I'd do it. I felt good the whole playoffs. I kind of got in the groove. Sometimes too much rest messes you up."

In one of the most difficult decisions of his managerial career, McKeon hesitated only slightly before naming him to start. Would it be better to hold Beckett back a day and use him with full rest in a potential Game 7? Or, would it be wiser to go for the gold right away and risk a one-game showdown without the ace of the staff?

"There are no guarantees," McKeon said. "This is the game we want to win. Forget pitch counts, rest, innings pitched, and all that. If he's throwing good, I'll leave him in there for nine innings."

Throughout the playoffs, the well seasoned manager had shown a distinct disdain for statistics, sabermetrics, and computer-generated strategems. Nor did he flinch when reporters pointed out that starters working on such short rest over the last five postseasons had gone 5-16 with a 6.30 ERA.

Acting more like a cigar-smoking poker player than a cyber-savvy manager, McKeon proved a master of the bluff. His decisions sometimes seemed impulsive, even impetuous, but he beat the house every time. Before Game 6, he not only went with his gut but predicted before the game that the Marlins would win by a 6-0 score.

You win some and you lose some.

McKeon picked the right result, a shutout, and got it by flaunting conventional strategy. But the final score was 2-0.

Florida gave Beckett all the runs he needed with single tallies in the fifth and sixth innings. With two outs in the fifth, Gonzalez and Pierre hit consecutive singles to right against Andy Pettitte, a left-hander trying to overcome a personal Game 6 jinx.

That brought up Luis Castillo, mired in a zero-for-15 skid. He was hitting .130 in the World Series and .206 in the postseason. He had already struck out and grounded into a fielder's choice against Pettitte. The veteran Yankee got two quick strikes but couldn't get the third. Castillo barely connected on a couple of fouls, then took two balls. Batting righthanded against the lefthanded pitcher, he rifled the next pitch into right field.

"I knew I was in a huge slump," he said later. "I was feeling bad but I knew God had to have something good for me. Nobody put pressure on me or made me feel down. Tonight I responded."

Castillo's opposite-field single scored Gonzalez, with Pierre and Castillo advancing on Karim Garcia's throw home. The shortstop made a hook slide around Jorge Posada, who missed a swipe tag after fielding the perfect strike from right. Gonzalez barely scratched the surface of the plate with his fingernails but umpire Tim Welke was watching closely. He gave the safe sign.

"When the catcher leaves home plate open, you have a chance," Gonzalez said later.

The inning continued as the Yankees walked the veteran Rodriguez, loading the bases, to face Cabrera, the first rookie to bat cleanup in a World Series since Ty Cobb. Though Cabrera might have added a grand slam to the two-run, opposite-field homer he had hit against Roger Clemens in Game 4, he couldn't touch Pettitte. Although he already had four postseason home runs, the freshman fanned for the final out, leaving Beckett with the thinnest of leads.

The pitcher found a little more breathing room an inning later, when Jeff Conine's routine grounder was booted by the usually sure-handed Jeter at short. Mike Lowell walked but was out at second when Lee's attempted sacrifice was fielded by the pitcher. Had the Yankees succeeded in completing a double play, Encarnacion's fly ball would have been harmless. Instead, it was a sacrifice fly that scored Conine with the second run of the night.

Plating that insurance run pleased Encarnacion, who had sat out all three games at Pro Player Stadium so that Conine and Cabrera could man the corners while Lowell played third. He succeeded only after falling behind in the count, 0-2. He fouled one off, took a ball, then sent the next delivery to medium right field, far enough away for Conine to race home.

The Marlins weren't through yet. Gonzalez reached on a bunt single, sending Lee to second, but Pierre—the toughest man to fan in the majors last year—struck out, stranding two for a total of five left on base in a two-inning span. The Yankees had rebounded from much larger deficits, especially in their own ballpark.

But October 25, 2003 would be different.

Beckett, playing his role in the Bronx even better than Richard Burton had played it on Broadway, refused to cave. Even when Bernie Williams and Jorge Posada reached him for doubles, the righthander left them stranded. He allowed three singles and two walks but coaxed two double plays, including one that started on a Nick Johnson grounder to end the eighth inning.

"When we made that double play," said shortstop Alex Gonzalez, "I said to myself, 'That's it, we're world champs.' The way Beckett was pitching, they weren't going to hurt him."

Beckett got the last out himself, tagging Posada on a slow roller up the first base line. The seventh pitcher to eliminate the Yankees at Yankee Stadium, Beckett was the fourth to finish the game, joining Johnny Beazley (1942), Johnny Podres (1955), and Lew Burdette (1957). He was also the first starter to finish a World Series finale since Orel Hershiser in 1988.

The Marlin master faced 32 batters, never allowed a runner past second, and fanned nine, tying Randy Johnson's record of 47 postseason strikeouts. In a game that lasted a relatively quick two hours and 57 minutes, he needed only 107 pitches, including less than 10 in three different innings (fourth, sixth, and ninth). Four times, the Yankees got their leadoff man on. In three of those innings, Beckett retired the next three men.

Derek Jeter, author of the only three hits Beckett had yielded in Game 3, went zero for four with two strikeouts. He also went zero for two with runners on base, helping to ensure there would be no Game 7 at Yankee Stadium for the 46th consecutive year.

"They were the best team in the Series," said Jeter after his only hitless game in the Series. "They beat San Francisco, they beat Chicago, and they beat us. No one deserves it more than them."

While Jeter prepared to go home for the winter, Beckett basked in the postgame spotlight.

"I thought all three of my pitches were pretty good," he said with a touch of modesty rare for a 23-year-old who predicted at his August 1999 signing that he'd be an All-Star within two years. "I didn't throw quite as many changeups today as I did the last start against these guys but I thought my curveball was sharp and I felt I could locate it."

The hard-throwing righthander retired eight of the last nine men, throwing his mid-90s fastballs as hard at the end of the game as he did at the start. Only his curve seemed less lively in the late innings, according to the pitcher's father.

"Everything worked for him," said catcher Pudge Rodriguez. "I had to be ready because he's so tough and nasty. I told him before the game, 'You're going to pitch the biggest game of your career tonight. All you have to do is trust your stuff and trust yourself.'"

In his final four games, including three starts and a four-inning relief stint in the final playoff game, the righthander recorded a 0.92 earned run average over 29 1/3 innings.

"It's going to be a big turning point in his career," said Penny, the only Marlin to beat the Yankees twice. "I think he'll go out and be lights out for the rest of his career."

Florida scouting director Stan Meek agreed. "The baton was passed from one Texan to another that night," he said. "From Clemens to Beckett. Three days of rest, Yankee Stadium, 23 years old. All these things against him and he was still phenomenal."

Beckett became the youngest pitcher since Bret Saberhagen to win a decisive World Series game. The Florida flamethrower took the mound at age 23 years, five months, and 10 days, while Kansas City's 1985 hero won at 21 years, six months, and 16 days of age.

Beckett's performance was more memorable because of the short rest, low score, and venue. While Saberhagen, with five days of rest, won an 11-0 game against the Cardinals at home, Beckett, beating the Yankees in their own ballpark, quieted a Yankee Stadium crowd of 55,773.

The 19th shutout in a World Series clincher and the fourth since divisional play started in 1969, it was the first since Jack Morris of the Minnesota Twins went 10 innings in Game 7 to beat the Atlanta Braves, 1-0, in 1991.

Beckett's win made the Marlins the first visiting team to win a World Series at Yankee Stadium since the 1981 Los Angeles Dodgers, as well as the first team of the expansion era (dating back to 1961) to win two world titles in its first 11 seasons.

"Who's going to be the first one to ask me if Beckett can pitch on three days' rest?" McKeon asked in the postgame press conference. "The guy has the guts of a burglar. He's mentally tough. And I knew he had the confidence to go out there and do the job he did tonight. I was not about to take him out. He went into the ninth inning with only 99 pitches (thrown). You are looking at a possible All-Star next year and a 20-game winner.

"Maybe you'll believe me now. Anything can happen."

Pettitte believes. The Yankee southpaw, a loser in two previous Game 6 appearances, retired 14 of the first 17 men he faced before

Gonzalez singled in the fifth. Until the shortstop scored, he had worked 12 2/3 scoreless innings against Florida. But even though he worked seven strong innings, Pettitte was no match for Beckett.

Yankee hitters went zero for seven with runners in scoring position, lowering their overall futility against Florida to seven-for-50, a success ratio of only 14 percent. That helped, since the Yankees had more runs (21-17), hits (54-47), and home runs (6-2) than their opponents over the six-game set. New York had a better batting average (.261 to .232) and a better earned run average (2.13 to 3.21).

Florida's fielding made the difference. The Marlins made two errors and yielded one unearned run, but the Yankees made five miscues (three by Aaron Boone) that seemed to come at critical times: they allowed four unearned runs, half of them during Florida's two-run win in Game 5.

"We haven't played a team like them all year," said Yankee pitcher Mike Mussina, who won his only start. "They're a throwback National League team."

Playing small ball had a big payoff for the Fish, who wound up with winners' shares of $303,894.84 per man, the highest since 1999. Six years earlier, Florida players received $188,467.55 each.

"They do the little things," said Yankee manager Joe Torre of the 2003 Marlins, "and they don't know what intimidation is. It was a helluva lesson for us."

The Marlins certainly taught the Yankees a lesson. They struck for 21 hits and 10 runs with two outs. All but 10 of their 47 hits in the Series were singles. And Florida's insurance run in the finale came without benefit of a hit, the result of an error, a walk, a bunt, and a sac fly.

"We don't have the big power of the Yankees or some other clubs," McKeon said in the Yankee Stadium interview room. "We just don't have that kind of firepower. You catch us down by five runs, it's pretty tough for us to catch up. But you keep the game close for us, we are going to give you some trouble.

"What happened with us in the postseason is that when one of our big guns goes south, somebody unexpected takes over. Cabrera was a big-game player before but didn't do anything (in Game 6). Castillo, who was struggling bad, gets a key hit to put us out front. Lee makes a good bunt. Then the sacrifice fly for the two-run lead. And Beckett took care of it. Small Ball has been part of our arsenal all year."

Even though he pitched four times in the final 14 days, Beckett made the Marlins virtually unbeatable. As George Steinbrenner said during Game 6, "That's one real tough kid."

The disappointment of the Yankee owner ran counter to the euphoria of the victors.

Pierre, the primary practitioner of the small ball philosophy, bounced around the winners' locker room with a glow. "All during the playoffs people doubted us," he told *USA Today*. "We didn't have the pitching or we didn't have enough power is what they kept saying. But they didn't know about our heart. Every day, we played with heart. That's something you can't scout."

Inside the clubhouse, players took turns pointing at the World Series trophy and posing for pictures. "We shocked the world again," the normally reserved Jeff Conine shouted above the din. "No one said we could do it. And look what it says right here: WORLD CHAMPIONS!"

A sea of hands carried the champagne-soaked trophy out onto the field, where Jeffrey Loria held it high above a group of family members smiling for photographers.

"I'm euphoric," he exclaimed as his players pranced around the diamond with champagne and cigars. "What could be more exciting than winning the World Series in your hometown, where you were born, where you spent a lot of years watching baseball? I can only tell you I felt fantastic."

The 58-year-old Florida owner had just completed a run around the bases, making him the oldest man ever to complete that circuit (with the possible exception of Satchel Paige). A New York

City art dealer with a home in South Florida, Loria had never felt so warm and fuzzy in Montreal, where baseball disinterest is a disease.

"All the kids in the world run the bases," said Loria, offering the same logic Sir Edmund Hillary gave for climbing Mt. Everest. "Why shouldn't I? I feel like a kid."

Loria's kids had scaled the Mt. Everest of the baseball world, taken a seat on Cloud 9, and relished the afterglow. But keeping the core of the team intact would pose a bigger challenge. The owner would address that issue later.

"I got to bed about 4 a.m.," he said. "I needed a few hours to return to earth and savor it all. I guess the word is elated. I guess there are no more discussions about whether baseball is alive in South Florida. There will be no more discussions about Fish fries."

The re-signing of third baseman Mike Lowell in December 2003, speaks volumes of
the Marlins' commitment to fielding a competitive team in 2004.
AP/WWP

Chapter 22

FISH FOR THE FUTURE

Jeffrey Loria came up to me during our victory celebration and said, "This is not 1997."

We are not dismantling. With the signing of Luis Castillo and Mike Lowell, we've got basically a huge core of guys coming back from this team that are still young. And I'm saying that as a player who went through that 1997 thing and saw everyone just cast off and shipped out of here so quickly it would make your head spin. Knowing that these guys want to grab ahold of South Florida and build something here as far as enthusiasm for baseball, they've done a great job.

—Jeff Conine

Three days after the end of the 1997 World Series, the owner of the Florida Marlins told his general manager heavy operating losses would force him to sell the team. H. Wayne Huizenga, a self-made billionaire, also ordered Dave Dombrowski to pare the top-heavy payroll.

No such edict came from Jeffrey Loria after his edition of the Marlins won another world title six years later. But the team's tradition of tying the purse strings tight, coupled with its inability to win approval for a weather-proof, all-baseball ballpark, scared the Florida faithful.

"I'm a different person (than Huizenga)," Loria insisted. "We are committed to South Florida. I am happiest when I see faces of young kids and new people who haven't been to the ballpark for awhile—or ever. We've made lots and lots of new fans."

Another fire sale would alienate that fragile fan base.

"For the sake of the baseball fans in South Florida," said third baseman Mike Lowell, nearly traded himself last season, "they need to bring back as much of the team as possible. They can't take another dismantling."

Marlins management would rather dismantle the team's ballpark.

Pro Player Stadium has been a thorn in the team's side since Day One. Designed for football, neither its dimensions nor location work well for baseball. Because few fans want to sit in the seats of the open-air stadium during Florida's hot, sticky summer nights, the team ranked third-from-worst in 2003 attendance, averaging only 16,000 per game during the regular season.

The message from fans was obvious: topless is okay on South Beach, but the Marlins need to cover their field.

That won't happen right away. With city, county, and state officials unable or unwilling to provide land or money for a new ballpark, the Marlins renewed their Pro Player Stadium lease through 2005. That won't add much to the team's coffers, since the Marlins receive little or no revenue from the suites, concessions, and parking at the ballpark.

Should a new stadium be built within the city limits, the Marlins would change their first name, substituting "Miami" for "Florida." It wouldn't be without precedent, since the Angels had previously subbed "Anaheim" for "California."

Florida's announcement came on October 30, when front pages trumpeting the club's world championship were still selling on the street.

According to team president David Samson, stepson of the team's owner, "It was something Jeffrey and I had no problem with. It was not a negotiating point. We need a baseball-only ballpark."

Finding financing for the 38,000-seat stadium is the hard part. Seattle's retractable-roof ballpark, Safeco Field, cost $517 million, far above figures proposed in talks with Miami, Miami-Dade County, and state officials. Florida Governor Jeb Bush, who once rejected a cruise tax designed to raise money for the ballpark, may also get involved.

In the meantime, the team faces the challenge of keeping its nucleus intact.

Even before the echoes of their World Series victory party had faded into the night, the Marlins realized their team would never be the same. Players eligible for free agency or arbitration would swell the payroll beyond affordable limits. The task for Loria, general manager Larry Beinfest, and their front-office advisers was to keep the core of the talented young team.

Keeping everyone would have cost an estimated $90 million, some $30 million more than Beinfest's projected 2004 budget. The Marlins had to make cuts somewhere.

Their first move came in November, when Florida first baseman Derrek Lee was dealt to the Chicago Cubs for Hee Seop Choi, a young player of promise at the same position. Lee, with 31 homers and a Gold Glove last year, could have earned $7.5 million in arbitration but eventually signed a one-year, $6.9 million deal with the Cubs.

"No one is going to take the place of Lee," McKeon said at the time. "You hate to see him go. But I think this move was an effort to see if they couldn't free up some money to enable us to keep as many other guys as we can."

Another regular left during the December winter meetings when the Marlins dealt Juan Encarnacion, their rightfielder most of last year, to the Dodgers. Although his 19 home runs, 19 stolen bases, and errorless defense will be missed, Encarnacion complained about being benched in World Series games that didn't have a DH. The team plans to open 2004 with the same outfield that started Game 5: Jeff Conine in left, Juan Pierre in center, and Miguel Cabrera in right.

While Choi, 25, brings a much-needed lefthanded bat to Jack McKeon's batting order, the remainder of Florida's infield looks familiar.

The Fish hooked the other regulars with new contracts for second baseman Luis Castillo, who had been courted by several clubs, and third baseman Mike Lowell, another Marlin mainstay since 1999, while shortstop Alex Gonzalez was given two years at $6.2 million.

Castillo, the first Marlin to sign a multi-year contract under Loria's ownership, inked a three-year, $16 million deal with a vesting option for a fourth. The Marlins believe the 28-year-old All-Star second baseman is worth the risk.

Lowell's contract, unlike Castillo's, hinges on the team finding financing for a new ballpark by November 1, 2004. He'll make $8 million a year through 2007 or, without new ballpark financing, $7 million during a one-year player option in 2005. He'll turn 30 during spring training.

Although retaining Pudge Rodriguez was also a Florida priority, the team came up empty. Refusing to take a cut from the $10 million he earned in 2003, the catcher rejected both an initial offer of four years at $7 million and a subsequent bid for four years at $8 million.

"I tried my best to remain a Marlin by not requesting a salary increase," said the veteran backstop, who was hoping for a four-year, $40 million pact. It never came, leaving the Marlins with a choice of holdovers Ramon Castro and Mike Redmond or the signing of another free-agent catcher. Since Castro hit five home runs in 53 at-bats, his potential is obvious.

In addition to I-Rod, the Marlins also lost closer Ugueth Urbina, set-up man Rick Helling, and outfielder Todd Hollandsworth, none of whom were offered arbitration, and hard-throwing Braden Looper, an arbitration-eligible reliever who was not tendered a contract. But they kept their bench strong by signing Mike Mordecai, who plays everything but the bass fiddle, and Lenny Harris, the lifetime leader in pinch hits.

Florida found a new closer in Armando Benitez, a 6'4", 225-pound righthander with 197 career saves and 764 strikeouts in 584 1/3 innings. The Dominican flamethrower, an NL All-Star in 2003, signed a one-year deal worth $3.5 million, well within the operating budget of the Marlins.

"We think this guy has a great arm," said Beinfest of Benitez. "Armando is an established closer, and we think he can flourish with our club. We think he will re-establish himself as one of the top closers in the game."

According to the general manager, Benitez should benefit from Florida's fine defense and its pitcher-friendly park.

He'll also have more leads to protect than he did with the Mets, a last-place team in both 2002 and 2003. Benitez, 31, had consecutive seasons of 40-plus saves in 2000-01 and has a lifetime ERA of 3.03.

After signing Benitez, Beinfest met reporters. "We are within our operating range," he said. "There are not big parts of this team to address."

The biggest question mark seemed to be the timetable for the return of A.J. Burnett. The author of a 3-0 no-hitter at San Diego on May 12, 2001, Burnett is a 6'4" righthander who has been on the disabled list for parts of the last four seasons. If his elbow, rebuilt by Tommy John ligament transplant surgery, is sound, Florida will have the league's most formidable rotation. Typical recovery time is 18 months.

Until Burnett is ready, the Marlins will use lefty Darren Oliver, a free agent signed in January, as their fifth starter behind Josh Beckett, Brad Penny, Carl Pavano, and Dontrelle Willis. A healthy Burnett would be far more powerful than a typical fifth wheel.

"He may have the best stuff of them all," Rick Helling told *Sports Illustrated* during the postseason. "That could be scary: four guys throwing 95-plus and Dontrelle (Willis) flinging from the left side. That could be something special. The nucleus is there to have a great team for a long time."

Burnett's projected return made Mark Redman expendable. The arbitration-eligible lefthander, a 14-game winner in his only Florida season, was swapped to Oakland for righthanded reliever Mike Neu, a University of Miami product six years his junior.

With nine free agents and 15 players eligible for arbitration, Beinfest hardly had time to rest on his laurels. Only Juan Pierre and Jeff Conine were signed beyond 2003. It was time for a reality check, not a blank check.

"If you have a team like this, you should keep it together for two, three, or four years," Pudge Rodgriquez said after the World Series. "If the team stays together, I think it can be like the Yankees. It can win pretty much every year in the playoffs and win more World Series.

"The team right now is what a lot of teams want to have, a team that can do everything—guys who can bunt, good pitching, guys who can move the guy over, power in the middle of the line-up."

According to Rodriguez, who will be tough to replace, good chemistry was a major factor for the team's success.

"If we didn't have the team unity that we had, we could have been eliminated," he said.

"But we stayed strong, stayed positive as a team. I like to talk to the pitchers, I like to talk to the young players. And we established a good relationship, all 25 players in the clubhouse, all together."

Losing Rodriguez was a setback for Florida.

"He was terrific for us, but we were not able to get a deal done," Beinfest said. "It's unfortunate. I thought Pudge was a good fit here. We needed to be creative and I think we were creative. Jeffrey was open to a lot of things. I think we were all hopeful of bringing Pudge back."

Keeping competitive within the confines of a tight budget requires creative thinking but also requires some gut-wrenching decisions, like the failed Rodriguez negotiations.

"We want to remain as competitive as possible," Samson said, "but everything has to fit right. A lot of good decisions and tough decisions had to be made. Very few teams have the same 25 guys year after year."

The team president admitted the turnover was tough on fans.

"I'm attached to players too," he said in a *Baseball America* interview, "but I'm more attached to the franchise. I'm more attached to making sure the Marlins are going to be here. The truth is, in 10 or 15 years, it won't be about Luis Castillo. If you've got players who are paid too much for what they deliver, you can't have them. That is the reality of baseball."

Finding a new formula won't be easy. But Larry Beinfest believes he's up to the task.

Step One was retaining the bulk of Jack McKeon's coaching staff: Jeff Cox (bullpen), Doug Davis (bench), Perry Hill (first base), Bill Robinson (hitting), and Wayne Rosenthal (pitching), along with bullpen coordinator Pierre Arsenault. He succeeded there.

Step Two was keeping the club's youthful core. For the most part, he did that too.

"You always want to stay strong and we need to stay strong," the GM said. "It doesn't mean the cupboard is bare, but each year we need to fill back in through the draft, through acquisitions, through our Latin program.

"We have a pretty clear vision of the team and how it will look. But you always try to remain as flexible as possible."

A big part of that flexibility is finding quality homegrown players.

"If you're a small-market club, you can only be successful if you are developing players within your system," explained Jim Fleming, Florida's scouting director. "We can't survive on free agents. So we have to produce.

"Since Jeffrey (Loria) has taken over, we've advanced scouting and player development.

"We're efficient. We've improved both our scouting and player development staffs since we came to Florida. And I think it's because Larry, David, and Jeffrey understand the importance of player development and scouting."

So does Jack McKeon.

"I think the nucleus is there for a winning team," he said, "but I can't say we'll get to the World Series again. That's pretty tough to do.

"We had a tremendous attitude on our club. The chemistry we had, I don't think anybody in the game will ever have that again."

The 2004 Marlins won't have the likes of Ugie Urbina and Pudge Rodriguez punctuating wins with a kiss. Or Derrek Lee providing dynamic defense at first base. Or Mark Redman leading the team in complete games. Or Ozzie Guillen waving runners around third base.

All are gone but not forgotten as the Marlins try to streamline their model for another title run. What's not gone is the optimism left by the most recent miracle team.

Maybe the Fish can fly again. Mr. Marlin will be there for the full year. Ditto Dontrelle Willis and Miguel Cabrera, the rookie raves of 2003. Castillo and Lowell, who nearly left last year, are happy with their new contracts. If Beckett feeds off October's momentum, Benitez thrives in the summer heat, and Burnett bounces back from surgery, McKeon might find another miracle under his hat.

At least, Florida fans have hope. Ticket sales spiked in September, when fans realized the Fish were in serious contention for a playoff berth, and peaked during the postseason, when Pro Player Stadium was packed. Attendance at the fifth game of the World Series was 65,075. Fans looking forward to next year even purchased several hundred 2004 season tickets within days of the last victory parade.

"We're the only team that won the last game," David Samson said. "On the field, I think Jeffrey and Larry have earned the right to say nothing could be improved on.

South Florida baseball fans rediscovered their devotion to Marlins baseball in 2003.
Thousands of fans lined the streets for the team's victory parade and rally.

AP/WWP

"Off the field, we could do better in expanding our fan base. That's very important to us. There's never any business operator who says he's home free. You're never there."

Another winning season, or several, would help.

Just ask McKeon. "Ownership has been great," the manager said. "Mr. Loria has been super in telling the fans that he was sincere about putting a winner in South Florida. He put up a lot of extra money to secure those players at the trading deadline.

"The fans supported us and they've energized South Florida baseball again. It's a compliment to the players and all the people in the organization. I think you're going to see that for years to come."

Jeffrey Loria couldn't agree more.

"We're going to keep doing more exciting things," he said. "We will do good things for baseball and good things for the fans.

"We've reconnected with our fans. The one thing I am confident about is that we'll have great baseball in South Florida for a long, long time."

Chapter 23
MARLIN MARVELS

Things to remember about The Miracle Marlins

LONE-STAR DISSENTER

George W. Bush of the Texas Rangers was the only major league club owner to vote against the three-division format that introduced the wild-card concept.

FEDERAL OFFENSE

Forgetting that defacing currency is a federal offense, the Florida Marlins ordered 75,000 dimes to be painted in the club's black-and-teal logo. The idea was to distribute them to schools, then allow recipients to trade them for tickets. Though the government agreed to ignore the situation, many kids kept the coins as collector's items.

LONG ODDS

On the eve of the 2003 season, Las Vegas odds against the Marlins winning the World Series were 150-to-1.

PRIDE OF PUERTO RICO

Backup catcher Ramon Castro, who hails from the same hometown as Pudge Rodriguez, was the first Puerto Rican high school player ever drafted in the first round. The Houston Astros took him with the 17th pick of the June 1994 amateur draft.

BATHING BEAUTIES

Florida fans found an extra added attraction last season: 15 women hired by the club to serve as "Mermaids." They hung out at The Oasis, the first inside-the-ballpark Jacuzzi in the big leagues. Spots, sold only in groups of 20-30, went for $35 per person during the regular season and $145 in the postseason. An extra added attraction was the chance to talk to Florida relievers, since the hot tub sat adjacent to the bullpen.

CHANGE FOR BETTER

Before the Marlins' in-season manager switcheroo in 2003, the last team to change managers and win a world championship in the same season was the 1978 New York Yankees (Bob Lemon replaced Billy Martin).

SPEED DEMONS

Juan Pierre and Luis Castillo combined for 86 stolen bases, more than 12 of the other 15 National League teams.

GRAND TIMING

The 2003 Florida Marlins did not hit a grand-slam home run.

GOOD GUESSWORK

In the movie *Back to the Future II*, made in 1989, Marty McFly (Christopher Lloyd) referred to a future World Series featuring a team from Miami. The Marlins started play four years after the film was released.

NO HITTER

Mark Redman may be the worst hitter in baseball. In his first National League season, he went one-for-61 and broke his thumb trying to bunt.

RETIRED NUMBER

The only retired number in Marlins history was never worn by a Florida player. It is the No. 5 worn by Yankee legend Joe DiMaggio, the favorite player of the late team president Carl Barger.

LORIA'S LONG MEMORY

The first time Jeffrey Loria went to a Yankee game by himself, he waited outside the players' gate for autographs. After everyone left, the young Loria was left with pitcher Eddie Lopat, who was waiting for a ride. They talked baseball for an hour and a half, giving the kid a thrill he would never forget. Years later, Loria spotted Lopat waiting for a traffic light and thanked him for those 90 memorable minutes.

GOOD LUCK CHARM

According to Jeff Miller in *ESPN The Magazine*, Florida had a good-luck charm in 80-year-old Spanish announcer Felo Ramirez. Several times during the 2003 season, the diminutive broadcaster rubbed bats of slumping players who immediately responded with big hits. "Felo changes the forces of nature," Mike Lowell told the magazine. "He's our Yoda."

MISTAKEN IDENTITY

When he was in the minors, Luis Castillo once pulled a fire alarm in the team hotel because he thought it was a shampoo dispenser.

REMEMBERING BECKETT

Said Dave Dombrowski, Florida GM when Josh Beckett was taken in the amateur draft: "From the day we scouted and signed him, we felt he was a special individual and had a chance to accomplish a lot. [Winning the World Series MVP award] was nice to watch, and it brought a smile to my face."

CHANGE OF COMMAND

During the three months between the departure of Dave Dombrowski and the hiring of Larry Beinfest, the Marlins had a troika in the general manager's chair. With the team about to be sold, the trio of John Westhoff, Scott Reid, and Al Avila were told to do nothing at the 2001 winter meetings.

STOP OR I'LL SHOOT

During his days as a minor league manager, Jack McKeon once fired a gun from his position as third-base coach to halt a runner who consistently ignored his stop signs. The gun was loaded with blanks.

HISTORY REPEATS

The last manager to pull two pitchers who had not retired a batter in the first inning—before Jack McKeon did it last June 27—was...Jack McKeon. As manager of the 2003 Marlins, he yanked Carl Pavano and Michael Tejera before they got an out during Boston's 14-run explosion at Fenway Park. McKeon had endured similar first-inning blues as a rookie manager with the Kansas City Royals in 1973, exactly 30 years earlier.

GIVE HIM A CIGAR

Florida manager Jack McKeon was named 2003 co-Sportsman of the Year by *The Sporting News* in December. He shared the honor with Kansas City Chiefs coach Dick Vermeil, whose NFL team also advanced to the playoffs.

HAPPY BLUES

The powder-blue Negro Leagues Hall of Fame T-shirts worn by Juan Pierre during his weight-room workouts help him remember those who paved his path in the big leagues.

LUIS THE LEADER

Luis Castillo has appeared in more games for the Marlins (856) than any other player.

STEALING THE TITLE

The Marlins were the first world champions since 1965 to lead the major leagues in stolen bases.

CAN'T CATCH ME

A Florida player has led the NL in stolen bases five times in the team's first 11 seasons: Chuck Carr in 1993, Quilvio Veras in 1995, Luis Castillo in 2000 and 2002, and Juan Pierre in 2003.

GOOD GLOVEWORK

Florida's .987 fielding percentage in 2003 was a team record. The Marlins made 78 errors in 6,004 chances.

PEDRO WHO?

Since Montreal traded Pedro Martinez to Boston for Carl Pavano and Tony Armas, Jr. in 1997, Pavano has more World Series starts (one) than Martinez (none).

TWO WEEKS LATE

Josh Beckett changed his number from 61 to 21 just two weeks after the Marlins staged a promotion in which they gave away 10,000 Beckett T-shirts bearing No. 61 on the back.

SILVER SI, GOLD NO

Brad Penny won a silver medal in the 1999 Pan Am Games but missed the gold when he lost to a Cuban team led by Jose Contreras, now with the Yankees.

OH, DEER

During the 2002 Texas hunting season, Josh Beckett won an award for shooting the largest deer—a 245-pound, 14-point buck.

NOT MUCH EXPERIENCE

The only 2003 Marlins with previous World Series experience were Jeff Conine, Lenny Harris, and Mike Mordecai.

GREAT AT GONZAGA

Before Bo Hart and Jason Bay reached the big leagues last year, Florida's Mike Redmond was the only Gonzaga University graduate in the majors. The school's most famous alumnus was not an athlete but an owner: singer Bing Crosby, who once owned a stake in the Pittsburgh Pirates.

THICK HIDE

Although the Jeffrey Loria regime was widely criticized during its first year in 2002, the Marlins' front office absorbed the shocks well. "We took all the shots everybody wanted to fire at us because what they were really doing was firing on history," he said. "We knew what we had to do."

YOUTH IS SERVED

In 2003, Dontrelle Willis became the youngest All-Star pitcher since Doc Gooden in 1984. Willis was 21 years and 184 days old when selected, as opposed to Gooden's 19 years and 237 days.

HARD TO HANDLE

Ugie Urbina held hitters to a .174 batting average during his 33 appearances with the Marlins.

GOOD COMPANY

Ty Cobb and Miguel Cabrera are the only players who hit cleanup in the World Series before their 21st birthdays.

BAD PITCH?

According to World Series MVP Josh Beckett, the double-play ball hit by Nick Johnson to end the bottom of the eighth inning in Game 6 was a hanging changeup.

BRADEN'S BONANZA

Braden Looper made the most of his first hit. Getting a rare chance to bat during a 2003 game against the Phillies, he stroked a single, motored to third on another hit, and scored the first run of his big-league career.

NOT INVITED?

Michael Tejera never told teammates he was getting married after a game in the middle of the 2002 season. They found out when one of them returned to the clubhouse and overheard the pending nuptials mentioned during the radio broadcast of the game. The Cuban defector pitched in relief the same day as his wedding.

THANKS, MOM

Ramon Castro didn't miss home cooking during his early years in the minors; his mother accompanied him.

BAD TIMING

Though Jeffrey Loria was in Yankee Stadium when New York clinched the 2003 AL pennant, he missed Aaron Boone's pennant-winning homer. "There was a lady in the restroom and it took forever for her to get out," he said. "As I was stepping in, I heard the crowd. That was Boone's home run."

TATTOO MAN

Tim Spooneybarger led the 2003 Marlins with 12 tattoos.

MANAGER'S IDOL

While growing up in South Amboy, NJ, Jack McKeon idolized hometown hero Allie Clark, who played for the 1947 Yankees.

TRIPLE THREAT

Braden Looper was his high school team MVP in baseball, basketball, and football. The National Honor Society member later won several academic awards at Wichita State, where he made the university's Hall of Fame.

BIG BAT

Jeff Conine tops the lifetime list of runs batted in by a member of the Marlins.

WHY JOSH WON

Josh Beckett said the Yankees helped him win Game 6 of the World Series with their anxiety at the plate. "They came out swinging," he said. "I thought they were more patient in my previous outing. It worked to my benefit. I didn't have to throw as many strikes because they were swinging at pitches that weren't necessarily strikes."

DOUBLEDAY FIELD?

Abner Doubleday, the alleged inventor of baseball, was stationed in South Florida late in his military career.

SLOPPY SUNDAYS

Sunday was the only day of the week in which the 2003 Marlins lost more games than they won. The team went 13-14 in Sunday games.

HAPPY AS A CLAM

Pitcher Chad Fox, a late-season pickup, couldn't figure out his new teammates. "You find yourself in a dogfight," he said. "You look around and the guys are smiling. Hey, they should be nervous. I've never been around a team like this."

COMEBACK KIDS

Florida's first four wins in the 2003 postseason were come-from-behind victories.

NEW RBI KING

With 10 RBIs in the 2003 NLCS, Pudge Rodriguez notched one more than previous record-holder Matt Williams of San Francisco in 1989.

SPEED + POWER

Derrek Lee was the only National Leaguer with at least 30 home runs and 20 stolen bases in 2003. He had 31 homers and 21 stolen bases, both career highs.

PENNY PERFECT

In 2003, Brad Penny became the only man to win both Game 7 of the Championship Series and Game 1 of the World Series. He won the playoff finale in relief, the Series opener as a starter.

BRONX BUST

Before the 2003 World Series, the Marlins had lost four of their five interleague games at Yankee Stadium.

AGE DIFFERENCE

Miguel Cabrera, whose first-inning homer helped beat Roger Clemens in the fourth game of the World Series, hadn't celebrated his second birthday before Clemens made his major-league debut in 1984.

TOUGH LOSS

Before their 3-2 defeat by Florida in the 2003 World Series opener, the Yankees had not lost a one-run World Series game at home since 1964.

STREAK STOPPED

The Yankees had won 10 straight World Series games at home, dating back to Game 6 in 1996, before losing the 2003 opener to Florida.

TERRIFYING TRIO

Florida power pitchers Josh Beckett, Brad Penny, and Carl Pavano went 3-1 with a 1.47 ERA in the 2003 World Series.

YANKEE DOODLE

World Series MVP Josh Beckett got his wish: he wanted to face the Yankees in the World Series. "They have 26 championships," he explained. "That's who we wanted to play, because if you are going to beat somebody, why not beat the best?"

WHAT'S NEXT?

After Josh Beckett's five-hit shutout ended the 2003 World Series, teammate Rick Helling did his best Yogi Berra in saying, "This is the beginning of the rest of his career."

APPENDIX

MAJOR LEAGUE STANDINGS

NL EAST	WON	LOST	PCT	GB
Atlanta	101	61	.623	--
*Florida	91	71	.562	10.0
Philadelphia	86	76	.531	15.0
Montreal	83	79	.512	18.0
New York	66	95	.410	34.5

NL CENTRAL	WON	LOST	PCT	GB
Chicago	88	74	.543	--
Houston	87	75	.537	1.0
St. Louis	85	77	.525	3.0
Pittsburgh	75	87	.463	13.0
Cincinnati	69	93	.426	19.0
Milwaukee	68	94	.420	20.0

NL WEST	WON	LOST	PCT	GB
San Francisco	100	61	.621	--
Los Angeles	85	77	.525	15.5
Arizona	84	78	.519	16.5
Colorado	74	88	.457	26.5
San Diego	64	98	.395	36.5

AL EAST	WON	LOST	PCT	GB
New York	101	61	.623	--
**Boston	95	67	.586	6.0
Toronto	86	76	.531	15.0
Baltimore	71	91	.438	30.0
Tampa Bay	63	99	.389	38.0

AL CENTRAL	WON	LOST	PCT	GB
Minnesota	90	72	.556	--
Chicago	86	76	.531	4.0
Kansas City	83	79	.512	7.0
Cleveland	68	94	.420	22.0
Detroit	43	119	.265	47.0

AL WEST	WON	LOST	PCT	GB
Oakland	96	66	.593	--
Seattle	93	69	.574	3.0
Anaheim	77	85	.475	19.0
Texas	71	91	.438	25.0

*NL Wild Card Winner
**AL Wild Card Winner

2003 MARLINS FINAL REGULAR SEASON STATS

PLAYER	G	AVG	AB	R	H	2B	3B	HR	RBI	BB	SO	SB	OBP	SLG
Allen	11	.208	24	2	5	1	1	0	0	0	5	0	.240	.333
Banks	90	.235	149	14	35	6	2	4	23	25	38	2	.348	.383
Beckett	21	.152	46	3	7	2	0	0	3	1	14	0	.170	.196
Bump	1	.000	0	0	0	0	0	0	0	0	0	0	.000	.000
Burnett	4	.143	7	0	1	0	0	0	0	2	3	0	.333	.143
Cabrera	87	.268	314	39	84	21	3	12	62	25	84	0	.325	.468
Castillo	152	.314	595	99	187	19	6	6	39	63	60	21	.381	.397
Conine	25	.238	84	13	20	3	0	5	15	13	10	0	.337	.452
Encarnacion	156	.270	601	80	162	37	6	19	94	37	82	19	.313	.446
Fox	65	.194	108	12	21	5	1	0	8	7	29	1	.269	.259
Gonzalez	150	.256	528	52	135	33	6	18	77	33	106	0	.313	.443
Harris	12	.286	14	3	4	0	0	0	1	3	1	0	.412	.286
Helling	2	.500	2	0	1	1	0	0	0	0	0	0	.500	1.000
Hollandsworth	91	.254	228	32	58	23	3	3	20	22	55	2	.317	.421
Lee	154	.271	539	91	146	31	2	31	92	88	131	21	.379	.508
Levrault	1	.000	2	0	0	0	0	0	0	0	1	0	.000	.000
Looper	3	1.000	1	1	1	0	0	0	0	0	0	0	1.000	1.000
Lowell	130	.276	492	76	136	27	1	32	105	56	78	3	.350	.530
Mordecai	58	.213	89	11	19	4	0	2	8	8	21	3	.276	.326

PLAYER	G	AVG	AB	R	H	2B	3B	HR	RBI	BB	SO	SB	OBP	SLG
Pavano	31	.098	61	4	6	2	1	0	1	2	27	0	.127	.164
Penny	30	.132	68	3	9	1	1	2	8	0	27	0	.132	.265
Phelps	8	.091	11	1	1	0	0	0	0	2	3	0	.231	.091
Pierre	162	.305	668	100	204	28	7	1	41	55	35	65	.361	.373
Redman	28	.016	6	1	0	1	0	1	0	1	1	31	.032	.016
Redmond	57	.240	125	12	30	7	1	0	11	7	16	0	.302	.312
Rodriguez	144	.297	511	90	152	36	3	16	85	55	92	10	.369	.474
Spooneybarger	3	.000	3	0	0	0	0	0	0	0	3	0	.000	.000
Tejera	11	.067	15	0	1	0	0	0	0	0	1	0	.067	.067
Urbina	2	.000	0	0	0	0	0	0	0	1	0	0	.000	.000
Wayne	1	.000	2	0	0	0	0	0	0	0	1	0	.000	.000
Williams	20	.129	31	5	4	1	0	0	3	2	5	3	.182	.161
Willis	25	.241	58	2	14	2	0	1	4	3	8	0	.279	.328
TOTAL	162	.266	5490	751	1459	292	44	157	709	515	978	150	.333	.421

PITCHER	W	L	ERA	G	GS	CG	SHO	SV	IP	H	HR	BB	SO
Almanza	4	5	6.08	51	0	0	0	0	50.1	59	10	25	49
Alvarez	0	0	3.09	9	0	0	0	0	11.2	8	2	8	6
Beckett	9	8	3.04	24	23	0	0	0	142.0	132	9	56	152
Borland	0	0	1.86	7	0	0	0	0	9.2	3	0	8	4

PITCHER	W	L	ERA	G	GS	CG	SHO	SV	IP	H	HR	BB	SO
Bump	4	0	4.71	32	0	0	0	0	36.1	34	3	20	17
Burnett	0	2	4.70	4	4	0	0	0	23.0	18	2	18	21
Fox	2	1	2.13	21	0	0	0	0	25.1	16	1	14	27
Helling	1	0	0.55	11	0	0	0	0	16.1	11	1	5	12
Levrault	1	0	3.86	19	0	0	0	0	28.0	38	3	15	21
Looper	6	4	3.68	74	0	0	0	28	80.2	82	4	29	56
Neal	0	0	8.14	18	0	0	0	0	21.0	38	2	9	10
Nunez	0	3	16.03	14	0	0	0	0	10.2	21	7	7	10
Olsen	0	0	12.75	7	0	0	0	0	12.0	25	2	4	12
Pavano	12	13	4.30	33	32	2	0	0	201.0	204	19	49	133
Penny	14	10	4.13	32	32	0	0	0	196.1	195	21	56	138
Phelps	3	2	4.00	27	7	0	0	0	63.0	70	3	23	43
Redman	14	9	3.59	29	29	3	0	0	190.2	172	16	61	151
Spooneybarger	1	2	4.07	33	0	0	0	0	42.0	27	1	11	32
Tejera	3	4	4.67	50	6	0	0	2	81.0	82	6	36	58
Urbina	3	0	1.41	33	0	0	0	6	38.1	23	2	13	37
Wayne	0	2	11.81	2	0	0	0	0	5.1	9	1	5	1
Willis	14	6	3.30	27	27	2	2	0	160.2	148	13	58	142
TOTAL	91	71	4.04	162	162	7	2	36	1445.1	1415	128	530	1132

2003 MARLINS LEADERS

Batting
Average: Luis Castillo, .314
Hits: Juan Pierre, 204
Doubles: Juan Encarnacion, 37
Triples: Juan Pierre, 7
Home runs: Mike Lowell, 32
Runs: Juan Pierre, 100
RBI: Mike Lowell, 105
Stolen bases: Juan Pierre, 65
On-Base percentage: Luis Castillo, .381
Slugging percentage: Mike Lowell, .530

Pitching
Wins: Dontrelle Willis, Brad Penny, Mark Redman, 14 each
Losses: Carl Pavano, 13
Won-Loss percentage: Dontrelle Willis, .700
ERA (100 IP): Josh Beckett, 3.04
Saves: Braden Looper, 28
Strikeouts: Josh Beckett, 152
Complete games: Mark Redman, 3
Shutouts: Dontrelle Willis, 2

MARLINS REGULAR SEASON LAST AT-BAT WINS

DATE	BATTER	GW-HIT	INNING	SCORE	OPPONENT
4/09	Rodriguez	RBI Single	Ninth	3-2	NY Mets
4/10	Pierre	2-Run Single	Ninth	4-3	NY Mets
4/19	Rodriguez	RBI FC	Ninth	6-5	at NY Mets
4/22	Rodriguez	2-Run HR	Eighth	4-2	Milwaukee
4/23	Encarnacion	RBI Single	Twelfth	5-4	Milwaukee
5/09	Encarnacion	Solo HR	Ninth	5-4	Colorado
6/20	Cabrera	2-Run HR	Eleventh	3-1	Tampa Bay
6/28	Lowell	3-Run HR	Ninth	10-9	at Boston
7/04	Lee	RBI Single	Ninth	2-1	at Philadelphia
7/11	Encarnacion	RBI Single	Ninth	5-4	at Montreal
7/23	Mordecai	Solo HR	Twelfth	5-4	at Atlanta
7/25	Encarnacion	Bases Loaded Walk	Eighth	11-5	Philadelphia

DATE	BATTER	GW-HIT	INNING	SCORE	OPPONENT
7/27	Pierre	RBI Single	Ninth	7-6	Philadelphia
8/12	Castro	Solo HR	Thirteenth	5-4	Los Angeles
8/13	Mordecai	Solo HR	Eleventh	2-1	Los Angeles
8/29	Banks	RBI Single	Ninth	3-2	Montreal
9/09	Gonzalez	2-Run Triple	Ninth	3-1	at NY Mets
9/12	Pierre	RBI Single	Ninth	5-4	Atlanta
9/20	Cabrera	Solo HR	Eleventh	6-5	at Atlanta

MARLINS REGULAR SEASON COMEBACK WINS (AFTER 6TH INNING)

DATE	INNING	SCORE	FINAL SCORE	OPPONENT
4/10	Sixth	0-2	4-3	NY Mets
4/19	Ninth	4-5	6-5	at NY Mets
4/23	Sixth	1-2	5-4	Milwaukee
4/26	Sixth	0-2	5-3	St. Louis
5/09	Eighth	3-4	5-4	Colorado
6/28	Ninth	6-9	10-9	at Boston
7/11	Ninth	3-4	5-4	at Montreal
7/25	Eighth	3-4	11-5	Philadelphia
8/16	Sixth	1-3	6-3	San Diego
8/29	Sixth	0-2	3-2	Montreal
9/01	Sixth	1-2	5-2	Montreal
9/09	Sixth	0-1	3-1	NY Mets
9/12	Sixth	2-3	5-4	Atlanta
9/23	Sixth	0-3	5-4	Philadelphia

MARLINS RECORDS SET IN 2003

Most Hits	203	Juan Pierre
Most Multi-Hit Games	60	Juan Pierre
Most Stolen Bases	65	Juan Pierre
Most At-Bats	668	Juan Pierre
Most Games	162 (tie)	Juan Pierre
Singles	168	Juan Pierre

CLUB HITTING - GAME

Most At-Bats	66	4/27 vs. STL (20 innings)
Most At-Bats, Nine Inning Game	50	4/5 at ATL
Most Runs	20	7/1 vs. ATL (20-1)
Most Hits	25	7/1 vs. ATL
Most Home Runs	4	19 times, last: 4/4 at ATL
Most Extra Base Hits	11	7/1 vs. ATL
Most Total Bases	43	7/1 vs. ATL
Most Base on Balls	16	4/27 vs. STL (20 innings)
Fewest Strikeouts	0	3 times, last: 5/31 vs. CIN
Most Runners Left on Base	21	2 times, last: 4/27 vs. STL (20 innings)

CLUB PITCHING - GAME

Most Hits Allowed	28	6/27 at BOS
Most Hits Allowed, Inning	14	6/27 at BOS
Most Runs Allowed	25	6/27 at BOS (25-8)
Most Runs Allowed, Inning	14	6/27 at BOS (1st inning)
Most Runs Allowed Before First Out	10	6/27 at BOS (1st inning)
Most Home Runs Allowed	6	6/29 at Boston
Most Home Runs Allowed, Inning	3	8 times, last: 4/7 at ATL (6th inning)

INDIVIDUAL - GAME

Most At-Bats	9	2 times, last: Pierre, Encarnacion, 4/27 vs. STL
Most Runs	4	10 times, last: Pierre, 5/11 vs.COL; Cabrera, 7/11 vs.ATL
Most Doubles	3	9 times, last: Lowell, 4/28 at ARI; Hollandsworth 5/10 vs. COL
Most Home Runs	2	71 times, last: Lowell 3 times; Lee 3 times; Gonzalez; Cabrera
Most Extra-Base Hits	4	2 times, last: Cabrera, 7/1 vs. ATL (2 2B, 2 HR)
Most Bases on Balls	5	Rodriguez, 4/8 vs. NYM

| Most Strikeouts | 4 | 27 times, last: Fox, 4/29 at ARI; Rodriguez, 5/30 vs. CIN |
| Most Home Runs Allowed | 4 | 3 times, last: Penny, 6/29 at BOS |

CAREER

Most Home Runs	129	Derrek Lee
Most Extra-Base Hits	305	Derrek Lee
Most Games Played	856	Luis Castillo
Most Runs Batted In	436	Jeff Conine
Most Total Bases	328	Derrek Lee

2003 MANAGER OF THE YEAR VOTING

Manager,	Team	1st	2nd	3rd	Total Points
Jack McKeon,	Florida	19	6	3	116
Dusty Baker,	Chicago	2	15	7	62
Bobby Cox,	Atlanta	6	5	11	56
Felipe Alou,	San Francisco	5	6	8	51
Frank Robinson,	Montreal	--	--	3	3

2003 POSTSEASON LINE SCORES

Division Series

Game 1 at San Francisco, Sept. 30
FLA   000 000 000 **0** 3 1
SF   000 100 01x **2** 3 2
W-Schmidt; L-Beckett.

Game 2 at San Francisco, Oct.1
FLA   100 033 110 **9** 14 0
SF   100 310 000 **5** 8 2
W-Pavano; L-Nathan; HR-Encarnacion

Game 3 at Florida, Oct. 3
SF   000 002 000 01 **3** 12 1
FLA   200 000 000 02 **4** 8 1
W-Looper; L-Worrell; HR-Rodriguez

Game 4 at Florida, Oct. 4
SF   010 004 001 **6** 9 2
FLA   012 200 02x **7** 12 0
W-Pavano; L-F.Rodriguez; SV-Urbina

Championship Series

Game 1 at Chicago, Oct. 7
FLA   005 001 002 01 **9** 14 1
CHI   400 002 002 00 **8** 11 1
W-Urbina; L-Guthrie; HR-Rodriguez, Cabrera, Encarnacion,
Lowell, Alou, Gonzalez, Sosa

Game 2 at Chicago, Oct. 8
FLA   000 002 010   **3** 9 1
CHI   233 031 00x **12** 16 1
W-Prior; L-Penny; HR-Lee, Cabrera, Sosa, Ramirez,
A.Gonzalez (Cubs) 2

Game 3 at Florida, Oct. 10
CHI   110 000 020 01 **5** 12 0
FLA   010 000 210 00 **4** 10 0
W-Borowski; L-Tejera; HR-Simon

Game 4 at Florida, Oct. 11
CHI   402 100 100 **8** 8 0
FLA   000 020 010 **3** 6 1
W-Clement; L-Willis; HR-Ramirez 2

Game 5 at Florida, Oct. 12
CHI   000 000 000 **0** 2 0
FLA   000 020 11x **4** 8 0
W-Beckett; L-Zambrano; HR-Lowell, Rodriguez, Conine

Game 6 at Chicago, Oct. 14
FLA   000 000 080 **8** 9 0
CHI   100 001 100 **3** 10 2
W-Fox; L-Prior

Game 7 at Chicago, Oct. 15
FLA   300 031 200 **9** 12 0
CHI   032 000 100 **6** 6 0
W-Penny; L-Wood; SV-Urbina; HR-Cabrera, Wood, Alou, O'Leary

World Series

Game 1 at New York
FLA   100 020 000 **3** 7 1
NY   001 001 000 **2** 9 0
W-Penny; L-Wells; SV-Urbina; HR-Williams

Game 2 at New York
FLA   000 000 001 **1** 6 0
NY   310 200 00x **6** 10 1
W-Pettitte; L-Redman; HR-Matsui, Soriano

Game 3 at Florida
NY   000 100 014 **6** 6 1
FLA   100 000 000 **1** 8 0
W-Mussina; L-Beckett; SV-Rivera; HR-Boone, Williams

Game 4 at Florida
NY   010 000 002 000 **3** 12 0
FLA   300 000 000 001 **4** 10 0
W-Looper; L-Weaver; HR-Cabrera, Gonzalez

Game 5 at Florida
NY   100 000 102 **4** 12 1
FLA   030 120 00x **6** 9 1
W-Penny; L-Contreras; SV-Urbina; HR-Giambi

Game 6 at New York
FLA   000 011 000 **2** 7 0
NY   000 000 000 **0** 5 1
W-Beckett; L-Pettitte

2003 MARLINS POSTSEASON STATS

PLAYER	G	AVG	AB	R	H	2B	3B	HR	RBI	BB	SO	SB	OBP	SLG
Banks	4	.000	3	1	0	0	0	0	0	1	0	0	.250	.000
Beckett	5	.182	11	0	2	0	0	0	0	1	6	0	.250	.182
Cabrera	17	.265	68	11	18	2	0	4	12	4	19	0	.315	.471
Castillo	17	.211	71	6	15	4	0	0	4	8	12	3	.291	.268
Conine	17	.367	60	10	22	2	1	1	5	9	5	0	.437	.483
Encarnacion	15	.184	38	3	7	1	0	2	3	3	12	0	.238	.368
Gonzalez	17	.161	62	6	10	4	0	1	6	1	16	0	.175	.274
Harris	5	.250	4	0	1	0	0	0	0	1	0	0	.400	.250
Helling	3	.000	1	0	0	0	0	0	0	0	0	0	.000	.000
Hollandsworth	9	.500	8	3	4	1	0	0	2	1	3	0	.556	.625
Lee	17	.208	72	6	15	3	0	1	8	3	17	2	.269	.292
Lowell	15	.196	46	6	9	1	0	2	5	5	8	0	.275	.348
Mordecai	3	.200	5	1	1	1	0	0	3	0	0	0	.200	.400
Pavano	7	.000	4	0	0	0	0	0	0	0	2	0	.000	.000
Penny	6	.500	4	0	2	0	0	0	2	0	1	0	.500	.500
Pierre	17	.301	73	12	22	4	2	0	7	8	4	3	.378	.411
Redman	3	.000	4	0	0	0	0	0	0	1	1	0	.200	.000
Redmond	2	.000	1	1	0	0	0	0	0	1	0	0	.500	.000
Rodriguez	17	.313	67	10	21	5	0	3	17	9	12	0	.390	.522
Willis	6	1.000	3	1	3	0	1	0	0	0	0	0	1.000	1.667

PITCHER	W	L	ERA	G	GS	CG	SHO	SV	IP	H	HR	BB	SO
Beckett	2	2	2.11	6	5	2	2	0	42.2	21	3	12	47
Bump	0	0	6.00	2	0	0	0	0	3.0	3	1	0	3
Fox	1	0	3.97	9	0	0	0	0	11.1	12	2	9	9
Helling	0	0	7.27	4	0	0	0	0	8.2	11	3	6	7
Looper	2	0	5.14	8	0	0	0	1	7.0	8	2	3	5
Pavano	2	0	1.40	8	2	0	0	0	19.1	17	0	3	15
Penny	3	1	5.73	7	4	0	0	0	22.0	29	3	9	13
Redman	0	1	6.50	4	4	0	0	0	18.0	25	3	9	10
Tejera	0	1	6.75	2	0	0	0	0	1.1	2	0	0	1
Urbina	1	0	3.46	10	0	0	0	4	13.0	8	1	4	14
Willis	0	1	8.53	7	2	0	0	0	12.2	15	1	10	10

HIGHLIGHTS OF MARLINS HISTORY

Aug. 8, 1985   MLB's new basic agreement allows the NL to expand by two teams to match AL's 14.

Mar. 7, 1990   H. Wayne Huizenga buys half of Joe Robbie Stadium and 15% of NFL Miami Dolphins, says he will pursue baseball expansion franchise.

Sept.13, 1990   Dade County repeals ordinance limiting Joe Robbie Stadium to 18 events per year.

Sept.18, 1990   NL expansion committee hears presentations from four South Florida groups.

Dec. 18, 1990   NL reveals six possible expansion sites, picks Huizenga group from S. Florida.

Mar. 30, 1991   Yankee-Oriole exhibition game held at Joe Robbie draws 67,654 fans, a spring training record.

June 10, 1991   Baseball names Denver and South Florida as sites of new franchises.

July 18, 1991   Marlins unveil first team logo.

Sept. 18, 1991   Montreal GM Dave Dombrowski is hired as Marlins GM.

June 1, 1992   University of Miami catcher Charles Johnson is Marlins' first amateur draft choice.

Oct. 23, 1992   Rene Lachemann becomes first Florida manager; brother Marcel is named pitching coach.

Nov. 17, 1992   Marlins pick 36 players, including Jeff Conine, in expansion draft.

Dec. 8, 1992   Marlins sign first free agent, knuckleballer Charlie Hough.

Dec. 9, 1992   Carl Barger, club's first president, dies from ruptured abdominal aortic aneurysm during winter meetings.

Mar. 5, 1993   Marlins beat Astros, 12-8, in first spring training game.

Apr. 5, 1993   Hough thrills 42,334 in first Florida opener with 6-3 win over Dodgers.

Apr. 12, 1993   Benito Santiago hits first home run in Marlins history.

July 13, 1993   Gary Sheffield and Bryan Harvey are Marlin All-Stars; Sheffield homers in first All-Star at-bat by a Marlin.

Oct. 2, 1993   Marlins pass 3,000,000 in attendance.

Jan. 24, 1994   Huizenga buys other half of Joe Robbie Stadium.

Mar. 4, 1994   Marlins open Space Coast Stadium as new spring home with 9-6 win vs KC.

July 11, 1995   Jeff Conine's solo homer wins All-Star Game, All-Star MVP award.

May 11, 1996   Al Leiter pitches first Marlins no-hitter.

Aug. 26, 1996   Joe Robbie Stadium renamed Pro Player Stadium after sports apparel brand of Fruit of the Loom.

Oct. 4, 1996   Jim Leyland named new manager of Marlins.

June 10, 1997   Florida's Kevin Brown no-hits San Francisco, 9-0.

Sept. 23, 1997   Marlins clinch wild card with 6-3 win in Montreal.

Oct. 3, 1997   Marlins complete Division Series sweep versus Giants.

Oct. 14, 1997   Florida beats Braves, four games to two, in Championship Series.

Oct. 26, 1997   Edgar Renteria's single in 11th inning of Game 7 wins World Series for Florida.

Oct. 2, 1998   John Boles becomes first man to manage Marlins twice.

Jan. 13, 1999   Owners approve sale of Marlins to John W. Henry.

Aug. 7, 1999   Henry unveils six possible sites for new ball park: Miami River, Miramar, Lauderill, Bicentennial Park, Davie, or downtown Fort Lauderdale.

Dec. 15, 1999	Marlins pick Bicentennial Park, downtown Miami, for new ballpark.
Mar. 1, 2000	David Dombrowski is named president as well as general manager.
Mar. 4, 2000	Marlins announce funding plan for retractable-roof ballpark in downtown Miami but plan needs voter approval.
May 12, 2001	A.J. Burnett no-hits San Diego, 3-0.
May 28, 2001	Tony Perez becomes fourth Marlins manager.
Nov. 5, 2001	Dombrowski resigns to take similar position with Detroit Tigers.
Feb. 16, 2002	Jeffrey Loria completes purchase of Marlins from John W. Henry.
June 21, 2002	Luis Castillo completes 35-game hitting streak, a franchise record.
Nov. 16, 2002	Marlins get centerfielder Juan Pierre from Rockies in three-team trade.
Jan. 11, 2003	Florida obtains lefthanded starter Mark Redman from Tigers.
Jan. 22, 2003	Marlins sign free-agent catcher Ivan Rodriguez .
Apr. 27, 2003	Marlins lose longest game in franchise history, 7-6 in 20 innings versus Cardinals.
May 9, 2003	Dontrelle Willis makes first major-league start.
May 11, 2003	Jack McKeon replaces Jeff Torborg as manager.
May 20, 2003	Miguel Cabrera hits 11th-inning walkoff homer in big-league debut.
June 16, 2003	Willis one-hits Mets, 1-0, for fifth straight win.
June 25, 2003	Marlins yield 14 runs in first inning, lose at Boston, 25-8.
June 26, 2003	Marlins rebound from 9-2 deficit to beat Bosox, 10-9, in Fenway.
July 1, 2003	Marlins beat Braves, 20-1, establishing club records for runs, hits, and victory margin.

July 11, 2003	Marlins trade three prospects to Texas for closer Ugueth Urbina.
July 22, 2003	Mike Mordecai's surprise homer in 12th beats Braves.
July 25, 2003	Eight-run Florida eighth sparks 11-5 win vs Phils.
Aug. 31, 2003	Florida acquires Jeff Conine from Baltimore.
Sept. 1, 2003	Marlins complete four-game sweep of Expos, who had been tied for wild-card spot.
Sept. 15, 2003	Phils beat Florida, 14-0, and pull within one-half game of wild-card lead.
Sept. 23, 2003	Five-run seventh helps Florida beat Phils, 5-4, take two-game wild-card lead.
Sept. 26, 2003	Marlins clinch NL wild-card berth with 4-3 win over Mets.
Oct. 4, 2003.	Marlins beat Giants, 7-6, in four-game Division Series.
Oct. 15, 2003	Marlins defeat Cubs, 9-6, in seventh game of Championship Series.
Oct. 18, 2003	Brad Penny wins World Series opener at Yankee Stadium, 3-2.
Oct. 22, 2003	Alex Gonzalez homers in 12th to beat Yanks, 4-3, in World Series Game 4.
Oct. 23, 2003	Penny pitches and hits his way past Yanks, 6-4, in WS Game 5.
Oct. 25, 2003	Beckett blanks Yanks, 2-0, to clinch World Series.

Bibliography

The following books and periodicals provided vital reference information for this book:

Baseball America

Baseball America Almanac 2004 (Baseball America, Durham, NC)

Baseball America Almanac 1998 (Baseball America, Durham, NC)

Baseball: the Biographical Encyclopedia (Total Sports Illustrated, Kingston, NY, 2000), edited by Michael Gershman, David Pietrusza, and Matthew Silverman.

2004 Baseball Register (Sporting News Books, St. Louis).

The Bill James Handbook 2004 (ACTA Publications, Chicago).

ESPN: The Magazine (ESPN, New York).

Florida Marlins: World Series Champions (Sports Publishing LLC, Champaign, IL).

2003 Florida Marlins Media Guide (Florida Marlins, Miami, FL).

2003 Florida Marlins Postseason Media Guide (Florida Marlins, Miami, FL).

The Miami Herald

MLB.com

2003 National League Championship Series Official Program (Major League Baseball Publications, New York).

2003 Official Major League Baseball Fact Book (Sporting News Books, St. Louis).

South Florida Sun-Sentinel

The Sports Encyclopedia: Baseball 2003 (St. Martin's Griffin, New York), edited by David S. Neft, Richard M. Cohen, and Michael L. Neft

Sports Illustrated Presents: World Champs 2003 Florida Marlins (Time Inc., New York)

USA Today Sports Weekly Commemorative Issue: 1997-2003 World Champions (Gannett Company, McLean, VA).

USA Today Sports Weekly

USA Today

Celebrate the Heroes of Baseball
in These Other Releases from Sports Publishing!

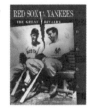